M000286401

Militarizing Culture

green press
INITIATIVE

Left Coast Press is committed to preserving ancient forests and natural resources. We elected to print this title on 30% post consumer recycled paper, processed chlorine free. As a result, for this printing, we have saved:

3 Trees (40' tall and 6-8" diameter)
1 Million BTUs of Total Energy
273 Pounds of Greenhouse Gases
1,317 Gallons of Wastewater
80 Pounds of Solid Waste

Left Coast Press made this paper choice because our printer, Thomson-Shore, Inc., is a member of Green Press Initiative, a nonprofit program dedicated to supporting authors, publishers, and suppliers in their efforts to reduce their use of fiber obtained from endangered forests.

For more information, visit www.greenpressinitiative.org

Environmental impact estimates were made using the Environmental Defense Paper Calculator. For more information visit: www.papercalculator.org.

Militarizing Culture
Essays on the Warfare State

Roberto J. González

Left Coast
Press Inc.

Walnut Creek, CA

Left Coast Press, Inc.
1630 North Main Street, #400
Walnut Creek, CA 94596
http://www.LCoastPress.com

Copyright 2010 by Left Coast Press, Inc.

All rights reserved. No part of this publication may be reproduced, stored in a retrieval system, or transmitted in any form or by any means, electronic, mechanical, photocopying, recording, or otherwise, without the prior permission of the publisher.

ISBN 978-1-59874-559-7 hardcover
ISBN 978-1-59874-560-3 paperback
eISBN 978-1-59874-561-0

Library of Congress Cataloging-in-Publication Data
González, Roberto J. (Roberto Jesús), 1969–
  Essays on the warfare state / Roberto J. González.
    p. cm.
  Includes bibliographical references and index.
  ISBN 978-1-59874-559-7 (hardcover : alk. paper) — ISBN 978-1-59874-560-3 (pbk. : alk. paper) — ISBN 978-1-59874-561-0 (eISBN)
1. United States—Civilization—21st century. 2. War and society—United States. 3. Popular culture—United States. 4. Afghan War, 2001—Social aspects—United States. 5. Iraq War, 2003—Social aspects—United States. I. Title.
  E169.12.G637 2010
  303.6'60973—dc22
                        2010025902

Printed in the United States of America

♾™ The paper used in this publication meets the minimum requirements of American National Standard for Information Sciences—Permanence of Paper for Printed Library Materials, ANSI/NISO Z39.48–1992.

An earlier version of chapter 3, "Towards Mercenary Anthropology?" was published in *Anthropology Today* 23, vol. 3: 14–19. Copyright © 2007 by the Royal Anthropological Institute, London.

An earlier version of chapter 5, "Human Terrain," was published in *Anthropology Today* 24, vol. 1: 21–26. Copyright © 2008 by the Royal Anthropological Institute, London.

An earlier version of chapter 7, "Going 'Tribal'," was originally published in *Anthropology Today* 25, vol. 2: 15–19. Copyright © 2009 by the Royal Anthropological Institute, London.
Figure 0.1: Copyright © 2009 by Sean M. Haffey/San Diego Union Tribune/ZUMA Press. Reprinted by permission.
Figure 0.3: Copyright © 2010 by Terese Hart. Reprinted by permission.
Figure 1.2: Copyright © 2008 by Trevor Paglen. Reprinted by permission.
Figure 1.3: Copyright © 2010 by Heidi Stambuck. Reprinted by permission.
Cover design by Allison Smith

Cover illustration: Children of an Iraqi farmer watch as US soldiers conduct operations in the town of Aqur Quf (northwest of Baghdad) on March 29, 2010. (Photo courtesy of Manhea Kim/US Department of Defense.)

FOR ROBERT, KATE, AND JOAQUÍN

Contents

Illustrations

Acknowledgments

The following people generously provided encouragement, criticism, comments, or assistance in the preparation of various portions of this book: Rochelle Davis, Matthew Engelke, Samuel Freeman, Roberto González, Jr., Imelda González, Hugh Gusterson, Karen Holmes, Gustaaf Houtman, Dahr Jamail, Heidi Kao, Tony Lagouranis, Kanhong Lin, Ron Loewe, Catherine Lutz, Laura McNamara, Laura Nader, Luis Plascencia, Kamala Platt, David Price, Adam Rodríguez, Robert Rubinstein, and Alisse Waterston. Two anonymous reviewers helped me improve the manuscript, for which I am grateful.

A sabbatical leave in Fall 2009 at San José State University allowed me to complete the final phase of this work.

Introduction
Militarizing Culture

For seven-year-old Justin Velázquez, Wednesday had been a big day—possibly the biggest day of his life. The slender, wide-eyed boy from San Diego had won a nationwide contest, and he and his family were awarded a special prize: the opportunity to attend an advance screening of a Hollywood action movie.

The judges chose Justin's letter from hundreds that had poured in during the summer of 2009 for a "Hometown Hero" contest sponsored by Paramount Pictures. Justin told the world about his father José, who had recently returned from military deployment overseas. In a 200-word essay, Justin movingly described the pain of sacrifice, the value of giving, the strength of love, and the power of family relationships:

> I am Justin my dad name is José. I am writing because my dad is a Real American Hero he has been through so much my dad is in the Navy I was just born in 2002 of Feb. my dad went on deployment when in July he was involved in a helo [helicopter] crash where the helo crashed on the ship and into the water (gulf). My dad was injured from what he told me. He had 2nd degree burns, back, shoulder injuries. My dad was helo out to the hospital where he stayed. Later he was sent back to Japan to go to therapy for his injuries.
>
> My dad didn't leave the Navy instead he stayed because of me. My dad in 2007 was motored and rpg [rocket propelled grenade] when he went to Iraq to support the war my dad did it not just for me but for all of us. I love my dad so much and so does Raul he's my brother. My dad has been through a lot but he has always come back for us. My Dad A Real American Hero.
>
> I went to give something back to my dad for all he has done for us.

On a sunny August afternoon, Justin, his parents, and his younger brother Raúl climbed into a military Humvee and were escorted in a motorcade led by police cars and a fire truck. Also present in the procession were the film's stars, director Stephen Sommers, state assemblywoman Lori Saldaña, and a group of uniformed men and women from the California

National Guard. Once the motorcade arrived at the theater, the San Diego State University marching band greeted the party. The out-of-town guests made speeches, the local media interviewed the Velázquez family, and then Justin met a special guest from Washington representing Susan Davis, the Velázquez family's congresswoman in the US House of Representatives. He gave Justin an American flag, a certificate, and a set of plastic action figures.[1]

Then all entered the theater to watch *GI Joe: The Rise of Cobra*.

Marketing Militarism

The story of Justin and José Velázquez resonates deeply—a triumphant and unusual case in which bonds of love and affection between father and son, between parent and child, are publicly recognized and celebrated.

At the same time, there is something profoundly unsettling about the entire episode, for it illustrates the intricate means by which militarism

Figure 0.1: Justin and Jose Velázquez attend a special advance screening of *GI Joe: The Rise of Cobra*, August 2009. (Photo courtesy of Sean M. Haffey/San Diego Union-Tribune/ZUMA Press.)

is designed, manufactured, packaged, and marketed in America today. It also reveals how human connections—including family relationships—are easily infiltrated by what President Dwight D. Eisenhower once called the "military-industrial complex."[2]

Paramount Pictures' movie is the latest product of the long running GI Joe franchise. For nearly half a century, the Hasbro toy company has sold its movable plastic doll to millions of American boys. (First introduced in 1964, GI Joe's creators were motivated to compete with Mattel's wildly popular and lucrative Barbie doll.) Its commercial success was due in large part to hundreds of additional accessories, such as uniforms, weapons, vehicles, and battle stations that Hasbro developed and sold to enthusiasts. Today there are dozens of official and unofficial GI Joe fan clubs and collectors' clubs, and original action figures and accessories sometimes sell for hundreds of dollars at antique shops. Some film critics were upset by the crass commercialism of Paramount's blockbuster: "It's More Toy Commercial Than Movie," declared the *Miami Herald.*[3]

The Hometown Hero contest—and the Velázquez family—were, in a sense, extensions of a broad marketing assault designed to promote *GI Joe: The Rise of Cobra* to American servicemen, servicewomen, their relatives, and others living in the American heartland. Just a few days before the San Diego event, Paramount invited 1,000 military personnel and their families to a screening at Andrews Air Force Base in Maryland. The movie's stars (Channing Tatum, Sienna Miller, and Marlon Wayans) attended and were treated to a helicopter tour and a meeting with the base commander.[4]

In an interview with the *Los Angeles Times*, Paramount vice chairman Rob Moore was blunt about the company's marketing strategy: "Our starting point for this movie is not Hollywood and Manhattan but rather mid-America," he said. "There are a group of people we think are going to respond to the movie who are normally not the first priority. But we're making them a priority."[5] Moore revealed that Paramount hoped to lure European audiences by having much of the action take place in France, and to attract Asian audiences by casting South Korean star Lee Byung-hun in a supporting role.

Paramount also launched a series of tie-ins including partnerships with Burger King and the 7-Eleven chain of convenience stores. Burger King introduced a Kids Meal with GI Joe "gadgets, action figures, and vehicles that offer the ultimate adventure." In the hyper-active, hyper-hyphenated language typical of corporate press releases, Burger King global marketing executive Russ Klein remarked, "Partnering with Paramount has allowed us to go beyond the typical tie-in property sponsorship to create all-encompassing entertainment and promotions that offer our restaurant guests a real piece of the action—in-restaurant, on their televisions, and online...the creativity and innovation we bring to the partnership add value to the studios' movie marketing effort."[6]

During the same week, 7-Eleven introduced a "GI Joe-themed true-blue Slurpee® flavor—Liquid Artillery" created by the Coca-Cola Company and a Go Joe cappuccino drink flavored with three "natural energy ingredients—taurine, guarana, and caffeine." Liquid Artillery and Go Joe were served in cups featuring GI Joe characters. Jay Wilkins, 7-Eleven brand manager, stated in a press release that GI Joe "is probably the best-known boy's toy in the world.... The movie has a ready-made audience of boys and men who played with GI Joe, and we want to bring back some of those great childhood memories."[7]

As if these "value added" initiatives were not enough to promote the "boy's toy" franchise, in 2009 Paramount and Hasbro created additional officially licensed tie-ins with Electronic Arts for a video game, with Del Ray Books (a division of Random House) for an "Essential Guide to GI Joe vs. Cobra," and with IDW Publishing for *We Are GI Joe*, a children's book "specifically written and illustrated for developing readers." Paramount also placed various products in the film, including Cisco Systems' Telepresence video conferencing services, Dubble Bubble gum, and Norton anti-virus computer software.[8]

But the biggest tie-in of all was the partnership between Paramount and the US Department of Defense. As in the case of many recent Hollywood war films (from *Top Gun* to *Iron Man*), the Pentagon loaned a great deal of equipment and personnel for the making of *GI Joe: The Rise of Cobra*, including Apache helicopters, Humvees, and even members of the Army's 21st Cavalry Brigade and the California National Guard.[9] Paramount had already experimented with this relationship in its 2007 movie *Transformers*, another film based upon a line of Hasbro toys. According to a report published by the Bloomberg news service, "Pentagon officials and weapon makers say they've found a savvy way to make US military service seem attractive to teenage boys": by placing the weapons of war on the big screen. The synergies of the Paramount-Pentagon partnership were simple but powerful—free high-tech stage props in exchange for a two-hour recruitment advertisement for the military. Weapons manufacturers enjoyed the added benefit of product promotion. The Bloomberg report quoted Scott Lusk, spokesman for Lockheed Martin, who provided a candid assessment of including F-22 fighter planes in Paramount films. Lusk declared that such appearances "help promote the state-of-the-art, high-tech products that are designed, developed and manufactured" by Lockheed Martin for the US military.[10]

Even before its partnership with Paramount, the Pentagon was involved in a symbiotic relationship with toy companies. In an eye-opening report that followed the United States-led invasion of Iraq in 2003, journalist William Hamilton revealed how Mattel, Hasbro, and other companies inspired state-of-the-art weaponry:

> "The M-16 rifle is based on something Mattel did," says Glenn Flood, a spokesman for the Pentagon, which is looking to toys and electronic games for parts, prototypes and ideas that can be developed effectively and inexpensively as battlefield tools. Inspiration has come from model planes (reconnaissance drones), "supersoaker" water guns (quick-loading assault weapons), cheap cellular phones for teenagers (video-capable walkie-talkies) and gaming control panels (for unmanned robotic vehicles).... Today's troops effectively received basic training as children.[11]

Given these connections, *GI Joe: The Rise of Cobra* could be described as a massive joint venture between Paramount Pictures, Hasbro, the Pentagon, the Pentagon's contract firms (Boeing, Lockheed Martin, AM General), Burger King, 7-Eleven, Random House, Cisco, Norton, and other firms and organizations set to benefit from box office sales, action figure

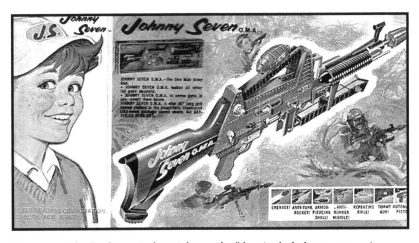

Figure 0.2: The "military-industrial complex" has included toy companies, video game manufacturers, and other organizations that have maintained a symbiotic relationship with the Pentagon over the years. (Photo courtesy of John Eaton/Wikimedia Commons.)

sales, weapon systems sales, junk food sales, video conferencing system sales, and the like. Despite the high price tag—$175 million in production costs plus an additional $150 million in marketing expenses—the film turned a huge profit. It earned Paramount more than $55 million in the United States and Canada during its opening weekend, and another $45 million abroad, making it among the year's most successful Hollywood box office debuts.[12]

The Story of Us All

But such endeavors can be measured in more than dollars and cents. The social and psychological consequences are also important considerations, for people and families sometimes get caught in the cross hairs. Cultural anthropologist Hugh Gusterson has explored the deeper meanings of films like *GI Joe: The Rise of Cobra*, and the wider processes by which military values are imposed upon young people:

> Hollywood's movie industry...churns out films, from *Rambo* to *Saving Private Ryan*, that glamorize soldiers, projecting them as archetypical American men whose struggles define the quest to come of age and find meaning in life.... The film makers behind such films routinely submit their scripts to the Pentagon and rewrite them, in exchange for access to military hardware and military locations, if the Pentagon objects to particular scenes.... Just in case teenagers are insufficiently brainwashed by their constant marinating in this pro-military mass culture, under the No Child Left Behind Act high schools lose all their federal funding if they do not give the names, addresses, and phone numbers of their students to military recruiters. [13]

Like any cultural product, *GI Joe: The Rise of Cobra* reveals much about our own society, including the powerful role played by the complex linking the Pentagon, Hollywood, weapons manufacturers, toy companies, and other industries; the mechanisms by which such institutions succeed in diffusing militaristic ideologies widely and effectively; and the disproportionately large effects of these projects on youth.[14] Apart from the web of corporations and government agencies connected by symbiotic business relationships, and apart from the economics of profit-making, there is the question of attitudes and values. What are the consequences of a culture industry that produces war films, toys, clothing, video games, and comic books year after year, in lockstep with the Pentagon's military adventures abroad? How can we better understand the long-term effects of what anthropologist Catherine Lutz has called the "military normal"—a condition in which science, entertainment, business, and even high fashion deeply reflect militaristic values?[15] In short, what are the costs of militarizing culture?

The screening attended by Justin Velázquez and his family might be viewed as a human interest story with a heart-warming ending, a media event that has the effect of making us feel good about fighting wars that create hometown heroes.

But from a more critical perspective, it might be viewed as an illustration of how today's military-industrial complex is powerful and sophisticated enough to infiltrate and mediate intimate social relationships—between parent and child, between family and community, between civilian and soldier—while exploiting those who can help it further its own ends. The Hometown Hero contest certainly does not lead most Americans to question whether our servicemen and women should be occupying Iraq and Afghanistan at all, or what happens to hundreds of thousands of children—American, Afghan, and Iraqi—who, unlike Justin, *have* lost their fathers or mothers.

What makes the Justin Velázquez story troubling—even tragic—is that it reveals how in our society, heroism, valor, and love are often expressed in the idiom of a military-industrial-entertainment complex whose architects have altogether different motives. What does it mean when gratitude, honor, and affection between parent and child are effectively expressed through a contest organized by one of the biggest entertainment corporations in the world, with support from the most powerful military in world history?

I begin with the story of Justin Velázquez and *GI Joe: The Rise of Cobra* because it is in many ways the story of us all. It is emblematic of themes that run throughout this book: the prevalence of militaristic ideologies in our society, the processes by which military organizations and ideas subtly invade our daily lives and relationships, and the cultural strip-mining (of science, education, art, and artifacts) practiced by the Pentagon, the "intelligence community" of spy agencies, and their contract firms.

What exactly is militarization? What is militarism? How are they connected?

Historian Richard H. Kohn defines militarization as a wide-ranging process that describes "the degree to which a society's institutions, policies, behaviors, thought, and values are devoted to military power and shaped by war." He argues that for nearly seventy years, the United States has "experienced a degree of militarization heretofore unknown in American history." What concerns Kohn even more is the possibility that American militarization will blur into *militarism*, which he defines as "the domination of war values and frameworks in American thinking, public policy, institutions, and society to the point of dominating rather than influencing or simply shaping American foreign relations and domestic life." For Kohn—who served for ten years as the US Air Force's chief historian and has held various academic positions at the US Army War College—militarism is the more acute condition. Kohn's analysis of the post-9/11 era and the subsequent open-ended "war on terror" raises the question of "whether the very character of the American people changes [as a result], with the emphasis on freedom and individualism displaced by obedience, discipline, hierarchy, collectivism, authoritarianism, pessimism, and cynicism."[16] Our government's frequent invocation of terrorism as a justification for military intervention, invasion, and occupation makes this question all the more relevant.

It is striking that a scholar with career-long connections to military institutions would issue such a warning, but others have echoed Kohn's concerns. Andrew Bacevich, a professor of international relations and a Vietnam War veteran who graduated from West Point, argues that "today as never before in their history Americans are enthralled with military power." He warns that "America will surely share the fate of all those who in ages past have looked to war and military power to fulfill their destiny. We will rob future generations of their rightful inheritance. We will wreak havoc abroad. We will endanger our security at home. We will risk the forfeiture of all that we prize."[17] By examining increases in defense spending, the growing size of our country's military arsenal, the worldwide expansion of American military bases, a greater propensity for our leaders to use force as a foreign policy tool, and a "new aesthetic of war" manifested through a sanitized "public enthusiasm for the whiz-bang technology of the US military," Bacevich convincingly argues that the rise of American militarism represents a threat to our country's long-term viability.

More recently, anthropologist Catherine Lutz has noted that "the ascendance of the military came about only relatively recently in US history," since America's founders were suspicious of standing armies and used the Constitution as a means of ensuring civilian control over the military. Until World War II, most Americans generally "saw the military as a burden in peacetime and at best very occasionally necessary.... Middle class families were reluctant to send their children into a military they saw as a virtual cesspool of vices." Like Kohn and Bacevich, Lutz describes America's most recent phase of militarization as a process that began taking shape seven decades ago. She reminds us that militarization consists of more than just overseas bases and economic links. It includes "all of the institutions and groups who benefitted from a large military budget":

> Not only weapons manufacturers but companies like Proctor & Gamble and the Disney Corporation came to enjoy and rely on immense military contracts. US universities were drawn up in a concerted government campaign to put much of the nation's scientific talent and university training at the disposal of the military, to the point where 45 percent of all computer science graduate students with federal support get it from the Pentagon, and 25 percent of all scientists and engineers work on military projects. The military-industrial-Congressional-media-entertainment-university complex is a massively entangled system.[18]

In her ground-breaking book *Homefront*—an ethnography of Fayetteville, North Carolina, a town located near one of the largest US military bases in the world—Lutz observes that "there are many places like Fayetteville in America, from its nearly nine hundred other domestic military bases in such towns as Norfolk, Virginia, New London, Connecticut, and Killeen, Texas, to the thousands of places from Seattle, Washington, to Binghamton, New York, where weapons and equipment are made." Our country's economy, its geography, its customs, its fashions, its forms of entertainment, and even its values, have been shaped by military institutions that developed as instruments of conquest and control of Native Americans in the so-called Indian Wars, which began in the late 1700s and continued for more than a century. Lutz notes: "In an important sense, we all inhabit an army camp, mobilized to lend support to the permanent state of war readiness that has been with us since World War II." American militarization truly affects us all.[19]

Warrior Cultures: Spartan, Mongolian, Aztec

Ours is not the first society to follow a military imperative. Others have also placed a high value on military prowess and war fighting, but at a cost. Archaeologists and cultural anthropologists have researched the rise and fall of warrior cultures in various regions of the world. Although there are many differences among them, they hold in common several characteristics that give insight into the consequences of militarism.

The ancient Greek city-state of Sparta is among the most famous. It was the dominant military power in Greece for nearly three centuries, beginning in approximately 650 BC. A citizen's primary obligation was to be a good soldier, and Sparta rose to prominence on the strength of its infantry.

According to Plutarch, Spartan mothers bathed their newborn sons in wine rather than water to test their resilience, and did not swaddle them as was customary in other parts of Greece. Even more remarkable was the extraordinary dominance of the Spartan state and its institutions. Unlike its rival Athens (and many other Greek city-states), Sparta was a society in which children, particularly boys, were separated from their parents at an early age. All boys were required to undergo a lengthy, physically challenging collective upbringing called the *agoge*, supervised by the city-state's most prestigious officers. Historian Mark Golden provides a glimpse of what childhood was like in this society:

> From the age of seven, Spartan boys spent at least part of the day in the company of their agemates...[focusing] on physical training.... The groupings of the agoge were called "herds" and "flocks," the official immediately responsible for it the *paidonomos* (boyherd). Boys lived close to the land—going shoeless, stealing from the fields to supplement scant rations, making their own beds with river rushes cut by hand. Recalcitrance or failure met brutal punishment, beating, or a distinctive form of discipline, biting of the thumb.[20]

The Spartans placed little importance on literature, the arts, or commerce. Instead, education focused upon strength, discipline, and austerity. By the age of twelve, when most Greek boys had completed their schooling, the agoge made ever greater demands upon young Spartans:

> Boys lived in barracks under the constant watch of leaders they chose themselves and of the community's elders as well as of the paidonomos and his whip bearers.... Besides this everyday scrutiny, boys faced frequent tests, from massed brawls and dancing under the midsummer sun at the Gymnopaediae festival to stealing cheeses from the altar of the goddess Orthia, in order to pass from one stage of the agoge to the next. Only those who proved their fitness could eventually earn election to one of the common messes where Spartan males lived from the ages of twenty to thirty and ate their main meal for thirty years more. The agoge aimed to instill soldierly virtues: strength, endurance, solidarity.[21]

Perhaps it is for this reason that the great Athenian statesman Pericles once noted that Spartan youth had no childhood at all.

A striking effect of this prolonged training was a severed bond between fathers and sons; indeed, Spartan fathers had no significant role in raising their children: "The boy belonged, effectively, not to his own family but to the state, and the goal was to produce a strong and efficient military machine whose men were loyal only to each other and to Sparta."[22]

The nomadic peoples of Mongolia were another society that placed great importance upon war fighting and military expansion. Prior to the thirteenth century AD, localized raids between different nomadic groups in that region were not unusual, but Genghis Khan managed to either unite or subdue the various groups by 1206. Then he and his descendants led the Mongol confederation on a series of conquests that would lead to the creation of the largest empire the world had ever seen.

The Mongol army was organized in a strict hierarchy, and its fighters were ruthless. As it expanded across Asia (and eventually into Europe), the army laid siege to towns and cities. Those who refused to surrender were often massacred, and surviving soldiers incorporated into the Mongol military. Genghis Khan earned the loyalty of his growing army by distributing the spoils among his warriors, and by promoting officers based on merit rather than kinship. He demanded absolute allegiance.

These tactical and political strategies were grafted onto the nomadic pastoral culture of the Mongols:

> To be a Mongol man was to be a Mongol warrior. There is no word in the Mongol language for "soldier," and it is no exaggeration to say that the whole of a Mongol warrior's daily life was a preparation for war. The same techniques that were learnt for survival, for herding or for hunting had direct application in the Mongol campaigns.... The Mongol army may alternatively be regarded as a Mongol society arranged on a war footing.[23]

An essential part of childhood, particularly for boys, included herding and hunting with bow and arrow. These things were commonly done on horseback; consequently, Mongolian men were experts in horsemanship by the time they were conscripted into the army at the age of fifteen. The Mongol army relied heavily on its cavalry, which allowed it to move, strike, and if necessary withdraw from battle quickly.

But perhaps what is most remarkable about thirteenth century Mongol warfare is the fact that the entire family—and the entire society— was mobilized in support of the Khan's wars of conquest. In the words of historian John Masson Smith, Jr., "The Mongol armies were the Mongol people in arms: all adult males were soldiers, and all women, children of age to do herding, and animals served as the logistical 'tail' of an army," resulting in a constantly moving "citizens' army."[24]

As the Mongol Empire was disintegrating into smaller entities in the 1400s, Aztec society was beginning to take shape on the other side of the world. It offers yet another example of a culture in which warfare was a central part of the identity of a people. Eric Wolf has described Aztec society, also known as the Mexica, as one of Mesoamerica's "militaristic" societies (as opposed to "theocratic") because warfare was much more widespread in the last few centuries of the pre-Hispanic period. Furthermore, within Aztec society warriors had more power and influence compared to ancient cultures of the Olmec, Maya, Zapotec, or Mixtec.[25]

The Aztecs settled on an island in the lagoon of Texcoco, situated in central plateau of Mexico, in the 1340s. Here they established the famed Tenochtitlán, a sophisticated city connected to the mainland by a series of causeways. Some have suggested that the Aztecs served as mercenaries for other indigenous groups in the region before their ascent to imperial power in the late 1400s.[26]

Warfare was a defining feature of Aztec life. It was the means by which they established political and economic hegemony over their empire. Warfare also had religious significance, for most of the victims that the Aztecs sacrificed to their gods were captured in battle.[27]

Military service was mandatory for all Aztec men. Commoner families, who made up the majority of the population, prepared their sons for the military by having them do hard physical work and by strictly rationing their food. Such hardships were designed to instill discipline. By the time they were fifteen years old, boys were required to undergo rigorous military training at an institution called the *telpochcalli*. Here the lessons of home were reinforced and expanded: teams of youth were expected to complete public works projects such as the cleaning and repairing of causeways and aqueducts, and to carry firewood over long distances. Veteran warriors trained youth in a series of exercises which eventually culminated in battlefield experience:

> War captains...taught the young men to handle weapons, including shooting arrows from a bow, throwing darts with an *atlatl* (spearthrower), and holding a shield and a *maquahuitl* (a kind of saw-sword carved of wood and affixed with an edge of sharp obsidian razor blades). Youths were taken as apprentices to carry supplies and arms for the instructing warrior when he went to war.... Eventually, they would be allowed to participate fully in battle and to attempt to capture enemy prisoners for sacrifice.[28]

Mock battles between groups of boys—organized as competitions— were valued highly in Aztec society. Youth who deviated from *telpochcalli* training were publicly humiliated. Those who excelled might one day join the ranks of the elite warriors: the military orders known as the eagles (*cuacuauhtin*) and jaguars (*ocelomeh*). Aztec emperors granted special rights and privileges to the members of the orders: "the right to wear otherwise proscribed jewelry and daily military attire, to dress in cotton and wear sandals in the royal palace, to eat human flesh and drink *octli* (pulque) in public, to keep concubines, and to dine in the royal palaces."[29]

As in many militaristic societies, women were profoundly affected by warfare. Although they were not allowed to become warriors, Aztec women defended their families from external attacks, even if that meant jeopardizing their own lives. But as in any society undergoing constant warfare, women were most directly affected by the reality and the effects of death. Aztec women frequently lost their husbands, their brothers, and their children in battle, and the burdens of everyday life were much heavier as a result.

A range of experiences differentiates Spartan, Mongol, and Aztec societies. At the same time, certain commonalities appear: the dominance of state or empire over personal relationships; child-rearing and educational practices characterized by hard physical training and harsh discipline; the extraordinary role of military symbols in songs, rituals, and art; a cult of masculinity; and absorption of the family unit into the warfare state. It is worth considering the degree to which militarization has shaped our own society in similar ways.

War, Human Nature, and Anthropology

So many societies have engaged in warfare that it is tempting to ask: Is war a part of human nature? Are militarism and warfare inevitable?

A recent poll conducted by Zogby International reveals that nearly three out of five Americans agreed that "waging war is a part of human nature," which would imply that a majority of people in our country think that warfare is rooted in *Homo sapiens'* evolutionary past.[30] However, overwhelming anthropological evidence indicates that this is not true. In fact, it appears that "warfare is only an invention"—and a relatively recent one at that.[31] In 1940, Margaret Mead argued that organized armed conflict between rival groups—that is, the institution of warfare—had never been invented by some societies. Mead noted that some contemporary hunting and gathering groups, such as the Inuit of the Arctic region and the Lepchas of the Himalayas, did not engage in war, but instead resolved conflicts through other means. The ethnographic record reveals that humans

Figure 0.3:
Although the Mbuti
are avid hunters,
they are a non-
warring society.
(Photo courtesy of
Terese Hart.)

have been creative when it comes to ending conflicts: mediation, duels, ordeals, games and contests, court systems, self-help, and other means have all functioned as alternatives to war.

More recently, others have expanded upon Mead's hypothesis. In his book *Beyond War*, anthropologist Douglas Fry identifies seventy-four "nonwarring" societies, mostly hunter-gatherers such as the Mbuti of the Democratic Republic of Congo and the Semai of the Malay peninsula. (Many of these societies are not completely free from violence, but have used means other than organized armed conflict for settling disputes.) The evidence is clear: human warfare does not have evolutionary roots, and Fry argues that *Homo sapiens* has "a substantial capacity for dealing with conflicts non-violently." He suggests that this might help humanity pave the way towards a future in which warring is less common.[32]

Another anthropologist, R. Brian Ferguson, has conducted more than thirty years of research on war (in which he has attempted to develop a rigorous and testable theory to explain war in materialist, political, and historical terms by synthesizing many anthropological studies) and has reached similar conclusions. He summarizes his findings in an essay entitled "Ten Points on War," and notes that "Our Species Is Not Biologically Destined for War" and "War Is Not an Inescapable Part of Social Existence."[33] After presenting a devastating critique of those who argue that humans have an innate predisposition to violence, Ferguson systematically outlines six preconditions which make war more likely to occur, namely: (1) sedentary agriculture (which began approximately 10,000 years ago); (2) increased population density; (3) pronounced social hierarchies; (4) trade, particularly of prestige goods; (5) "bounded social

INTRODUCTION

groups"; and (6) "serious ecological reversals." War became common once a series of long-term processes was set in motion:

(1) as those preconditions became more common, war began in more places; (2) war spread, often quite gradually, into surrounding areas; (3) the rise of ancient states projected militarism deep into their peripheries and along trade routes; and (4) Western expansion since the late fifteenth century often generated or intensified war in contact zones.[34]

War is a relatively recent human invention that has spread as humanity has become more agricultural, more organized into hierarchical state societies and expanding empires, and more involved in cross-cultural conquest and trade.

Ferguson concludes with a disturbing point: "people have the *capacity* to learn, even to enjoy, war and build it into their social lives and institutions." Furthermore, he argues, "once a given society is internally adapted for war, making war becomes much easier—a necessity, even, for the reproduction of existing social relations. Commentators have often compared war to a disease, but a more apt analogy is an addiction."[35]

About This Book

This book is a collection of essays that diagnoses the symptoms of America's addiction to war and examines the effects of this addiction. It is a critique of the ways in which our own society has become "internally adapted for war," making it possible for some people to enjoy militarism, to profit from it, and to build it into family life, schooling, the professions, and other parts of our society. In short, it is an inquiry into what it means to live and work in a warfare state.[36] I have written the book to critically explore the processes by which American militarization has come to influence and in some cases dominate US scientific research, educational centers, political systems, economic life, and popular culture. For half a century our society has largely ignored President Eisenhower's prescient warning about the unwarranted influence of the military-industrial complex, and now we are left to confront the consequences.

The first part of the book, "Basic Training," examines two instances in which militaristic values have transformed social norms and attitudes in our own society. Chapter 1, entitled "Spy Camp for Kids," considers the ways in which education is being reshaped to meet the needs of military intelligence agencies. The following chapter, "Shattered Taboo," dissects the processes by which popular attitudes about torture and other forms of "extreme interrogation" are shifting in the context of the so-called war on terror.

The next part of the book, "Enlisting Culture," analyzes how elements within the US military establishment—and corporations that do its contract work—are seeking to recruit "cultural knowledge" experts, particularly social scientists, for war fighting. To illustrate how this is occurring, chapter 3 (entitled "Towards Mercenary Anthropology?") focuses upon the US Army's new counterinsurgency field manual, which relies heavily upon social scientists' work. This is followed by "*The Arab Mind* and Abu Ghraib," a chapter that reviews the alleged use of an ethnography about Arabs by American interrogators at Iraqi prisons. Chapter 5, entitled "Human Terrain," explores the genesis and development of the Human Terrain System, a $250 million Pentagon program to embed social scientists with combat brigades in Iraq and Afghanistan.

The last part of the book, "Controlling Behavior," can be read as a critical analysis of American and British methods of counterinsurgency and imperial policing in colonial and neocolonial settings. Chapter 6, "Counterinsurgency in the Colonies," focuses upon United States efforts in the Philippine Islands in the period immediately following the Spanish-American war of 1898 and British methods of indirect rule in the Middle East and Africa in the early twentieth century. The next chapter, "Going 'Tribal'," examines how the Pentagon is deploying "tribal engagement" strategies in Iraq and Afghanistan today.

Throughout the essays, several themes emerge: public acceptance of (or passive acquiescence to) the widespread presence of the military in US society; the rise of obedient technical experts and simultaneous disappearance of critical thinkers and generalists; frequent dehumanization of people in other societies; a naive belief in American exceptionalism; the prevalence of marketing and public relations approaches to dealing with complex social problems; the drift to imperialism (though with a different label); an apparent willingness on the part of scientists and other professionals to abandon ethical principles; a reappearance of "dissociated persons" out of touch with their own capacity to transcend violence;[37] the artistic, academic, and cultural embrace of militarism; and the predominance of apathy, triviality, and escapism in American life.

None of these trends is inevitable or irreversible. It is my hope that this collection of essays might play a small role in helping to change the drift.

Notes

1. For an account of the event see Leonel Sánchez, "Hero Worship Puts Focus on Sailor Dad," *San Diego Union-Tribune*, August 6, 2009.

2. Nick Turse has recently expanded Eisenhower's concept by calling it "America's military-industrial-technological-entertainment-academic-media-corporate" complex. Nick Turse, *The Complex: How the Military Invades Our Everyday Lives* (New York: Metropolitan Books, 2008).

3. Rene Rodríguez, "*GI Joe: The Rise of Cobra*: It's More Toy Commercial Than Movie," *Miami Herald Blog*, August 7, 2009, http://miamiherald.typepad.com/reeling/2009/08/review-gi-joe-the-rise-of-cobra.html (accessed March 15, 2010).

4. Paramount's marketing strategy is analyzed in Claudia Eller and Ben Fritz, "Paramount Pictures Waves the Flag for 'GI Joe,'" *Los Angeles Times*, August 3, 2009.

5. Rob Moore quoted in ibid.

6. Russ Klein quoted in Burger King Corporation, "Burger King Corp. Beams Up Movie Tie-Ins with Paramount Pictures," May 4, 2009, http://investor.bk.com/phoenix.zhtml?c=87140&p=irol-newsArticle&ID=1283540&highlight= (accessed March 15, 2010).

7. Jay Wilkins quoted in Margaret Chabris, "'GI Joe: The Rise of Cobra' Advances on 7-Eleven Stores," *7–11 News Room*, June 30, 2009, http://www.7-eleven.com/NewsRoom/GIJoeTheRiseOfCobraAdvancesOn7Eleven/tabid/316/Default.aspx (accessed March 15, 2010).

8. For descriptions of product placement in the *GI Joe* movie, see Electronic Arts Inc., "EA Calls All GI Joe Fans to Report for Duty," August 4, 2009, http://investor.ea.com/releasedetail.cfm?releaseid=400911 (accessed March 15, 2010); Jim Goldman, "Cisco Reports for Duty in 'GI Joe,'" *CNBC Business News*, August 11, 2009, http://www.cnbc.com/id/32375230 (accessed March 15, 2010); and "Dubble Bubble Product Placement in GI Joe," *Product Placement News*, September 9, 2009, http://www.productplacement.biz/200909103220/News/Movies/dubble-bubble-product-placement-in-gi-joe.html (accessed March 15, 2010).

9. Accounts of National Guard and Army involvement in the *GI Joe* movie can be found in Kimberly Holman, "Yo, Joe! Guard Adds Real-Life Heroes to GI Movie," *Grizzly: Official Newsmagazine of the California National Guard*, September 2009, 4; and in Gary Sheftick and Grafton Pritchartt, "Face of Defense: Soldiers Bring Life to 'GI Joe,'" *American Forces Press Service*, August 11, 2009, http://www.defenselink.mil/news/newsarticle.aspx?id=55441 (accessed March 15, 2010).

10. Scott Lusk quoted in Edmond Lococo, "Lockheed, Sikorsky Grab Villain's Roles in Film 'Transformers,'" *Bloomberg News Service*, July 3, 2007, http://www.bloomberg.com/apps/news?pid=20601109&sid=aeNvfvWH13yY&refer=news (accessed March 15, 2010).

11. William Hamilton, "Toying with War," *The Age* (Melbourne, Australia), May 4, 2003, http://www.theage.com.au/articles/2003/05/03/1051876901536.html (accessed March 15, 2010).

12. Ben Fritz, "'GI Joe' Opens to $100 Million Worldwide, But Will It Hold?" *Los Angeles Times,* August 9, 2009.

13. Hugh Gusterson's research on cultural militarization includes more that a year of participant-observation conducted in Livermore, California, where he interviewed hundreds of people who worked in one of the world's largest nuclear weapons laboratories. See Hugh Gusterson, *Nuclear Rites: A Weapons Laboratory at the End of the Cold War* (Berkeley: University of California Press, 1998). A more recent book includes a textual analysis that explores the meanings of Hollywood films from multiple perspectives. See Hugh Gusterson, *People of the Bomb* (Minneapolis: University of Minnesota Press, 2004). Gusterson wrote the quoted passage as part of a longer chapter co-written with David Price and I. See Roberto J. González, Hugh Gusterson, and David Price, "Introduction: War, Culture, and Counterinsurgency," in *The Counter-Counterinsurgency Manual,* ed. Network of Concerned Anthropologists (Chicago: Prickly Paradigm Press, 2009), 6–7. For more research on violence in media and movies, see Paul Virilio, *War and Cinema* (New York: Verso, 1989) and James Der Derian, *Virtuous War: Mapping the Military-Industrial-Media-Entertainment Network* (New York: Routledge, 2001).

14. Turse, *The Complex*. See also Dave Grossman and Gloria DeGaetano, *Stop Teaching Our Kids to Kill* (New York: Crown, 1998); Chris Hedges, *War Is a Force That Gives Us Meaning* (New York: Anchor, 2003); Robertson Allen, "Games without Tears, Wars without Frontiers," presented at the annual meetings of the American Anthropological Society (December 6, 2009), Philadelphia, PA.; Beatrice Jauregui, "Military Communitas? Re-centering the Citizen-Soldier Interface at the US Army Experience Center," presented at the conference "Reconsidering American Power" at the University of Chicago (April 24, 2009).

15. Catherine Lutz, "The Military Normal: Feeling at Home with Counterinsurgency in the United States," in ibid., 23. For a typical example of *haute couture* military chic, see the March 2010 edition of the US *Vogue,* particularly the photo spread by Mario Testino, "Military Issue," *Vogue,* March 2010, 446–458. Twelve full-page photos feature svelte models wearing khaki and olive drab blouses, coats, hats, shoes, and accessories by Louis Vuitton, Max Mara, Ralph Lauren, Gaultier, Balmain, and Chloé among many others. Among the products is a $300 dog tag necklace by Gucci. For similar photo collections, see Matt Jones and Isabel Dupre, "Military Tactics," *Marie Claire,* March 2010, 160–169; Jean-Baptiste Mondino, "Combat Ready: Fashion Deploys for Action, Ready March!" *T-Magazine,* March 2010, 162–167; Anne Monoky, "Utilitarian Chic," *Harper's Bazaar,* January 2010, 142–143.

16. Richard H. Kohn, "The Danger of Militarization in an Endless 'War' on Terrorism," *Journal of Military History,* January 2009, 177–208. Kohn's qualitative analysis focuses upon the ways in which political institutions, the US legal

system, and shifts in cultural mores have changed in the post-World War II period, and the post-9/11 period in particular. Another troubling trend is the militarization of our county's southern border, which more and more resembles a low-intensity conflict zone claiming thousands of casualties each year. See Timothy Dunn and José Palafox, "Militarization of the Border," in *Oxford Encyclopedia of Latinos and Latinas in the United States, Volume 3*, ed. Suzanne Oboler and Deana J. Gonzalez, (Oxford, UK: Oxford University Press, 2005), 150–155.

17. Andrew J. Bacevich, *The New American Militarism: How Americans Are Seduced by War* (New York: Oxford University Press, 2005), 1, 255. In May 2007, Bacevich's own son was killed by an improvised explosive device in Iraq.

18. Lutz, "The Military Normal," 28–29.

19. Catherine Lutz, *Homefront: A Military City and the American 20th Century* (Boston: Beacon Press, 2001), 3.

20. Mark Golden, "Childhood in Ancient Greece," in *Coming of Age in Ancient Greece*, ed. Jenifer Neils and John H. Oakley (New Haven, CT: Yale University Press, 2003), 20.

21. Ibid.

22. H.A. Shapiro, "Fathers and Sons, Men and Boys," in ibid., 107.

23. Stephen Turnbull, *Mongol Warrior 1200–1350* (London: Osprey Publishing, 2003), 26.

24. John Masson Smith, Jr. quoted in ibid., 26.

25. Eric R. Wolf, *Sons of the Shaking Earth* (Chicago: University of Chicago Press, 1957), 130–151.

26. Manuel Aguilar-Moreno, *Handbook to Life in the Aztec World* (Oxford, UK: Oxford University Press), 100.

27. Wolf, 132. See also David Carrasco, *Daily Life of the Aztecs: People of the Sun and Earth* (Westport, CT: Greenwood Press, 1998).

28. Wolf, 145–147.

29. Aguilar-Moreno, 105.

30. John Zogby, "War, Peace, and Politics," *The Way We'll Be*, September 26, 2009, http://www.zogby.com/blog2/index.php/category/war/.

31. Margaret Mead, "Warfare Is Only an Invention—Not a Biological Necessity," *Asia* 40 (August 1940): 402–405.

32. Douglas Fry, *Beyond War: The Human Potential for Peace* (New York: Oxford University Press, 2007), 2. See also Leslie E. Sponsel, "Reflections on the Possibilities of a Nonkilling Society," in *Toward a Nonkilling Paradigm*, ed. Joam Evans Pim (Honolulu: Center for Global Nonkilling, 2009), 35–72.

33. R. Brian Ferguson, "Ten Points on War," *Social Analysis* 52, no. 2 (2008): 33–34.

34. Ibid., 35.

35. Ibid., 34, 40.

36. The term "warfare state" was used as early as the 1960s to describe US society. See Fred J. Cook, *The Warfare State* (New York: Macmillan, 1962).

37. Stanley Diamond, "War and the Dissociated Personality," in *War: The Anthropology of Armed Conflict and Aggression*, ed. Morton Fried, Marvin Harris, and Robert Murphy (Garden City, NJ: Natural History Press, 1968), 188.

INTRODUCTION

Part I
Basic Training

Chapter 1
Spy Camp for Kids

In July 2005, a select group of fifteen- to nineteen-year-old high school students participated in a week-long summer program called "Spy Camp" in the Washington DC area. The program included a field trip to the CIA's headquarters in Langley, Virginia, an intelligence simulation exercise, and a visit to the $35 million International Spy Museum. According to the Spy Museum's web site, visiting groups have the option of choosing from three different scavenger hunts in which teams are pitted against one another in activities ranging "from code-breaking to deceptive maneuvers.... Each team will be armed with a top secret bag of tricks to help solve challenging questions" whose answers can be found in the museum.[1]

On the surface, the program sounds like fun and games, and after reading about the program one might guess that it was organized by an imaginative social studies teacher. But for some, Spy Camp was more than just fun and games—it was very serious business. The high school program was carried out by Trinity University of Washington DC—a predominantly African-American university with an overwhelmingly female student population—as part of a pilot grant from the US Office of the Director of National Intelligence (DNI) to create an "Intelligence Community Center of Academic Excellence" (or IC Center).

According to the Office of the DNI, the goal of the IC Center program is to increase the pool of future applicants for careers in the CIA, the FBI, the Defense Intelligence Agency (DIA), and the dozen or so other organizations that make up the US intelligence community—in less euphemistic terms, America's spy agencies.

The idea for IC Centers came about in the wake of the September 11, 2001, plane hijackings, when both the US Senate and House of Representatives held hearings about how the country's spy agencies missed clues that might have foiled the World Trade Center and Pentagon attacks. As part of the response, Congress passed a sweeping law called the Intelligence Reform and Terrorism Prevention Act (S 2845). In the House Intelligence Committee hearings prior to the bill's passage, California representative Jane Harman (Democrat from California and chair of the

House Intelligence Committee) put it bluntly: "We can no longer expect an Intelligence Community that is mostly male and mostly white to be able to monitor and infiltrate suspicious organizations or terrorist groups. *We need spies that look like their targets*, CIA officers who speak the dialects that terrorists use, and FBI agents who can speak to Muslim women that might be intimidated by men."[2]

For this reason, the IC Center program wasn't aimed at students attending Harvard, Yale, Princeton, or other Ivy League schools, or internationally renowned universities like Stanford or Berkeley or University of Chicago. The program's architects consciously directed it at schools where minority students are the majority—predominantly African-American and Latino universities which are chronically underfunded. Perhaps this reflects the shape of "multiculturalism" in a militarized society: the government's spy agencies and armed forces recruit minority students from low-income regions in order to "monitor and infiltrate" people ("targets") that look and speak like them.

Figure 1.1: The CIA, the DIA, and other spy agencies are aggressively recruiting minority youth with advertisements, scholarship programs, and university "centers for academic excellence." (Image courtesy of Central Intelligence Agency.)

Since 2005, Trinity's IC Center has had its funding renewed, and Spy Camp has continued every summer since. In fact, beginning in 2006 the Director of National Intelligence dramatically expanded the IC Center program (of which the Spy Camp is only one part), and today there are a total of twenty-one such centers throughout the country. These are located at California State University-San Bernardino, Carnegie-Mellon University, Clemson University, Clark Atlanta University, Florida A&M University, Florida International University, Howard University, Miles College (Alabama), Norfolk State University (Virginia), North Carolina A&T University, Pennsylvania State University, Tennessee State University, Trinity University, University of Maryland-College Park, University of Nebraska, University of New Mexico, University of North Carolina-Wilmington, University of Texas-El Paso, University of Texas-Pan American, University of Washington, Virginia Tech, and Wayne State University (Michigan). Significantly, most of these universities have large numbers of minority students, which corresponds with the original objectives of the IC Center program's architects. Tens of millions of dollars have been appropriated for the programs, with some centers receiving individual grants of up to $750,000. According to the *Washington Post*, the DNI planned to expand the program to twenty universities by the year 2015. Apparently, it has met this goal far ahead of schedule.[3] (Since 2008, the DNI has included universities with significantly higher percentages of "white" students.)

This is not the first time that US military and intelligence agencies have funneled large sums of money into universities to advance their interests. The 1958 National Defense Education Act led to the creation of dozens of language and area studies programs focused upon Russia, Latin America, and Southeast Asia, but those centers generally did not limit scholars' ability to pursue a wide range of research, including critical social science research building upon anti-imperial and leftist scholarship.[4] By contrast, it appears that the IC Centers and other new recruitment programs have much more focused and narrow objectives: curriculum to "build the skill sets needed in the IC professions," "pre-collegiate outreach," and the hosting of conferences "to heighten IC issues and careers" are the priorities spelled out by the Director of National Intelligence.

Judging from some students' responses, it seems that the DNI programs are making an impact. News reports from college newspapers begin to tell the story. Najam Hassan, a nineteen-year-old student at Trinity University, said that "It's a good opportunity. I have interest in the FBI." Reagan Thompson, who is seventeen, told a reporter, "I want to be a spy when I grow up. You learn different perspectives and it opens your mind." Meriam Fadli, also seventeen, said: "I was like 'Oh my God, I am so joining the FBI'.... She (the speaker) made it seem so interesting. It's not like a dull office job." Leah Martin, a twenty-one-year-old, decided that she wanted an intelligence career after getting involved in the program: "You get to travel, to do something different every day, you're challenged in your work and you get to serve your country. How cool is that?"[5] The picture that emerges from these and other comments is that students are drawn to the IC Centers because they offer exciting, challenging experiences that will serve the country—not unlike the reasons that many young people decide to enlist in the armed forces. TV series that glorify law enforcement agents (*CSI: Crime Scene Investigation*), intelligence operatives (*24*), and military personnel (*JAG*) have greatly romanticized these careers.

University administrators and faculty like the IC Centers for other reasons. Obviously there are the issues of funding and job placement for graduating students. But some also emphasize the importance of building an ethnically and culturally diverse pool of intelligence agents who might blend in more easily abroad. Norfolk State University geology professor David Padgett told the journal *Diverse Online*, "When a lot of higher education funding shifted after September 11 into defense, a lot of Black colleges weren't in a position to take advantage of it. We saw an opening. In order to have a diverse work force in the intelligence arena, you have to get to minority-serving institutions. In intelligence, people have to go to areas populated by people of color."[6]

Economist Dennis Soden, who is executive director of the Institute for Policy and Economic Development, a University of Texas-El Paso unit that was awarded an IC Center grant, had this to say:

> In the intelligence community before, it was really a white male, Ivy League, Big-10 kind of place. All these guys who went to Harvard, Wisconsin, and Yale looked like America and they got the jobs and ended up just slapping each other on the back telling each other how great they were. Of course, we found out they weren't very good because they couldn't find WMDs and they couldn't figure out what was going on. There is a real sense that the agencies were just recruiting from the same places all the time and getting the same people over and over again—it was like a type of inbreeding.... The US-Mexico border is now a national security interest, but who really understands it? A guy at Yale who takes Spanish for a few years doesn't really understand it. The idea is to get people both for domestic and international intelligence purposes who reflect the country and understand all of its nuances.[7]

The Office of the Director of National Intelligence promoted the IC Center program heavily during its first few years of existence. The original IC Center program plan is a twenty-five-page document that clearly lays out goals and procedures. Under the title "Pre-College/High School Outreach" is the subheading "Summer Camp (for elementary and junior high students)." The program plan notes: "Institutions may consider coordinating summer camps for junior high students. The camps should be at least one week in duration with high energy programs that excite the participants.... They should focus on developing the critical skill of 'thinking before you act.'"[8]

Though it is not clear whether or not elementary and junior high students have been included in IC Center programs so far, the Office of the DNI clearly supports this idea. (The CIA, the FBI, the Department of Homeland Security, the National Security Agency, and the Defense Intelligence Agency all have "Kids' Page" websites that include games, puzzles, and occasionally, sanitized histories of the agencies.) Nearly all universities that have received funding for IC Centers have created high school outreach programs. For example, Norfolk State's program included a simulation exercise in which faculty asked Nashville-area high schoolers to locate ten simulated "weapons of mass destruction" hidden in the city using GPS locators.[9]

The name "Spy Camp" was only used once, at Trinity University. Now, the high-school outreach programs are known in many places as "Summer Intelligence Seminars."

Recruiting Intelligence?

Though there are numerous differences from one school to the next, all twenty-one universities appear to be involved in three kinds of activities apart from high-school outreach programs like Spy Camp.

Curriculum development—especially the creation of new classes—is a common process for IC Center schools. Many participating universities are creating new majors and minors in "intelligence studies," and developing new courses to meet the demands of spy agencies. For example, Trinity University developed a new course entitled, "East vs. West: Just War, Jihad and Crusade, 1050–1450." While the title itself is benign (though it conjures up images of the "clash of civilizations" popularized by historian Samuel Huntington), the syllabus reportedly states that the course "seeks to develop the critical/analytical and writing skills that are particularly important to the intelligence community."[10] (We are left to wonder what the costs of favoring some kinds of writing—perhaps intelligence briefs and PowerPoint presentations—over others might be.) In some cases new masters' programs are also being developed, which might result in faculty hiring. New classes in languages deemed important to US security are being established as well (particularly in Arabic and Mandarin), and many campuses are purchasing books and films to support these new courses.

Another group of activities includes organized events such as academic colloquia and guest lectures. Like all university special events, these can be intellectually stimulating, particularly when a thought-provoking or controversial speaker is invited to speak. But what should occur when a guest lecture or other campus event becomes a recruiting pitch for spy agencies?

Finally, nearly all of the IC Centers include scholarship and travel abroad programs. The same law that brought the IC Centers into existence also created the new "Intelligence Community Scholarship Program" (ICSP). Scholarship fellows take required intelligence-related courses and are typically eligible for study abroad experiences and internships with spy agencies. According to the law, ICSP students who do not take jobs with US intelligence agencies after graduating are required "to repay the costs of their education plus penalties assessed at three times the legally allowed interest rate."[11] Like PRISP (the Pat Roberts Intelligence Scholarship Program, a $25,000 one-year scholarship for undergraduate and graduate students which requires them to work for the CIA after graduation), the identities of students are not publicly announced. Congress established PRISP in 2004 as a kind of academic version of the ROTC (Reserve Officer Training Corps) program: it was designed to combine intelligence training skills with academic areas of expertise, such as anthropology or political science. Since its creation PRISP has placed hundreds of students in an unknown number of university classrooms. Although critics have referred to such programs as "debt bondage to constrain student career choices," President Barack Obama's director of national intelligence, Dennis Blair, announced in 2009 plans to make PRISP permanent.[12]

In and of themselves, these activities sound benign, even desirable. After all, who could argue against funding for new courses, films, guest speakers, conferences, and scholarships, particularly during this period of chronic underfunding of higher education? But there is a subtle danger posed by the deluge of funds reaching universities through IC Centers—a danger similar to that posed by military funding. Anthropologist Hugh Gusterson has written eloquently about the ways in which this can twist the education process over time. A wide range of problems comes into focus:

When research that could be funded by neutral civilian agencies is instead funded by the military, knowledge is subtly militarized and bent in the way a tree is bent by a prevailing wind. The public comes to accept that basic academic research on religion and violence "belongs" to the military; scholars who never saw themselves as doing military research now do; maybe they wonder if their access to future funding is best secured by not criticizing US foreign policy; a discipline whose independence from military and corporate funding fueled the kind of critical thinking a democracy needs is now compromised; and the priorities of the military further define the basic terms of public and academic debate.[13]

In short, the IC Centers could further threaten the notion of the classroom as a free marketplace of ideas—a threat that is proving to be very real due to the powerful influence exerted on college campuses by multinational corporations and other commercial interests. The fact that the intelligence community includes heavy representation from Pentagon agencies (such as DIA and Marine Corps Intelligence, to name but two) and is closely linked to military contract firms further underscores the significance of Gusterson's words.

Close to Home

For me, learning about the IC Centers struck close to home—literally. I first found out about IC Centers from an anthropology professor at a participating university, the University of Texas-Pan American (UTPA), located along the United States-Mexico border deep in south Texas. The professor was interested in seeing an article I had written in which I criticized the "military-anthropology complex"—a web connecting US social scientists to the Pentagon and military contract firms for counterinsurgency work. I learned that some of the key players at UTPA's IC Center were anthropologists (including a college dean), and to their credit, they were interested in learning more about the history of such relationships and ethical dilemmas that might arise as a result. I sent my article to the anthropology professor, along with a request to interview the dean of the College of Social Sciences—a request which was rapidly granted.

UTPA is located seven miles away from my childhood home, and my parents both graduated from the university when it was called Pan American College. My first academic job was at UTPA more than twenty years ago. I tutored local high school students as part of the Texas

Pre-Freshman Engineering Program. Now I planned a trip to the university's anthropology department that would coincide with a summer visit to my hometown.

Arriving at the university brought back many memories. As I walked toward the social science building in the sweltering tropical heat of a south Texas summer afternoon, the sprawling campus, the long arched corridors connecting its buildings, and the beautiful palm trees lining its perimeter made a renewed impression on my mind.

UTPA is not a small university—it has about 30,000 students, nearly 90 percent of whom are Latino. More than one out of three faculty are Latino, and it has more full-time Latino faculty members than any other Texas university. I learned that like many other universities around the country, UTPA has not grown quickly enough to meet local demand. Administrators and donors have tended to give strong support to UTPA's engineering, health science, and business schools, while social science and humanities departments have sometimes struggled.

For these reasons, the IC Center grant was especially attractive to the College of Social Sciences. The applicants were able to get faculty from each of the colleges to support the grant proposal and letters of support from the university president and a local school district superintendent. Their efforts paid off handsomely: in October 2006, the DNI awarded UTPA a grant of $500,000 a year for five years, for a total of $2.5 million.

Within a year, UTPA's IC Center staff organized a high-school outreach program—a five-day camp involving twenty local students—which took place in August 2007. They called it "Got Intelligence?" (students wore black T-shirts with the phrase silk-screened across the chest), and according to the UTPA magazine *Los Arcos*, students "heard from speakers from intelligence community agencies, such as the CIA and FBI."[14] Other activities included workshops for geographic information systems training, resume preparation, and a solar-powered vehicle competition.

Just two months earlier, a smaller group of UTPA students had an even more dramatic experience: a one-month all expenses paid study abroad trip to Qingdao, China. This was reportedly the first trip ever taken by a UTPA group to China. Accounts of the trip in the *Monitor* (the local daily newspaper) did not mention the word "intelligence," nor the Office of the Director of National Intelligence. Instead, the "Center for Academic Excellence" was described as "promot[ing] international research and analytical thinking skills."[15] Later, the study abroad program was expanded to include Morocco.

The dean was very optimistic about the future of the IC Center. He described ongoing efforts to create a new minor in intelligence and, eventually, a masters' degree program in "global security studies and leadership." He noted that courses in Mandarin Chinese would soon be offered for the first time at UTPA, and there were plans to introduce Arabic language courses in the near future. When I asked about whether he was concerned about the possibility that students might be corralled into dangerous careers with agencies that have a record of human rights abuses, the dean emphasized that this was primarily a program for better global understanding, not an intelligence gathering program. (In fact, the IC Center eventually changed its name to the "Integrated Global Knowledge and Understanding Collaboration" or IGKNU.) Even so, he acknowledged that the IC Center offered many opportunities for dialogue with "agency people" for internship opportunities and career placement for college graduates.

The UTPA IC Center staff were cordial to me, but they seemed to have a benign view of spy agencies, maybe even a naive view given headlines in recent years. For example, they expressed the idea that in future generations, more ethnically diverse intelligence agencies will likely lead to better policies. Others seemed convinced that they would be able to keep the program focused on sharpening students' critical thinking and other skills not limited to spy work. They repeatedly emphasized the idea that in a period of scarce resources, the IC Center grant was beneficial because of the generous funds that were made available to students and faculty. There was little concern that UTPA's base of knowledge might be "bent in the way a tree is bent by a prevailing wind."

Dissenting Voices

Not everyone at UTPA approved of the IC Center. A group made up of students from the university's chapter of MEChA (a nationwide Chicano student organization) and faculty members voiced opposition to UTPA's participation in the DNI grant before it had been awarded, and I contacted several of them.

These critics brought up a wide range of concerns. Some expressed concern that the Center might lead to bias in the classroom, or a biased orientation of books and other materials purchased in the library. In the words of a professor opposed to the IC Center, "I don't think they're going to be buying history books that examine the CIA's crimes in Central America or the abuses of graduates of the School of the Americas." (I heard later that some university staff designated one section of the main library the "spy room" because it houses a large number of intelligence-related journals and books acquired for the IC Center.) The professor noted that IC Center personnel appeared to suffer from a lack of awareness of the dark history of the CIA, the FBI, and other intelligence agencies.

UTPA political science professor Samuel Freeman argued that "just as intelligence agencies are penetrating our universities today with phony 'Intelligence Community Centers of Academic Excellence'—like the center recently established at UTPA unfortunately—the CIA, in the 1950s and 1960s conspired with unethical university professors and administrators."[16] Freeman's concerns linked intelligence agencies' current recruiting efforts to a broader history of co-option on university campuses.

Some critics were concerned about the way in which the intelligence agencies might be manipulating diversity to meet their own interests, rather than the interests of students. A graduate student I spoke with was particularly galled by the cloak of multiculturalism used by the DNI and the IC Center to promote the program.

Another student, Nadezhda Garza, reportedly said of the UTPA program: "At this point, you have to decide if opportunity is really opportunity.... The [intelligence community] isn't pushing you academically, it's pushing you to recruitment. The [intelligence community] has its own agenda."[17] A report in the *San Antonio Express-News* appeared to confirm Garza's words, noting that "CIA recruiters were on [the UTPA] campus visiting mainly with students in the program who are earning an intelligence studies certificate."[18]

Still another concern expressed by critics of the program had to do with the safety of UTPA students participating in study abroad programs. "What kind of risk are students in China going to face if that country's government knows that they are connected to the Office of the Director of National Intelligence?" asked a professor. He argued that Chinese officials might view them as spies.

Finally, both students and professors were alarmed at the possibility that academic freedom at UTPA might be threatened by the IC Center. What would happen to students or faculty who refused to go along with the current produced by waves of IC Center funding? How would university administrators (or campus police) deal with students or faculty who actively protested guest speakers from the CIA or FBI? According to the minutes of an April 2006 UTPA faculty senate meeting, a group of MEChA students expressed concerns over the proposed IC Center ranging from "possible restrictions to academic freedom" to "exploitation of UTPA

CHAPTER 1

students by intelligence communities."[19] When local media ran a handful of stories on the UTPA IC Center in 2007, reporters generally ignored the many criticisms that had been raised by concerned faculty and students. The CIA, FBI, and other spy agencies appeared to be scoring a silent coup at UTPA, a pattern that would be repeated at other universities as the IC Center program diffused throughout the country.[20]

Ignoring the Elephant in the Room

Once I began combing through dozens of documents, articles, government reports, websites, and interview transcripts, it became clear that many university administrators, Congressional representatives, and educators were ignoring the elephant in the room: outrageous and illegal actions that US spy agencies have been involved with over the last sixty years. In particular, I found no discussion of the ethical implications of involving universities with the CIA and other intelligence agencies. I began to ask: "What happened to teaching critical thinking skills at the IC Centers?"

As Stephen Kinzer has noted in his book *Overthrow*, the CIA has been deeply involved in orchestrating coups, assassinations, and civil wars in such diverse places as Iran, Guatemala, Chile, Indonesia, and El Salvador, among many others over the past century.[21] We now know that the CIA supported social science research throughout the 1950s and 1960s to perfect psychological torture techniques that were outsourced to Vietnam, Argentina, and other countries. [22] Phillip Agee was so shocked by the CIA's covert operations in support of Latin American dictatorships that in 1968 he quit the Agency and spent the rest of his life criticizing it.[23]

In recent years many people have exposed illegal acts carried out with impunity by United States intelligence agencies. Here are a few that illustrate the scope of operations:

- December 2002: The *Washington Post* runs a front-page story describing how CIA operatives are sending suspected members of al Qaeda to third countries for brutal interrogations.[24] The report includes a chilling quote from a US official involved in capturing and transferring accused terrorists: "If you don't violate someone's rights some of the time, you probably aren't doing your job."

- November 2005: Investigative journalist Dana Priest reveals the presence of a secret CIA network of overseas prisons in Eastern Europe, southeast Asia, and other regions. The prisons (called "black sites" by CIA officials) are located in countries whose police and intelligence agencies are infamous for their egregious human rights violations, which have been extensively documented by human rights organizations.[25]

- March 2006: Former CIA analyst Ray McGovern returns his Intelligence Commendation Award to protest the CIA's involvement in torture—a gross violation of the Geneva Conventions—and declares that the Agency altered its reports on weapons of mass destruction in Iraq under pressure from the White House.[26]

- April 2006: Former AT&T technician Mark Klein issues a public statement in which he describes AT&T's cooperation in a secret National Security Agency (NSA) operation that would allow it to conduct "vacuum-cleaner surveillance of all the data crossing the internet," a form of wiretapping prohibited by the US Constitution.[27] (The NSA is among the agencies making up the intelligence community.)

- December 2005: The *New York Times* describes the NSA and Defense Intelligence Agency's use of illegal wiretapping at the request of the Bush administration. The report is based in part on leaks from NSA whistleblower Russell Tice. In a letter to Congress, Tice wrote, "It's with my oath as a US intelligence officer weighing heavy on my mind that I wish to report to Congress acts I believe are unlawful and unconstitutional."[28]

- February 2007: An Italian court indicts twenty-six US intelligence agents, most of them from the CIA, for the 2003 kidnapping of an Egyptian cleric, Usama Nasr. Nasr was taken to Egypt where he was held for four years and reportedly tortured before being freed by an Egyptian court that ruled his detention to be "unfounded."[29]

- January 2007: A German court issues arrest warrants for thirteen US intelligence agents (mostly CIA) involved in the 2003 kidnapping of a German citizen, Khaled el Masri. Masri was taken to Afghanistan, jailed for five months, and physically and psychologically tortured before being released without charges.[30]

- June 2007: Following a Freedom of Information Act request filed in 1992, the CIA releases to the public a set of reports detailing illegal Agency activities from the 1950s to the mid-1970s. The report includes revelations of illegal wiretapping, domestic surveillance, assassination plots, and experimentation on human subjects.[31]

Figure 1.2: After kidnapping Khaled el Masri, CIA agents are thought to have taken him to a secret prison complex known as the "Salt Pit," near Kabul, Afghanistan. (Photo courtesy of Trevor Paglen.)

Although these events (and many other similar violations) were making headlines at the time the IC Centers were established, few of the news articles about the Centers mentioned any dilemmas that might be posed by university collaboration with the agencies in question. Nor did they ask whether it was appropriate for institutions of higher education to be accepting money linked to such sources. It was as if the 1975–1976 Church Committee reports of the US Senate—which famously and publicly exposed the legal and political abuses carried out by US intelligence agencies—had never existed.

Some scholars did make these connections, and raised questions that were inconvenient for proponents of the program. For example, independent scholar and writer Kamala Platt noted that in south Texas, "decades of being among the poorest and most underserved regions of the country have laid the groundwork" for the program. In many ways, student participation in IC Centers resembles participation in JROTC programs. As anthropologist Gina Pérez argues, JROTC is "deeply rooted in notions of citizenship [and service to country]...[and] informed by the realities of a local political economy with extremely limited employment opportunities for working-class youth." Consequently, both IC Centers and JROTC might be seen as programs in which "notions of exceptional citizenship [are] anchored in a distinctive and particularly valorized military culture."[32]

But a militarized culture can lead to intellectual, moral, and ethical dilemmas. According to Kamala Platt, a range of contradictions inherently accompany such initiatives:

> Underlying ICC's interest in these [academic] fields is the identification, fear, and domination of "enemies" and the blowing up of bridges of communication.... The intelligence community's interest in these disciplines defiles them, and I could never in good conscience (i.e. with intellectual or moral integrity) participate in these junctures of university and IC-CAE. I could never teach a Chicana novel in a classroom where I knew some of the students were being trained to read the literature for knowledge that might endanger sister barrios.[33]

It seems likely that once critics started to raise such points, some IC Centers began to drop Intelligence Community from their names. Now

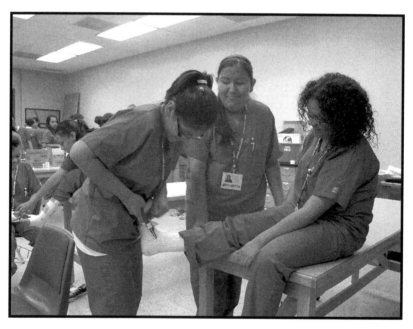

Figure 1.3: Junior high school students from Springdale, Arkansas, learn about the medical professions at a week-long summer program sponsored by the University of Arkansas. (Photo courtesy of Heidi S. Stambuck/University of Arkansas.)

many are known simply as "Centers for Academic Excellence." Similarly, the Spy Camp at Trinity became "Summer Intelligence Seminar," while UTPA's version became the "Got Intelligence?" camp.

It may be that the DNI's primary goal in creating the IC Centers is to increase the pool of minority youth seeking employment in spy agencies. But an important secondary goal appears to be a public relations goal: to give an extreme makeover to the CIA, the FBI, the NSA, and other agencies for a generation too young to know about the agencies' past abuses, and too overworked and distracted to be aware of their current ones. Only by whitewashing the past can the Director of National Intelligence hope to normalize spy work.

Learning from Fulbright

Is the IC Center program as benign and generous as its proponents claim? Is it really the "win-win relationship for everyone involved," to quote a sympathetic article?[34] Or somewhere down the line does someone lose?

From one point of view, the program appears to be creating new opportunities for young people, especially African-American and Latino students who are excited at the possibility of challenging, adventurous work in service of country. But on the other hand, we might ask: Couldn't these young people play a more constructive role in our society if they were aggressively recruited into careers in medicine, engineering, or education?

We might also ask ourselves: What kind of a society is it whose citizens define "serving your country" in terms of employment with the military or intelligence agencies, as if other institutions didn't matter? This propaganda strategy in the DNI's effort to recruit intelligence—modeled after the military's techniques for recruiting soldiers—deserves much criticism, whether such methods are targeted at minorities and recent immigrants to our country or to the general populace.

It is clear that many of the IC Centers expose students to unrealistic scenarios if not outright deception. Like many recruitment processes— whether for messianic cults, the military, or other totalistic institutions— there is an element of undue influence, what psychologists call "coercive persuasion": the creation of behavioral and ideological changes by exerting psychological pressure or by taking advantage of a position of power over another person.[35] If these centers soften children up through obligatory scavenger hunts and other activities that their powerful patrons are coordinating, we might ask whether children are being given the chance to freely explore other options. If a charismatic CIA analyst or military intelligence officer pumps up junior high or high school kids with stories about their global travels, many are easily convinced that it "beats having an office job!" In the official IC Center literature from the DNI, the histories of the agencies are sanitized. Full disclosure is nonexistent. Nowhere are CIA assassination plots mentioned, nor COINTELPRO (the FBI's illegal domestic surveillance program), no mention of secret prisons in the "war on terror." This is not much different from the military recruiter who promises high school students money for college and the chance to see the world without mentioning that they might be sent to the front lines of Afghanistan or Iraq for a year or two. Such techniques are egregious, but they are even more egregious when children are the victims.

UTPA professor Samuel Freeman observes, "The [IC] Spy Center is part of nothing less than an attempt to legitimize the illegitimate, to manipulate us into condoning the unpardonable, and to accept the crimes of US intelligence agencies as actions that are legitimate, acceptable, and even respectable.... Hopefully, protests raised by students and faculty will send a message to other UTPA organizations that consorting with IC-CAE/IGkNU is not worth the cost."[36]

Will students and faculty eventually mobilize themselves against intelligence agencies on America's college campuses? It is still too early to tell. The IC Centers have largely succeeded because local resistance efforts have tended to be isolated from each other. David Price has noted that those opposed to IC-CAE are more likely to succeed if they forge alliances nationwide to make common cause: "Something like an 'IC-CAE Watch' or 'CIA Campus Watch' website could be started by a faculty member or grad student on an IC-CAE campus, providing forums to collect documents, stories, and resistance tactics from across the country."[37] In addition, Price recommends that concerned students, faculty, and staff make use of state public records laws and the national Freedom of Information Act to request records related to IC-CAE, and that tenured professors at IC-CAE funded universities take a leading role in asking tough questions about the program.

But in the meantime the IC Centers are spreading, while students are getting lured into scholarship programs like PRISP that require mandatory service to intelligence agencies. Another initiative, the Stokes Program (sponsored by the CIA, the FBI, and the NSA), targets high school seniors with the promise of paid tuition and a government salary in exchange for mandatory employment with these agencies. In the case of most of these programs, the cloak of secrecy surrounding the scholarships is extremely troubling. Typically, students secretly receive money from the DNI and no one—neither peer, nor professor, nor administrator—knows that they are receiving financial support. Under these circumstances, what is to keep the intelligence agencies from demanding that PRISP or Stokes Program participants monitor political student groups, international students from the Middle East or central Asia, or professors for "subversive" activities such as participating in anti-war rallies or demonstrations opposing torture? The very possibility that these scenarios might play out is enough to have a chilling effect at a time when college campuses are already under pressure as the result of the Patriot Act and the proposed HR 1955 (the so-called Violent Radicalization and Homegrown Terrorism Prevention Act) currently being debated in Congress.

Perhaps it is not surprising that in a speech delivered to the Association of American Universities on April 14, 2008, Defense Secretary Robert Gates announced the creation of the $60 million "Minerva Consortium" project which would provide Defense Department funding for new social science research projects related to national security. (The project is named after the Roman goddess of wisdom and warfare.) Gates outlined four areas of interest: Chinese military studies, religious studies, "Iraqi and Terrorist Perspectives," and the "New Disciplines Project," the latter of which would help the Pentagon develop expertise in anthropology, history, and sociology. But the very idea of a Minerva Consortium is ill-conceived. There are many urgent priorities that could be addressed instead. The $60 million spent on Minerva could pay for the annual tuition and fees of approximately 15,000 students at a public university, or to hire more than 1,000 new professors, or to update the library collections of many colleges.

IC Centers, PRISP, the Minerva Consortium, and their like will likely erode academic freedom and distort the education of university students. Classes that support the needs of intelligence agencies and the Pentagon will likely have ample funding; those that expose the historical crimes of the CIA, FBI, and other spy agencies will not. Professors who accept the goals and perspectives of the DNI will likely be supported in their efforts to secure tenure, internal grants, and facilities; those who don't accept them will not. Similar situations in the past—in which universities or professional associations have succumbed to the pressures of commercialization—have tended to produce these results. Late nineteenth-century US economists (such as Henry Carter Adams and Richard Ely) who proposed ideas for radical economic reform faced tremendous pressure to conform to the dictates of conservative administrators who sought to please industrial magnates. They and many others buckled under the pressure, until eventually, economic "studies and findings tended to be internal recommendations hedged with qualifiers, analyses couched in jargon that was unintelligible to the average citizen."[38]

The reform advocates became impotent professionals. In the early years of the twentieth century, radical engineers such as C. E. Drayer, F. W. Ballard, and Morris Cooke called for public control of utilities, but were then reprimanded by professional associations that were dominated by corporations. Sometimes, the engineers were forced to give up engineering practice.[39] As a new wave of intelligence-based commercialization hits, we need to be wary of the dangers that it poses to academic freedom and the core principles of higher education.[40] The university itself runs the risk of selling its soul for a quick financial fix that, in the end, does a disservice to the students and the entire society.

In many ways, the stage was set as early as the 1980s, when public universities began shifting to a profit-driven corporate model. As state governments began cutting back public funding for higher education, universities came to rely more and more upon external funding, especially from corporations, alumni, and other private sources. The private finance model is rapidly replacing our country's public university system. Indeed, public funding for higher education in the US has dropped to two-thirds of what it was in 1980.[41] This process has inflicted widespread damage to a part of American society that is still greatly admired around the world. A striking example comes from our country's medical schools, where pharmaceutical companies have stepped in to fill the void created by decreased public higher education funding. As noted by University of California, Santa Barbara professor Christopher Newfield, it is common practice for "corporate representatives [to]…recommend speakers paid for at company expense and help shape the content and format of continuing education courses by giving ample subsidies that help medical schools operate at a profit…. [Such speakers] cannot be assumed to be as objective and disinterested as university instructors ought to be."[42]

As noted earlier in this chapter, this is not the only time that military and intelligence agencies have aggressively infiltrated college and university campuses. However, the structures of the IC Center programs, PRISP, and other initiatives that threaten to constrain free and open intellectual inquiry on our campuses should concern us all.

Universities in the United States have strayed far from their core values: academic freedom, open scientific inquiry not subject to secrecy, and commitment to high-quality education for the benefit of students, not for some ulterior motive.[43] But there is still time to turn things around. In this context it is worth remembering the words of Senator William Fulbright (for whom the Fulbright Fellowship program was named). Just over forty years ago, in the midst of the Vietnam War, he said the following on the floor of the Senate:

More and more our economy, our government, and our universities are adapting themselves to the requirements of continuing war.... The universities might have formed an effective counterweight to the military-industrial complex by strengthening their emphasis on the traditional values of our democracy, but many of our leading institutions have instead joined the monolith, adding greatly to its power and influence.... Among the most baneful effects of the government-university contract system, the most damaging and corrupting are the neglect of its students, and the taking into the government camp of scholars, especially those in the social sciences, who ought to be acting as responsible and independent critics of their government's policies.... When the university turns away from its central purpose and makes itself an appendage to the government, concerning itself with techniques rather than purposes, with expedients rather than ideals...it is not only failing to meet its responsibilities to its students; it is betraying a public trust.[44]

Fulbright's words are as relevant today as when he first spoke them in 1967. The senator understood that when educators and students succumb to these pressures, then our society spirals ever more quickly into a state of militarism. It is left now to students, faculty, and citizens of conscience to ensure that wisdom and good judgment will prevail over a marriage of convenience between universities and spy agencies.

Notes

1. "Special Events: Scavenger Hunts," *International Spy Museum*, http://www.spymuseum.org/special/hunts.php (accessed August 2, 2008).

2. Jane Harman, quoted in US House Intelligence Committee, "Building Capabilities: The Intelligence Community's National Security Requirements for Diversity of Language, Skills, and Ethnic and Cultural Understanding," November 5, 2003, http://www.fas.org/irp/congress/2003_hr/110503hpsci.pdf (accessed August 2, 2008).

3. US Office of the Director of National Intelligence, "Intelligence Community Centers of Academic Excellence Program," *Intelligence Community Centers of Academic Excellence*, http://www.dni.gov/cae/institutions.htm. See also Walter Pincus, "Howard, Virginia Tech Join US Intelligence Program," *Washington Post*, September 7, 2009.

4. See, for example, Bruce Cumings, "Boundary Displacement: Area Studies and International Studies during and after the Cold War," *Bulletin of Concerned Asia Scholars* 29, no. 1 (1999): 6–26. See also *Universities and Empire: Money*

and *Politics in the Social Sciences during the Cold War*, ed. Christopher Simpson (New York: The New Press, 1999).

5. Joshua Garner, "University's 'Spy Camp' Lets Teens Learn about Intelligence Gathering," *Catholic News Service*, July 17, 2007, http://www.catholicnews.com/data/briefs/cns/20070717.htm (accessed August 2, 2008); Richard Willing, "Intelligence Agencies Invest in College Education," *USA Today*, November 27, 2006.

6. Peter Galuszka, "Black Colleges Involved in Efforts to Boost Intelligence Community Talent Pool," *Diverse Online*, January 11, 2007, http://diverseeducation.com/article/6874/black-colleges-involved-in-efforts.html (accessed August 2, 2008).

7. Ryan Poulous, "UTEP Camp Shows the World of Intelligence," *El Paso Inc.*, July 4–10, 2008, http://www.elpasoinc.com/showArticle.asp?articleId=1471 (accessed March 12, 2010).

8. US Office of the Director of National Intelligence, *United States Intelligence Community Centers of Academic Excellence in National Security Studies: Program Plan for Fiscal Years 2005–2015* (Washington DC: Office of the Director of National Intelligence, 2005), 6–7, http://www.trinitydc.edu/programs/intel_center/IC CAE Application April05 seal.pdf (accessed August 2, 2008).

9. Galuzka, "Black Colleges Involved."

10. "Cloak and Gown," *Texas Observer*, April 21, 2006, http://www.texasobserver.org/archives/item/14790-2188-political-intelligence-marchers-mccain-y-mas (accessed August 10, 2008).

11. Hugh Gusterson and David Price, "Spies in Our Midst," *Anthropology News* 46, no. 6 (September 2005): 39–40.

12. Ibid. See also David Price, "Obama's Classroom Spies," *CounterPunch*, June 23, 2009, http://www.counterpunch.org/price06232009.html (accessed March 12, 2010).

13. Hugh Gusterson, "The US Military's Quest to Weaponize Culture," *Bulletin of the Atomic Scientists*, June 20, 2008, http://www.thebulletin.org/web-edition/columnists/hugh-gusterson/the-us-militarys-quest-to-weaponize-culture (accessed March 12, 2010).

14. "Center for Academic Excellence Creates New Opportunities for Valley Students," *Los Arcos: The University of Texas Pan-American*, Fall 2007: 18.

15. Daniel Perry, "The China Connection: UTPA Students Experience Chinese Culture, Academics," *The Monitor* (McAllen, Texas), July 24, 2007, http://www.themonitor.com/articles/china-4002-students-center.html (accessed August 2, 2008).

16. Samuel Freeman, "Intelligence Agencies Are Penetrating Our Universities Today," *Rio Grande Guardian* (McAllen, Texas), April 10, 2007, http://www.riograndeguardian.com/index.asp (accessed March 12, 2010).

17. Jesse Bogan, "Intelligence Grants in Valley Rile Some," *San Antonio Express-News,* December 2, 2006, http://www.mysanantonio.com/news/MYSA120306_04B_intelligencealert_2715c86_html8625.html (accessed March 12, 2010).

18. Ibid.

19. "University of Texas-Pan American Faculty Senate Minutes," April 26, 2006, https://portal.utpa.edu/portal/page/portal/utpa_main/daa_home/senate_home/senate_imagesfiles/fs_060426_lm.pdf (accessed March 12, 2010). It is not clear whether the students' concerns materialized.

20. David Price, "Silent Coup: How the CIA Is Welcoming Itself Back onto American University Campuses," *CounterPunch*, January 16–31, 2010: 1–4; David Price, "The Spook School Program," *CounterPunch*, February 1–15, 2010: 7–8.

21. Stephen Kinzer, *Overthrow: America's Century of Regime Change from Hawaii to Iraq* (New York: Times Books, 2007).

22. Alfred McCoy, *A Question of Torture: CIA Interrogation from the Cold War to the War on Terror* (New York: Metropolitan Books, 2006).

23. Phillip Agee, *Inside the Company: CIA Diary* (New York: Bantam, 1984).

24. Dana Priest and Barton Gellman, "US Decries Abuse but Defends Interrogations," *Washington Post*, December 26, 2002.

25. Dana Priest, "CIA Holds Terror Suspects in Secret Prisons," *Washington Post*, November 2, 2005.

26. Margot Patterson, "The Mission of Ray McGovern," *National Catholic Reporter,* October 27, 2006.

27. Shayana Kadidal, "NSA Surveillance: More Muck from the Bowels of AT&T," *Huffington Post*, April 14, 2006, http://www.huffingtonpost.com/shayana-kadidal/nsa-surveillance-more-muc_b_19128.html (accessed March 12, 2010). See also Ellen Nakashima, "A Story of Surveillance," *Washington Post*, November 7, 2007, http://www.washingtonpost.com/wp-dyn/content/article/2007/11/07/AR2007110700006.html (accessed March 12, 2010).

28. James Risen and Eric Lichtblau, "Bush Lets US Spy on Callers without Courts," *New York Times*, December 16, 2005. See also "NSA Whistleblower Warns Domestic Spying Program Is Sign the US Is Decaying into a 'Police State,'" *Democracy Now!* (syndicated by Pacifica Radio), January 3, 2006, http://www.democracynow.org/2006/1/3/exclusive_national_security_agency_whistleblower_warns (accessed March 12, 2010).

29. Tracy Wilkinson and Maria De Cristofaro, "Italy Indicts CIA Agents in Kidnapping," *Los Angeles Times*, February 17, 2007.

30. Mathias Gebauer, "Germany Issues Arrest Warrants for 13 CIA Agents in El-Masri Case," *Spiegel Online*, January 31, 2007, http://www.spiegel.de/international/0,1518,463385,00.html (accessed March 12, 2010).

31. Karen DeYoung and Walter Pincus, "CIA Releases Files on Past Misdeeds," *Washington Post*, June 27, 2007, http://www.washingtonpost.com/wp-dyn/content/article/2007/06/26/AR2007062600861.html (accessed March 12, 2010).

32. Gina Pérez, "JROTC, Citizenship, and Puerto Rican Youth in Lorain, Ohio," (presentation, annual meetings of the American Anthropological Association, Philadelphia, PA, December 6, 2009). See also Gina Pérez, "JROTC and Latina/o Youth in Neoliberal Cities," in *Rethinking America*, ed. Jeff Maskovsky and Ida Susser (New York: Paradigm Publishers, 2009), 31–48. For analysis of the legal and political implications of Latino non-citizens in the military (and their conversion to citizens), see Luis F. B. Plascencia, "The Military Gates of Non-Citizenship: Latino Aliens and Non-citizen Nationals Performing Military Work in the US Homeland," (presentation, annual meetings of the American Anthropological Association, Philadelphia, PA, December 6, 2009).

33. Kamala Platt, "How Can We Sleep? The Birthing of an Intelligence Center on University Grounds," *La Voz de Esperanza* (San Antonio, Texas), May 2007, 6–7. See also Kamala Platt, "Latino/a Students and Covert 'Securities': The Integration of Academic and Intelligence Communities," *Latino Studies* 6: 456–465.

34. "Intelligence Studies Initiative," *Trinity Magazine* (Fall 2005), http://www.trinitydc.edu/news_events/mags/fall05/intelligence_studies_initiative.php (accessed August 2, 2008).

35. Edward H. Schein, *Coercive Persuasion* (New York: H.H. Norton, 1971).

36. Samuel Freeman, "PACE and the 'Spy Center's' Shills," *Rio Grande Guardian* (McAllen, Texas), January 30, 2009, http://www.riograndeguardian.com/index.asp (accessed March 12, 2010).

37. David Price, "Silent Coup," 4.

38. Mary O. Furner, *Advocacy and Objectivity: A Crisis in the Professionalization of American Social Science, 1865–1905* (Lexington: University of Kentucky Press, 1975), 128–142; 154–162; 324.

39. David Noble, *America by Design: Science, Technology, and the Rise of Corporate Capitalism* (New York: Oxford University Press, 1979), 62–63.

40. Christopher Newfield, *Unmaking the Public University: The Forty-Year Assault on the Middle Class* (Cambridge, MA: Harvard University Press, 2008), 265.

41. Ibid., 230, See also Henry A. Giroux, *The University in Chains: Confronting the Military-Industrial-Academic Complex* (Boulder: Paradigm Publishers, 2007); Gaye Tuchman, *Wannabe U: Inside the Corporate University* (Chicago: University of Chicago Press, 2009).

42. Derek Bok, *Universities in the Marketplace: The Commercialization of Higher Education* (Princeton, NJ: Princeton University Press, 2004).

43. J. William Fulbright, "A Point of View," *Science*, December 22, 1967, 1555.

Chapter 2
Shattered Taboo

In 1984, anthropologist Lisa Peattie developed the idea of "normalizing the unthinkable" by comparing the roles played by men and women operating Nazi death camps and those working in US nuclear weapons labs and production facilities.[1] Peattie examined the processes of routinization in these settings—that is, the way in which the creation of monstrous situations became routine—and found that in each case, an elaborate division of labor functioned as a distancing mechanism, shifting the responsibility for mass murder away from those who were participating in it. Each society's willingness to accept a previously unthinkable scenario was thus facilitated by compartmentalization of tasks. And so, normalization of the unthinkable came to pass in each case.

Compartmentalization and *routinization* are but two examples of "controlling processes," dynamic components of power that anthropologist Laura Nader has proposed for study. According to Nader, controlling processes refers to "the transformative nature of central ideas...that emanate from institutions operating as dynamic components of power.... It is the study of how individuals and groups are influenced and persuaded to participate in their own domination or, alternatively, to resist it."[2]

Controlling processes are widespread and deeply entrenched in many societies, including our own. For example, Michael Panasitti and Natasha Schull, in their 1994 essay "Re-articulating the Moral Economy of Gambling," examine how over the course of the twentieth century attitudes towards gambling shifted 180 degrees in the United States, as it went from vice to family entertainment to, finally, a nationwide system of state-sanctioned lotteries—a form of taxation that regressively takes more from the poor than it does from the rich. Control shifted from small-scale back room gambling to corporate casinos and the rise of the "gaming industry."[3]

Another example comes from the work of historian Stuart Ewen, who uncovers the ways in which the *Captains of Consciousness* undermined the idea of thrift as a virtue—widely held in the United States before the

1920s—and replaced it with the idea of thrift as a negative trait, as miserliness. Advertising men, bankers issuing credit and installment plans, and multinational corporations all played a part. The effect was to create "fancied needs" among the working classes where few had existed before. Quite suddenly, millions of Americans felt that they *needed* mouthwash, cosmetics, automobiles, kitchen appliances, and other gadgets. Consequently, the "captains of consciousness" transformed citizens into mass consumers—an entire country was persuaded to need new things.[4]

These examples illustrate a special type of controlling process, one which Laura Nader has called "ideological control":

> Ideological control deals with pressures outside of individuals or groups that result in the formation of a control that becomes culturally set over time. Ideals and principles affecting the behavior of individuals are developed, penetrating and linking together different social domains and spheres of action, thought, and influence.... Ideological controls are the most indirect and pervasive in modern society...they are less vulnerable to abrupt change.[5]

In this chapter I shall be concerned with a situation that might be leading to a similar transformation in the United States today: a shift in popular attitudes regarding torture, as the result of incremental controlling processes in the legal sphere, in mass entertainment culture, and in the academic world. Specifically, I am interested in examining how ideas about torture are being transformed in the United States today as the result of "ideals and principles...penetrating and linking together different social domains and spheres of action, thought, and influence" over the past nine years.[6] This is of particular relevance for those concerned about militarization in American life, since torture has frequently been used as a means of control in militaristic societies. In particular, I ask: Are we witnessing before our very eyes the shattering of a taboo—the long-standing cultural taboo against torture?

To investigate this question, I have relied upon an eclectic range of materials including a declassified memo from the Office of Legal Counsel at the US Department of Justice, investigative reports on torture and violence in the media from non-governmental organizations such as Human Rights First and the Parents Television Council, and data from public opinion polls. Although none of these sources alone gives a complete picture, together they provide preliminary data that may serve as starting points for further research.

It is not yet possible to definitively state whether or not popular attitudes about torture in the United States have significantly changed, any more than it would have been possible in 1920 to have definitively stated whether or not popular attitudes about thrift had significantly changed. To state this in somewhat different terms: I am not suggesting that this chapter is a definitive study of whether or not attitudes about torture have become more acceptable in the United States over time. Instead, I hope to provide a few data points that might provide insight and perhaps inspire others to undertake more comprehensive analyses. Long-term controlling processes are often difficult to detect in real-time since the anthropologist is only observing a single moment in time. But a potentially enlightening means of monitoring controlling processes might be to analyze multiple discursive fields in which ideological transformations are playing out. If we take seriously the notion that our society has become deeply militarized over the past seventy years (a point argued by numerous historians, political scientists, and anthropologists—see the Introduction to this book), then the question of the public's acceptance of torture should be an especially salient concern.

An Acceptance of Torture?

Before approaching the question of whether a more permissive attitude towards torture has developed in the United States in recent years, it is important to distinguish two distinct but related topics: (1) transformations in the popular acceptance of torture; and (2) more broadly, the transformation of the definition of "torture" itself.

Transformations in the popular acceptance of torture in the United States could be tentatively examined by means of polling data. Although public opinion polls are a notoriously problematic means of understanding social phenomena, carefully worded polls can provide us with a starting point into public attitudes regarding torture.[7] Among the most revealing polls are those that have been designed to gauge public opinion around this question.

In October 2005, the Pew Center conducted a poll within the United States which had troubling results: it indicated that 46 percent of Americans thought that torture is often or sometimes justified. (Another 17 percent said it was rarely justified.) The Pew Center poll was consistent with several polls it had carried out since July 2004. The BBC conducted a similar poll in October 2006. It indicated that in the United States, 36 percent of the respondents approved of torture in certain cases, making it among the highest of the twenty-five countries surveyed. Only Israel, Indonesia, the Philippines, Kenya, and China had higher rates of approval.[8]

More recent polls conducted in the United States have led to similar results. In April 2009, Gallup found that more than half of those polled thought that "harsh interrogation techniques" (presumably including sleep deprivation and waterboarding) were justified for terrorism suspects.[9] During the same month, the Pew Center reported that 71 percent of those polled said that torture was justified in at least rare cases.[10] Even more recently, a survey conducted by the Associated Press and GfK Roper Public Affairs (in late May and early June 2009) revealed that just over half of those polled said that torture was sometimes justified.[11]

Did the attacks of September 11, 2001, substantially change these attitudes? It would seem that the shock of that terrible event might have led to some Americans' greater willingness to permit torture by government agencies, but there is some indication that even before September 11, incremental changes were already in motion. Specifically, in 1993 the US Senate ratified the UN Convention Against Torture—which President Clinton then signed the following year—but the law included a provision that eliminated psychological torture from consideration, as we shall see shortly.[12]

This raises an important side note: the difference between physical forms of torture and psychological forms. Physical torture dates back to ancient times, but psychological torture is a much more recent creation. KGB interrogators employed it in the earliest stages of the Cold War. The CIA then conducted extensive research and experimentation in order to replicate these methods, and finally codified them in interrogation manuals in the early 1960s. Among the most devastating psychological torture techniques are sensory deprivation and sensory assault, self-inflicted pain, and isolation—simple methods that do not require torturers to administer drugs, to use specialized equipment, or even to have prolonged contact with their victims.[13] Psychological torture often leaves deep emotional scars that can last a lifetime, so it is significant that in discussions about torture that have taken place over the last fifteen years within the US government, psychological torture has largely disappeared from official discussion.[14] The lack of understanding of the seriousness of psychological torture is reflected in public attitudes which might not consider psychological torture as torture at all.

Legal Transformations; or, When Torture Is Not Torture

A common pattern in controlling processes is the subtle shift of legal norms, often accompanied by transformations in language. A trenchant example is that of the "harmony model" of law (settling or avoiding disputes by means of imposed ideologies of social harmony), evident in some parts of the United States as a preference for Alternative Dispute Resolution and other non-confrontational means of resolving disputes that in some cases places social harmony above justice.[15] The language of justice is replaced with the language of therapy, as Laura Nader notes in her book *Harmony Ideology*.

In the case of torture, significant shifts have occurred in US law. These began with Congress's incremental exclusion of psychological assaults as a form of torture in the 1980s and especially the 1990s.[16] This process of exclusion resumed with a series of severe restrictions in the kinds of physical manipulations defined as torture, with an extreme point being reached in August 2002 with the Bush administration's creation and circulation of the so-called Bybee memo, an internal government document prepared by Jay Bybee, then head of the US Justice Department's Office of Legal Counsel. The document defined torture as "equivalent in intensity to the pain accompanying serious physical injury, such as organ failure, impairment of bodily function, or even death."[17] After US newspapers published the Abu Ghraib photos of US soldiers abusing Iraqi prisoners, the Bush administration declared the Bybee memo inoperative, but the damage had been done.

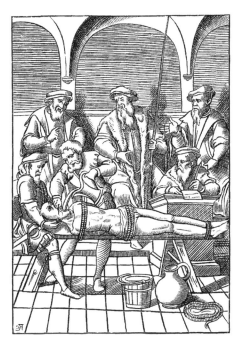

Figure 2.1: Many US officials (including former Attorney General Michael Mukasey) have declined to state whether the ancient technique of waterboarding constitutes torture. (Image in the public domain.)

It is tempting to interpret Abu Ghraib (and the steps leading up to it) as an illustration of a callous disregard for international law by an extremist Republican administration, but the political reality is more complex. As noted above, a Democratic-controlled Senate approved the UN Convention Against Torture in 1993 and (Democratic) President Clinton signed it into law in 1994. Although this might sound like a progressive act, the US version included four "reservations" focused around the term "mental." These changes excluded sensory deprivation and self-inflicted pain from the definition of torture—precisely those methods that had been perfected by the CIA over the previous thirty years.[18]

Although the narrow definition of torture expressed in the Bybee memo was repudiated by the White House following the publication of the Abu Ghraib torture photos in 2004, a great deal of legal ambiguity continues. For example, in October 2007, during his Congressional confirmation hearings, former Attorney General Michael Mukasey refused to state under oath whether he considered waterboarding to be constitutional—in other words, he refused to state whether waterboarding constituted torture.[19]

Rather than adopt the broadly accepted international standard of torture, Mulkasey, President Bush, and his legal team instead opted to define these actions not as torture but as "enhanced interrogation." In this case, controlling processes work through the relationship between language and law. Thus the president was able to make statements such as "we do not torture" with conviction. Such statements were eventually amplified by the mass media. It is to the media that we now turn.

From 24 to Iraqi Prisons: The Influence of Corporate Entertainment Culture

In addition to research pointing to the addictive nature of television, a great many studies indicate that media violence influences the behavior and attitudes of viewers, particularly young viewers.[20] Portrayals of torture on television programs and in Hollywood movies in recent years have also changed public attitudes—and behavior within the military and intelligence establishment. In fact, a report in the *New Yorker* magazine describes how in November 2006, West Point dean Brigadier General Patrick Finnegan, a team of experienced military and FBI interrogators, and representatives of Human Rights First requested a meeting with with the writers of the wildly popular Fox Television series 24, which at the time had a weekly audience of fifteen million viewers. They asked the program's creative team to stop broadcasting torture scenes because US soldiers were imitating the show's tactics.[21]

Each season of *24* depicts a day in the life of protagonist Jack Bauer, who has twenty-four hours to foil a terrorist plot that threatens the United States. Bauer often resorts to torture to force informants to divulge information. Some of Bauer's tactics include "drugging, waterboarding, electrocution or power drilling into a man's shoulder. In five seasons of the show there have been no less than 67 torture scenes...more than one every show."[22] In addition to *24*, a number of other shows have broadcast torture scenes, including ABC's programs *Alias* and *Lost* and NBC's program *Law and Order*. Still another series, Fox's *Solitary*, is a game show in which contestants are apparently held in solitary confinement without access to clocks, sunlight, or direct communication with the outside world. They are then subjected to physically and mentally challenging contests, occasionally forgoing food and sleep, until they are eliminated one by one.[23] The last remaining contestant wins $50,000.

David Danzig, director of Human Rights First's Prime Time Torture Project, was among those who visited with Fox's creative team. His research group examined portrayals of torture on television and found startling patterns. Before September 11, 2001, there were few incidents of torture—approximately four per year. After September 11, these gradually increased to more than one hundred per year. Danzig notes:

> What's particularly disturbing...is that when you look at who's doing the torturing, the people who are involved in it have changed. It used to be the bad guys were the ones who tortured, the Nazis or aliens or something like that, and torture never worked. But now it's people like Jack Bauer.... So the message that...soldiers in Iraq and Afghanistan get is that good guys use this stuff and it works.... They make you a hero.[24]

Consequently, Danzig calls *24* "an advertisement for torture" and notes that Brigadier General Patrick Finnegan was not only familiar with the series, but that

> He and...other people who taught interrogators...have told us that in their classes, Jack Bauer comes up all the time. When I first talked to a colonel at West Point about this, he said, "Oh, my God! *24* is one of the biggest problems I have in teaching my classes. Everybody wants to be like Jack Bauer. They all think that it may be possible or there are times when you should have to cross the line."[25]

Figure 2.2: The cast of the hit television series *24,* which features frequent interrogations of suspected terrorists by Jack Bauer (played by Kiefer Sutherland, *fourth from right*). (Photo courtesy of Kristin Dos Santos/ Wikimedia Commons.)

Among those who want to be like Jack Bauer is Supreme Court Justice Antonin Scalia, who in 2007 told a Canadian audience that "Jack Bauer saved Los Angeles.... He saved hundreds of thousands of lives," before he suggested that the legal system should not have "absolutes" on torture prohibitions.[26]

If a West Point dean is having such problems with future interrogators, and a Supreme Court justice approvingly references a TV torturer, then *24* and similar programs must be influencing the general public's ideas about the acceptability of torture as well, especially given the overwhelming evidence linking media violence to changes in viewers' behavior.

Comments from former Army interrogator Tony Lagouranis support Danzig's claim. Lagouranis has noted that in Iraqi prisons, interrogators were strongly influenced by what they saw on the screen:

> [Interrogators] were getting ideas from television.... Among the things that I saw people doing that they got from television was

water-boarding, mock execution, using mock torture. They wanted to hook up one of our translators to an electric generator and pretend that they were torturing him and allow prisoners to see that so that they thought that they would experience the same thing.[27]

In an interview conducted on the radio program *Democracy Now!*, Lagouranis also mentioned the impact on the general public of TV shows like *24*. He stated that such programming is "really affecting public opinion, too. I've been speaking about torture since I returned from Iraq, and people always bring up the ticking time bomb scenario, and they always bring up *24* as a reason why we need to legalize torture." He also said, "Where is this idea coming from that we need to torture to combat terrorism? It's coming from the media, in my opinion."[28]

Given these observations, it is worth asking the question: If TV viewers are exposed to frequent images of "good guys" torturing "bad guys," is it possible that these images are contributing to the shattering of a taboo against torture? In other words, are they helping to foster a greater popular acceptance of torture as a way of life? Are these images playing a part in "normalizing the unthinkable"? New research by anthropologists or psychologists—perhaps modeled after the many studies linking exposure to media violence with viewers' aggressive behavior—might lead to more definitive answers to these questions.

More Than Academic

The academic sphere is another domain in which torture questions have surfaced. Undoubtedly the most vocal proponent of the use of torture in interrogations is Harvard law professor Alan Dershowitz, who has argued that US judges should issue "torture warrants" in exceptional cases in which public safety is in grave danger—that is, in "ticking time bomb" scenarios in which detainees might have specific information that could prevent imminent terrorist acts.[29] Dershowitz describes Israeli policies that allowed its intelligence agents "to employ what it euphemistically called 'moderate physical pressure' to elicit information from terrorists" about future threats, and claims that "several attacks were prevented by this unpleasant tactic" (a dubious statement for which he provides no evidence). Though these policies were later banned by the Israeli Supreme Court, Dershowitz approvingly notes that the Court left open the possibility that in a ticking bomb case, "an agent who employed physical pressure [torture] could defend himself against criminal charges by invoking the 'law of necessity.'"[30]

For many, this argument is compelling because the period after September 11 in the United States has been marked by a sometimes desperate search for effective ways of preventing future terrorist attacks.

Less well-known in the United States is the work of Mirko Bagaric and Julie Clarke, two Australian law professors who maintain that government agents should be permitted to use torture "where the evidence suggests that this is the only means, due to the immediacy of the situation, to save the life of an innocent person." Their argument—outlined in the book *Torture: When the Unthinkable is Morally Permissible*—is that self-defense sometimes dictates torture.[31]

But Dershowitz, Bagaric, and Clarke have many critics, including historians, political scientists, legal scholars, and others, including even former interrogators. For example, historian Alfred McCoy has noted that the hypothetical ticking time bomb scenario proposed by Dershowitz "embodies our deepest fears and makes most of us quietly—unwittingly—complicit in the Bush administration's recourse to torture." His six-point critique is devastating:

1. "In the real world, the probability that a terrorist might be captured after concealing a ticking nuclear bomb in Times Square and that his captors would somehow recognize his significance is phenomenally slender."

2. "This scenario still rests on the critical, utterly unexamined assumption that torture can get useful intelligence from this or any hardened terrorist' even though professional interrogators often claim that 'brutalization doesn't work."

3. "Once we agree to torture the one terrorist…we admit a possibility, even an imperative, for torturing hundreds who might have ticking bombs or thousands who just might have some knowledge about those bombs."

4. "Useful intelligence perhaps, but at what cost? The price of torture is unacceptably high because it disgraces and then undermines the country that countenances it."

5. "If torture produces limited gains at such high political cost, why does any rational American leader condone interrogation practices 'tantamount to torture'?"

6. "The use of torture to stop ticking bombs leads ultimately to a cruel choice—either legalize this brutality, ala Dershowitz and Bush, or accept that the logical corollary to state-sanctioned torture is state-sponsored murder."[32]

Many other scholars have addressed this topic and have published books examining the issues that are at stake. A moral philosopher has analyzed *Torture and the Ticking Bomb*; another couple of philosophers have recently written about *The Ethics of Torture*; a human rights lawyer and colleagues have explored *Torture: Does It Make Us Safer? Is It Ever OK?*; a religious studies professor has written an inquiry into *Spirituality and the Ethics of Torture*; and a legal scholar has posed the question, *Why Not Torture Terrorists?*[33]

The mass media began to amplify these academic debates, which effectively helped the process of making torture appear to be something about which reasonable people could disagree. In 2005, *Newsweek* outlined "The Debate over Torture," shortly after ABC's TV news program *Nightline* dedicated one of its programs to the question of "When Is Torture OK?" Even the typically understated British magazine *Economist* asked in 2009: "Does Torture Work?"[34]

Although it is fascinating to delve into the philosophical, historical, spiritual, legal, and ethical dimensions of torture, the "torture debate" (particularly the debate over whether or not it is effective in gathering useful intelligence) has undeniably had the effect of raising the profile of the Dershowitz-Bagaric-Clarke argument. The fact that Dershowitz in particular has frequently appeared on CNN, Fox News, and other television news programs has transformed the ticking time bomb argument into a more or less respectable side in the debate—facts be damned.

The broader point is that these elements, in combination, may well signal an incremental transformation—a critical element of controlling processes which can be analyzed through fine-grained longitudinal analyses comparing concepts, attitudes, and practices over time. The changes are gradual enough for us to not be fully aware or cognizant of them. Yet today, academic discussions take place about the effectiveness of torture, the legality of torture, the politics of torture, and so forth—debates that would not have been imaginable in this country a decade ago. The debate has become more than academic. The unthinkable has become not only thinkable but normalized.

Understanding the "Ordinary Man"

Psychologist Roy Eidelson has recently written a thought-provoking essay in which he reflects upon how Americans think about torture. It is worth quoting part of his essay at length, for in it he stresses the importance of context:

It is easy at first to be surprised and troubled by the degree to which Americans have expressed support for the inhumane treatment and torture of detainees. But public sentiment on such matters does not emerge in a vacuum. Rather, it often reflects the influence of carefully orchestrated marketing campaigns by powerful vested interests eager to shape opinion in support of a specific agenda or facts on the ground.[35]

Eidelson reviews numerous elements that government officials have used to shape public opinion: an environment of paranoid fear, a belief in the effectiveness of torture, an insistence on the culpability of detainees, the notion of American exceptionalism (in other words, the idea that the United States is inherently different from other countries and morally superior), and the marginalization of critics. It is clear from Eidelson's essay that there is nothing in American culture or in the American psyche that is predisposed to accept torture, but rather a historically specific set of circumstances. He concludes by noting that "the combination of an outsized public relations budget, an overly accommodating mainstream media, and an unwary audience of millions is every marketer's dream," and that there is good reason to believe that these factors have helped to make torture permissible to many Americans today. This kind of critical research is essential for understanding how controlling processes related to torture are functioning in the United States today.[36]

Social scientists might be able to make an especially valuable contribution to this research by adding an ethnographic component. Such work might be modeled after Emily Martin's *Flexible Bodies*, a groundbreaking study which examined the metaphors that people use to describe the human immune system.[37] Martin asked open-ended questions, had her research participants sketch their impressions of how the immune system works, and combined this information with media reports to get rich ethnography. As I have tried to demonstrate in this chapter, a similar methodology incorporating the perspectives of lawyers, military interrogators, scholars, former detainees, and ordinary citizens might help us develop a more compete picture of what may well be a shattering taboo—a permissive attitude towards torture in the United States. In my own research, I began by searching for official reports, statements, interview transcripts, and memos written by those who were forging a new set of harsh interrogation policies in the post-September 11 period. I then searched for documents from those criticizing such policies. To supplement these materials I found various accounts from former interrogators and detainees. Examining this data gave me an opportunity to discover patterns that revealed shifts in official and unofficial discourses. Among the most striking shifts was a

CHAPTER 2

euphemistic transformation in language: torture became "enhanced inter-rogation"; kidnapping became "extraordinary rendition"; shackling limbs became "stress positions"; continuous sleep deprivation became "sleep adjustment"; starvation and force-feeding became "dietary manipulation."

Another contribution might include looking at torture from a cross-cultural perspective. How did different sectors of the general public accept (or reject) torture in Germany and Italy in the 1940s, Chile and Argentina in the 1970s, Iran in the 1980s, or Israel in the twenty-first century? How was torture defined in each of these cases? How did legal systems and ter-minology shift? Did academic discourses and "torture debates" develop in

Figure 2.3: Former US military personnel, such as these who are guarding captives at Guantánamo Bay in 2002, might provide insight into obedience and authority. (Photo courtesy of US Department of Defense.)

those societies, as in ours? Did TV programs or cinema reflect or motivate social transformations? Though several of these topics have been explored by social scientists, we need to begin the process of comparing and contrasting these societies with the contemporary United States.

Still another area that needs to be explored more thoroughly by social scientists is the question of obedience and authority. Social psychologists such as Stanley Milgram and Philip Zimbardo have written extensively about how easily most ordinary men can be persuaded to obey the orders of authority figures (even when those orders involve doing harm to other people), and others have examined the long-term effects that affect torture victims, but we still do not have a very complete picture of the torturers themselves.[38] Interviews with former interrogators who have participated in torture and harsh interrogations in Iraqi or Afghan prisons, Guantánamo Bay, or the CIA's black sites should be an essential topic for future social science research. This may seem like a difficult task, but the willingness of former interrogators (such as Tony Lagouranis and others) to speak on the record makes this a distinct possibility.

What other roles can social scientists play in the study of the taboo against torture? Since some are generalists, a potentially fruitful role might be an integrative one. For example, a savvy anthropologist might connect the work of legal scholars, historians, psychologists, former interrogators, activists, and media critics who are exposing various pieces of a very large puzzle: the dynamics of a systematized torture apparatus that has taken hundreds of suspected terrorists into custody (sometimes by kidnapping them) and subjected them to brutal interrogations in secret prisons, in violation of US and international laws.[39] Another role—a more public one—might involve publicly denouncing torture, as the American Anthropological Association did in 2007.

Finally, let us not forget that the social sciences are partly based upon history—and history tells us that that torture is *not* an effective way to collect intelligence, and that once established it tends to infect the legal system—and corrupt the entire society—over time. Like all controlling processes, the apparent normalization of torture in the United States is profoundly undemocratic, for it serves to strike fear into the American population as a whole—a form of state terror that government ultimately uses to control the citizenry itself. In spite of President Barack Obama's initial rhetoric about ending harsh interrogations, minimizing extraordinary renditions, and closing the Guantánamo detention facility, these practices appear to have not changed substantially. As this book goes to press, nearly 200 men are still imprisoned there.[40]

CHAPTER 2

We forget the lessons of history at our own peril. As Naomi Klein reminds us, the true purpose of torture isn't to collect information about ticking bombs, but rather "to terrorize—not only the people in Guantánamo's cages and Syria's isolation cells but also, and more important, the broader community that hears about these abuses. Torture is a machine designed to break the will to resist—the individual prisoner's will and the collective will" of the greater society.[41]

Notes

1. Lisa Peattie, "Normalizing the Unthinkable," *Bulletin of the Atomic Scientists,* March 1984, 32–36.

2. Laura Nader, "Controlling Processes: Tracing the Dynamic Components of Power," *Current Anthropology* 38, no. 5 (1997): 711–737.

3. Mike Panasitti and Natasha Schull, "Re-articulating the Moral Economy of Gambling," *Kroeber Anthropological Society Papers* 77 (1994): 65–102.

4. Stuart Ewen, *Captains of Consciousness: Advertising and the Social Roots of Consumer Culture* (New York: McGraw-Hill, 1976).

5. Laura Nader, "*1984* and *Brave New World*: The Insidious Threat of Covert Control," *Radcliffe Quarterly,* December 1983, 2–3.

6. Ibid., 3.

7. For an exploration of the reliability of opinion polls and surveys for social science research, see Howard Schuman, *Method and Meaning in Polls and Surveys* (Cambridge, MA: Harvard University Press, 2008).

8. Pew Research Center, *America's Place in the World 2005*, November 2005, http://people-press.org/reports/pdf/263.pdf (accessed July 12, 2007); BBC World Service, "World Citizens Reject Torture, Global Poll Reveals," October 19, 2006, http://www.globescan.com/news_archives/bbctorture06/BBCTorture06.pdf (accessed July 12, 2007).

9. Gallup, "Slim Majority Wants Bush-Era Interrogations Investigated," April 27, 2009, http://www.gallup.com/poll/118006/Slim-Majority-Wants-Bush-Era-Interrogations-Investigated.aspx (accessed March 4, 2010).

10. Pew Research Center, "Public Remains Divided over Use of Torture," April 24, 2009, http://people-press.org/reports/pdf/510.pdf (accessed March 4, 2010).

11. GfK Roper Public Affairs & Media, "The AP-GfK Poll," June 2009, http://www.ap-gfkpoll.com/pdf/AP-GfK_Poll_Supreme_Court_Final_Topline.pdf (accessed March 4, 2010).

12. Alfred McCoy, *A Question of Torture: CIA Interrogation from the Cold War to the War on Terror* (New York: Metropolitan, 2006).

13. Alfred McCoy quoted in radio broadcast, "Obama Reluctance on Bush Prosecutions Affirms Culture of Impunity," *Democracy Now!* (syndicated by Pacifica Radio), May 1, 2009, http://www.democracynow.org/2009/5/1/torture_expert_alfred_mccoy_obama_reluctance (accessed March 4, 2010).

14. McCoy, *A Question of Torture*.

15. Laura Nader, *Harmony Ideology: Justice and Control in a Zapotec Mountain Village* (Stanford, CA: Stanford University Press, 1991).

16. Alfred McCoy, "The US Has a History of Using Torture," *History News Network*, December 4, 2006, http://hnn.us/articles/32497.html (accessed July 6, 2007).

17. Jay Bybee, "Memorandum for Alberto R. Gonzales," August 1, 2002, http://news.findlaw.com/wp/docs/doj/bybee80102mem.pdf (accessed March 4, 2010).

18. McCoy, *A Question of Torture*, 100–102.

19. Ari Shapiro, "Mukasey Refuses to Call Waterboarding Torture," *All Things Considered* (syndicated by National Public Radio), October 18, 2007, http://www.npr.org/templates/story/story.php?storyId=15413635 (accessed March 4, 2010).

20. See Robert McIlwraith, "I'm Addicted to Television: The Personality, Imagination, and Watching Patterns of Self-Identified TV Addicts," *Journal of Broadcasting and Electronic Media* 42(3)(1998), 371–386; Craig A. Anderson et al., "The Influence of Media Violence on Youth," *Psychological Science in the Public Interest* 4(3) (December 2003): 81–110.

21. Jane Mayer, "Whatever It Takes: The Politics of the Man behind *24*," *New Yorker*, February 19, 2007, http://www.newyorker.com/reporting/2007/02/19/070219fa_fact_mayer (accessed March 4, 2010). See also Scott Horton, "How Hollywood Learned to Stop Worrying and Love the (Ticking) Bomb," *Harper's*, March 2008, http://www.harpers.org/archive/2008/03/hbc-90002531 (accessed March 4, 2010).

22. "Is Torture on Hit Fox TV Show '24' Encouraging US Soldiers to Abuse Detainees?" *Democracy Now!* (syndicated by Pacifica Radio), February 22, 2007, http://www.democracynow.org/2007/2/22/is_torture_on_hit_fox_tv (accessed March 4, 2010).

23. Michael Mechanic, "Voluntary Confinement," *Mother Jones*, March/April 2008, http://motherjones.com/politics/2008/03/voluntary-confinement (accessed March 6, 2010). For more information on torture and violence on television, see Parents Television Council, *TV Bloodbath: Violence on Prime Time Broadcast TV*, http://www.parentstv.org/PTC/publications/reports/stateindustryviolence/main.asp (accessed March 6, 2010).

24. David Danzig quoted in radio broadcast, "Is Torture on Hit Fox TV Show *24* Encouraging US Soldiers to Abuse Detainees?" *Democracy Now!*

(syndicated by Pacifica Radio), February 22, 2007, http://www.democra-cynow.org/2007/2/22/is_torture_on_hit_fox_tv (accessed March 4, 2010).

25. Ibid.

26. David Danzig, "An Open Letter to Antonin Scalia," June 27, 2007, http://www.humanrightsfirst.info/pdf/07622-etn-danzig-scalia-24.pdf (accessed March 4, 2010). See also Human Rights First, *Prime Time Torture Project*, http://www.humanrightsfirst.org/us_law/etn/primetime/index.asp (accessed March 4, 2010).

27. Tony Lagouranis, quoted in radio broadcast, "Is Torture on Hit Fox TV Show *24* Encouraging US Soldiers to Abuse Detainees?" *Democracy Now!* (syndicated by Pacifica Radio), February 22, 2007, http://www.democracynow.org/2007/2/22/is_torture_on_hit_fox_tv (accessed March 4, 2010).

28. Ibid.

29. Alan M. Dershowitz, "Want to Torture? Get a Warrant," *San Francisco Chronicle*, January 22, 2002.

30. Ibid.

31. Mirko Bagaric and Julie Clarke, *Torture: When the Unthinkable Is Morally Permissible* (Albany, NY: SUNY Press, 2007).

32. Alfred McCoy, "The Myth of the Ticking Time Bomb," *The Progressive*, October 2006, http://www.progressive.org/mag_mccoy1006 (accessed March 7, 2010).

33. Bob Brecher, *Torture and the Ticking Bomb* (San Francisco: Wiley-Blackwell, 2007); J. Jeremy Wisnewski and R. D. Emerick, *The Ethics of Torture* (London: Continuum, 2009); Kenneth Roth, Minky Worden, and Amy D. Bernstein, *Torture: Does It Make Us Safer? Is It Ever OK?* (New York: New Press, 2005); Derek S. Jeffreys, *Spirituality and the Ethics of Torture* (New York: Palgrave Macmillan 2009); Yuval Ginbar, *Why Not Torture Terrorists?* (Oxford, UK: Oxford University Press, 2008).

34. Evan Thomas and Michael Hirsh, "The Debate over Torture," *Newsweek*, November 21, 2005; ABC News, "When Is Torture OK?" *Nightline*, June 17, 2004; "Does Torture Work?" *Economist*, January 27, 2009.

35. Roy Eidelson, "How Americans Think about Torture—and Why," *Truthout*, May 11, 2009, http://www.truthout.org/051209C (accessed March 2, 2010). Eidelson's article is a subset of his broader work, which includes analyses of Americans' support for the "war on terror" and beliefs before and after 9/11. See Roy Eidelson, "Self and Nation: A Comparison of Americans' Beliefs Before and After 9/11," *Peace and Conflict* 11 (2005): 153–175; and Roy Eidelson, "An Individual-Group Belief Framework," *Peace and Conflict* 15 (2009): 1–26.

36. Ibid. Others have conducted important analyses of the multiple connections between humiliation and international conflict, including the corrosive effects of humiliating acts unleashed upon individuals. See Evelin Lindner, *Making Enemies: Humiliation and International Conflict* (Santa Barbara, CA: Praeger Security International, 2006).

37. Emily Martin, *Flexible Bodies* (Boston: Beacon Press, 1994).

38. Stanley Milgram, *Obedience to Authority: An Experimental View* (New York: Harper and Row, 1974); Philip G. Zimbardo, *The Lucifer Effect: Understanding How Good People Turn Evil* (New York: Random House, 2007).

39. For examples of such work, see McCoy, *A Question of Torture*; Eidelson, "How Americans Think about Torture—and Why"; Zimbardo, *The Lucifer Effect*; Scott Horton, "Carl Schmitt and the Military Commissions Act of 2006," *Balkinization* (October 16, 2006), http://balkin.blogspot.com/2006/10/carl-schmitt-and-military-commissions_16.html (accessed April 22, 2008); Jordan Paust, "Executive Plans and Authorizations to Violate International Law Concerning Treatment and Interrogation of Detainees," *Columbia Journal of Transnational Law* 43, no. 3 (2005), 811–812; Karen J. Greenberg and Joshua L. Dratel (eds.), *The Torture Papers: The Road to Abu Ghraib* (Cambridge, UK: Cambridge University Press, 2005); Jane Mayer, *The Dark Side* (New York: Doubleday, 2008); Tony Lagouranis and Allen Mikaelian, *Fear Up Harsh: An Army Interrogator's Dark Journey through Iraq* (New York: NAL Caliber, 2007). Anthropologist Laura McNamara has recently done some of this connecting work by analyzing many declassified documents and transcripts from interrogation sessions led by US military intelligence personnel since 2001. See Laura McNamara, "Culture, Torture, Interrogation, and the Global War on Terrorism," (presentation, annual meetings of the Society for Applied Anthropology, Santa Fe, NM, March 17–21, 2009), http://sfaapodcasts.net/2009/05/10/scholars-security-and-citizenship-part-i-sar-plenary/ (accessed March 19, 2010)

40. See, for example, Greg Miller, "Obama Preserves Renditions as Counterterrorism Tool," *Los Angeles Times*, February 1, 2009.

41. Naomi Klein, "Torture's Dirty Secret: It Works," *The Nation*, May 12, 2005.

Part II
Enlisting Culture

Chapter 3
Towards Mercenary Anthropology?

On December 15, 2006, the US Army released a new counterinsurgency manual, *Field Manual 3-24*. It was the first field manual dedicated exclusively to counterinsurgency in more than twenty years.

At least one anthropologist played a role in preparing the 282-page document: Montgomery McFate, an American cultural anthropologist, co-authored a chapter entitled "Intelligence in Counterinsurgency" with a military intelligence specialist. In addition, the Pentagon adapted the work of Australian infantry officer David Kilcullen for an appendix entitled "A Guide for Action." (Though the media has widely reported that Kilcullen is an anthropologist, he in fact holds a PhD from the School of Politics of the University of New South Wales.)[1] Together, the contributions of McFate and Kilcullen account for nearly fifty pages of *FM 3-24*.

Many observers were surprised when they discovered that these and other social scientists—trained to learn about and empathize with people in other societies—would be using their knowledge to support an occupying army engaged in counterinsurgency warfare in Iraq and Afghanistan.

Such involvement in the preparation of the counterinsurgency manual is but one development in a trend that has become evident since 2001: the use of "cultural knowledge" to wage the so-called war on terror, and the revival of militarized anthropology.[2]

These developments raise a number of questions. What exactly did social scientists contribute to *FM 3-24*? Why would military and intelligence officials express such interest in cultural knowledge in recent years? How are private contractors to the military—that is, companies like Xe Services (Blackwater), Lockheed Martin, and Science Applications International—seeking cultural expertise for counterinsurgency work? What are the ethical implications and other consequences of such work for Iraqis and Afghans living under military occupation? And how are social scientists responding? The answers to these questions indicate that by attempting to incorporate analytical concepts and methods (for example, the culture concept, social network analysis, and participant-observation), US counterinsurgency theorists are playing a leading role in militarizing the social sciences.

Anthropological Contributions to *FM 3-24*

Although the names of General David Petraeus (US Army) and Lieutenant General James Amos (US Marine Corps) appear prominently in the preface of *FM 3-24*, most of the material was written by others. In fact, dozens of contributors wrote the handbook, including many academics. "Cultural knowledge" is highlighted in the first chapter:

> Cultural knowledge is essential to waging a successful counterinsurgency. American ideas of what is "normal" or "rational" are not universal. To the contrary, members of other societies often have different notions of rationality, appropriate behavior, level of religious devotion, and norms concerning gender. Thus, what may appear abnormal or strange to an external observer may appear as self-evidently normal to a group member. For this reason, counter-insurgents—especially commanders, planners, and small-scale unit leaders—should strive to avoid imposing their ideals of normalcy on a foreign cultural problem.[3]

This is elaborated in chapter 3 (coauthored by Montgomery McFate), which begins by carving out an anthropological niche: "IPB [intelligence preparation of the battlefield] in COIN [counterinsurgency] requires personnel to work in areas like economics, anthropology, and governance that may be outside their expertise.... External experts with local and regional knowledge are critical to effective preparation."[4]

Chapter 3 defines terms including society, social structure, language, power, authority and interests. It also emphasizes the importance of culture, a "web of meaning...[that] influences how people make judgments about what is right or wrong, assess what is important and unimportant, categorize things, and deal with things that do not fit into existing categories."[5]

Another section highlights "rituals, symbols, ceremonies, myths, and narratives":

> The most important cultural form for counterinsurgents to understand is the narrative...a story recounted in the form of a causally linked set of events that explains an event in a group's history and expresses the values, character, or self-identity of the group.... Commanders should pay special attention to cultural narratives of the HN [host nation] population pertaining to outlaws, revolutionary heroes, and historical resistance figures. Insurgents may use these narratives to mobilize the population.[6]

In a subsequent chapter (entitled "Executing Counterinsurgency Operations"), readers are informed that they should "develop countermessages and counternarratives to attack the insurgents' ideology. Understanding the local culture is required to do this." In other words, understanding culture is the key to creating powerful propaganda. [7]

The final sections of chapter 3 review HUMINT (human intelligence), SIGINT (signal intelligence), OSINT (open source intelligence), IMINT (imagery intelligence), MASINT (measurement and signal intelligence), GEOINT (geospatial intelligence), and "intelligence collaboration" between US agents and host nation officials.

In anthropological terms, the chapter is not innovative. It is essentially a primer on cultural relativism and social structure. At times it resembles a simplified introductory anthropology textbook—though with few examples and no illustrations. (Anthropologist David Price discovered that *FM 3-24* contains more than twenty pilfered passages, including sentences and phrases lifted from social science textbooks![8]) Much of the material is numbingly banal. Some concepts are incomplete or outdated, notably the culture concept, which suggests that culture is:

> a system of shared beliefs, values, customs, behaviors, and artifacts that members of a society use to cope with their world and with one another; learned, through a process called enculturation; shared by members of a society: there is no "culture of one"; patterned, meaning that people in a society live and think in ways forming definite, repeating patterns; changeable, through social interactions between people and groups; arbitrary, meaning that soldiers and marines should make no assumptions regarding what a society considers right and wrong, good and bad; internalized, in the sense that it is habitual, taken for granted, and perceived as "natural" by people within the society.[9]

Entirely absent from this definition is the notion of culture as a product of historical processes—in spite of the fact that for at least the last quarter century many anthropologists have stressed that culture has been profoundly shaped by state capitalism, communism, colonialism, modernization schemes, and other political and economic forces on a global scale. Instead, chapter 3 treats cultures as internally coherent, easily bounded and one-dimensional—in a manner reminiscent of the structural-functionalists of an earlier era.

Appendix A of *FM 3-24*, adapted almost entirely from David Kilcullen's essay "Twenty-Eight Articles," is strikingly different in tone, content and purpose. It is inspired by T. E. Lawrence—the man immortalized as "Lawrence of Arabia" by the US media—who in 1917 published the piece "Twenty-Seven Articles" for *Arab Bulletin*, the intelligence journal of Great Britain's Cairo-based Arab Bureau.[10] (According to Kilcullen, the

Figure 3.1: David Kilcullen (*right*) briefs US Army officers in Iraq, June 2007. (Photo courtesy of US Army.)

title was intended to allude to Lawrence's essay, which is a well-known piece among counterinsurgency theorists.)

Although Lawrence wrote his essay as a practical guide for British officers employing Arabs in battle against the Ottoman army, Kilcullen's *FM 3-24* appendix is written for US troops seeking to win "hearts and minds." Lawrence wrote his articles as "commandments," and Kilcullen follows suit. Examples illustrate both form and content:

> *Lawrence*: Learn all you can about your Ashraf and Bedu. Get to know their families, clans and tribes, friends and enemies, wells, hills and roads. Do all this by listening and by indirect inquiry. (Article 2)

> *Kilcullen*: Learn about the people, topography, economy, history, religion, and culture of the area of operations (AO). Know every village, road, field, population group, tribal leader, and ancient grievance.[11]

Kilcullen, like Lawrence, counsels a patient approach, emphasizing co-option of locals:

> *Lawrence*: Go easy for the first few weeks. A bad start is difficult to atone for, and the Arabs form their judgments on externals that we ignore. When you have reached the inner circle in a tribe, you can do as you please with yourself and them. (Article 1)

> *Kilcullen*: Do not try to crack the hardest nut first. Do not go straight

for the main insurgent stronghold or try to take on villages that support insurgents. Instead, start from secure areas and work gradually outwards. Extend influence through the local people's networks. Go with, not against, the grain of the local populace.[12]

Like Lawrence, Kilcullen also emphasizes gift-giving as a way of winning people over, though Kilcullen is more interested in providing "social work":

Lawrence: If you can, without being too lavish, forestall presents to yourself. A well-placed gift is often most effective in winning over a suspicious sheik. Never receive a present without giving a liberal return, but you may delay this return (while letting its ultimate certainty be known) if you require a particular service from the giver. (Article 16)

Kilcullen: COIN operations can be characterized as armed social work. It includes attempts to redress basic social and political problems while being shot at. This makes CMO [civil-military operations] a central COIN activity, not an afterthought.[13]

At times, the wording is nearly identical, though Lawrence is explicit about who is to be "handled":

Lawrence: Handling Hejaz Arabs is an art, not a science. (Introduction)

Kilcullen: This is art, not science.[14]

Interestingly, Lawrence is never mentioned in the appendix. Kilcullen's other written work makes a passing reference, but does not acknowledge the degree to which Lawrence's ideas and style have been influential. Nor does it mention the dark side of Lawrence's career—for example, his reliance on terrorist techniques (repeated dynamite attacks upon the Hejaz Railway).

There are significant differences between Lawrence's "Twenty-Seven Articles" and Kilcullen's appendix. Lawrence includes information about how to dress, speak, and interact with Arabs. In contrast, Appendix A includes little such ethnographic detail. Kilcullen provides guidelines for how to "prepare," "execute," and "end the mission," noting that "engagements are often won or lost in moments; whoever can bring combat power to bear in seconds wins."[15]

Other guidelines are more specific. For example, a section advises counterinsurgents to "engage the women; be cautious around the children." Since homesick soldiers are often tempted to "drop their guard with kids," the appendix warns that insurgents might use children as agents;

therefore, children should be treated cautiously. The section also recommends "co-opting neutral or friendly women through targeted social and economic programs."[16]

The appendix advises counterinsurgents to "have local forces mirror the enemy, not US forces." Rather than train local police in US-style tactics, the appendix recommends that they be encouraged to imitate "the enemy's capabilities and seek to supplant the insurgent's role."[17] Still another section suggests that small-scale programs be given preference over large ones, since local conditions favor success.

Like chapter 3, the appendix emphasizes narrative: "most societies include opinion-makers—local leaders, religious figures, media personalities, and others...[whose] influence often follows a single narrative—a simple, unifying, easily expressed story or explanation that organizes people's experience.... Undercutting their influence requires exploiting an alternative narrative."[18]

Despite its energetic prose, the appendix includes little substantive cultural knowledge. At bottom, Appendix A is a collection of counterinsurgency guidelines for manipulating local social relationships in order to

Figure 3.2: These British officers helped to enforce a system of indirect colonial rule in Baghdad, October 1932. (Photo courtesy of US Library of Congress.)

CHAPTER 3

pry insurgents away from bases of support. (In fairness, Kilcullen has written several articles published in scholarly journals that examine theoretical aspects of counterinsurgency in greater depth.)

FM 3-24 generally reads like a manual for indirect colonial rule—though "empire" and "imperial" are taboo words, never used in reference to US power. The authors draw historical examples from British, French, and Japanese colonial counterinsurgency campaigns in Malaya, Vietnam, Algeria, and China. They euphemistically refer to local leaders collaborating with occupying forces as the "host nation" (rather than indirect rulers) and uniformly describe opponents as "insurgents." Yet they never mention *empire*—hardly surprising, since *FM 3-24* is a document written for the US Army and Marine Corps, and from a perspective ensconced within US military culture. Indeed, is it possible to imagine that any US Army field manual would ever use such terms?

Instead, *FM 3-24*'s authors imply that a culturally informed occupation—with native power brokers safely co-opted by US forces, imperial policing duties carried out by a culturally sensitive occupying army, development funds doled out to local women, etc.—will result in a lighter colonial touch, with less "collateral damage" and a lower price tag. The question of whether military occupation is appropriate is not addressed, nor is there any serious exploration of assessing the legitimacy of insurgents' grievances. This is not just a simple oversight. Because it ignores the broader context of US imperial power, it is incomplete, inadequate, and at times inane. Is it anthropology at all?

That McFate, Kilcullen and others have committed social science to goals established by the Pentagon—goals that include missions resembling colonial style police operations in the Middle East and Central Asia—is indicative of a rapidly evolving approach to counterinsurgency.

"Warrior-Intellectuals" as Counterinsurgency Experts

Military interest in culture coincides with a broad shift within the Pentagon—the rise to power of a clique ("a small band of warrior-intellectuals" in the words of *Washington Post* reporter Thomas Ricks)—in the post-Rumsfeld era.[19] Among this group's most influential members is US Army General David Petraeus, who served as the top commander in Iraq before being promoted to commander of the US military's Central Command. (He drew international attention after leading the US Army's 101st Airborne Division, charged with policing northern Iraq from 2003–2004.)

Beginning in 2005, Petraeus, who has a doctorate in international relations from Princeton, began assembling a team of social science PhDs who rose to prominence as the George W. Bush administration began desperately seeking to improve the situation in Iraq. This initiative received wide media coverage, including a sympathetic front-page *Washington Post* profile of Petraeus's inner circle, which included David Kilcullen, who was on loan to the US military from the Australian government.

The warrior-intellectuals depart from the Pentagon's conventional wisdom. For example, in his counterinsurgency writing, Kilcullen encourages troops to "lighten their combat loads and enforce a habit of speed and mobility," advocates "building trusted networks" by "conducting village and neighborhood surveys to identify community needs," and suggests that soldiers "win the confidence of a few villages, and then work with those with whom they trade, intermarry, or do business." He also urges military commanders to "remember small is beautiful.... Keep programs small."[20] Such tactics are apparently anathema to many in the Pentagon. *FM 3-24* features a foreword by Petraeus and US Marine Corps Lieutenant General James Amos which reveals much about their world view and interest in cultural knowledge: "conducting a successful counterinsurgency campaign requires a flexible, adaptive force led by agile, well-informed, culturally astute leaders.... Our Soldiers and Marines deserve nothing less," they write.[21]

Ironically, the "new" approach relies upon an antiquated culture concept (in the work of McFate) and a reinterpretation of Lawrence's counterinsurgency tips from the 1910s (in the work of Kilcullen)—perhaps not surprising for warrior-intellectuals seeking particular forms of cultural knowledge that might facilitate indirect rule over foreign lands. Like the colonial administrators of yesteryear, today's nation builders find practical use in a one-dimensional culture concept.

The fact that *Time* magazine could describe *FM 3-24* as "radical," "revolutionary," and "Zen tinged" is a sobering reminder of the intellectual impoverishment of a reactionary mass media. It also reveals a broader pattern of cultural militarization.[22]

The Military-Anthropology Complex

There are other connections between anthropologists, military counterinsurgency experts, and intelligence agencies. Journals such as *Military Review* (published by the US Army's Combined Arms Center) and the online *Small Wars Journal* have featured articles explicitly advocating a more "anthropological" approach to war fighting.[23]

Some retired generals have even called for "culture-centric warfare." Testifying before the US House Armed Services Committee in 2004, Major General Robert Scales argued that "during the present 'cultural' phase of the war...intimate knowledge of the enemy's motivation, intent, will, tactical method, and cultural environment has proven to be far more important for success than the deployment of smart bombs, unmanned aircraft, and expansive bandwidth."[24] Furthermore, Scales suggested, the US military could learn a lesson from the British:

> The British Army created a habit of "seconding" bright officers to various corners of the world so as to immerse them in the cultures of the Empire and to become intimate with potentates from Egypt to Malaya. Names like China [sic] Gordon and T. E. Lawrence testify to the wisdom of such a custom.... At the heart of a cultural-centric approach to future war would be a cadre of global scouts, well educated, with a penchant for languages and a comfort with strange and distant places. These soldiers should be given time to immerse themselves in a single culture.... They should attend graduate schools in disciplines necessary to understand human behavior and cultural anthropology.[25]

Shortly after Scales testified to Congress, the Pentagon created a new program called the Human Terrain System (see chapter 5 of this book). According to Montgomery McFate and Andrea Jackson, such teams might provide one part of a larger organizational solution to the Defense Department's "cultural knowledge needs." In an article published in *Military Review*, they stressed the need for a proposed organization to "augment the military's ability to effectively plan, train, and operate in the complex human terrain of weak states by conducting unbiased, accurate field research in countries of interest and administering related programs."[26]

At the same time that this proposal for "unbiased, accurate field research" was issued, one of the authors was arguing that the military needed to better understand an ambiguously defined "adversary culture" in Iraq composed of tribal warfare, blood feuds, and other customs typical of "an enemy so deeply moored in history and theology."[27] This remarkable conclusion was based not on participant observation, but largely on reports from the *New York Times*, the *Washington Post*, and the *Wall Street Journal*. The article did not provide even a minimal distinction between adversary culture, Arab societies, Islam in its various forms, Wahaabism, and the ideologies of al-Qaeda. Instead, it declared that al-Qaeda and Iraqi insurgent "adversaries neither think nor act like nation-states.... Their form of warfare, organizational structure, and motivations are determined by the society and the culture from which they came"—which begs the question of *which* society and *which* culture, given that al-Qaeda operatives come from perhaps sixty different countries?[28] Small wonder that facile "unbiased" notions of culture are preferred by soldier-scholars working for government agencies: they appear to provide ideological justifications for military occupation through appeals to orientalist stereotypes.

Apart from government agencies, contractors to the military are also employing many anthropologists. The following is a small sample of contractors that have recently recruited anthropologists to service military operations:

1. BAE Systems is advertising a "field anthropologist" position for deployment to Iraq and Afghanistan for what appears to be counterinsurgency support work. The job is "designed to dramatically improve the collection, interpretation, understanding, operational application, and sharing of local cultural knowledge.... [It] facilitates the collection, analysis, archiving, and application of cultural information relevant to the unit commander's operational decision making process."

2. Hicks & Associates (a subsidiary of the multinational Science Applications International Corporation) is advertising a "research assistant" position for a project that "investigates the evolution of subnational identities within and across states, and the implication of culture on attitudinal perspectives of other groups...[in] Tunisia and other North African nations.... The position requires a background in anthropology.... Arabic language skills are a plus."

3. L-3 Communications is advertising a position for "cultural expert—Middle East." Duties include "technical intelligence data gathering and analysis skills and abilities to manage, develop, implement, and administer intelligence analysis programs and policies for customer applications." Candidate "MUST be fluent in Arabic, Pashtu, or Persian-Farsi...MUST have knowledge of prevalent Sunni and Shia tribes in the Middle East.... US Citizens applying must hold PhD in History or Anthropology."

4. Military Professional Resources Incorporated (MPRI) is advertising a "COIN operations specialist" position in order to "provide Brigade Combat Team or Regiment, battalion and company-level leaders of Coalition units and brigade and battalion-level leaders of Transition Teams (MiTT/NPTT/BTT) and the Iraqi Security Forces (Iraqi Army and Iraqi National Police) with a fundamental understanding of COIN principles, lessons learned and TTPs required to

execute full-spectrum operations in the Iraqi Theater of Operations....
A Master's Degree in Military Science, Psychology, Cultural
Anthropology" is preferred and military experience is a requirement.

5. Booz Allen Hamilton is advertising a position for a "war on terrorism
analyst" who will conduct "research into adversary and target country elements of power, including political, military, economic, social,
infrastructure, and information (PMESII) systems to assist military
planners...conduct evaluations of terrorist adversary and target
country response to effects based activities...[and] work with joint
military planners and the inter-agency community to determine
planning options to achieve War on Terrorism efforts and objectives." Qualifications include a BA or BS degree, with "knowledge of
political science, economics, social anthropology, infrastructure, or
information operations preferred."

Figure 3.3: BAE Systems, one of the largest European military contractors,
produces the Bradley assault vehicle (pictured here) and also contracts social
scientists for counterinsurgency support work in Iraq and Afghanistan.
(Photo courtesy of BAE Systems.)

6. The Mitre Corporation is advertising a "Sr. artificial intelligence engineer" position "to play a role in applying modeling and simulation as an experimental approach to social and behavioral science problems of national significance...[and] to apply social sciences to critical national security issues." Desirable applicants will have a "PhD in a social science discipline (e.g. anthropology, sociology, sociolinguistics, medical anthropology, cultural geography, comparative social and cognitive psychology, cultural communication studies, science/technology studies, international labor/industrial relations, industrial/organizational psychology, comparative political science, public administration)."

Counterinsurgency consulting represents a reappearance of militarized anthropology, in which military and intelligence agencies employ social science as just another weapon on the battlefield. When such work is carried out covertly and without informed consent, it represents a grave breach of the American Anthropological Association's (AAA's) code of ethics. When it is carried out by anthropologists working as cultural mercenaries—hired to design or implement culturally specific counterinsurgency campaigns or other war making tactics—the ethical transgressions are graver still.

Oppositional Forces

The crass use of "cultural knowledge" in the military deserves fuller and deeper analysis. A preliminary approach might include exploration of the degree to which self-styled anthropologists who write military field manuals (as opposed to academic texts) have adhered to contemporary professional standards. Shouldn't anthropologists be responsible for conducting work that reflects current methodological, theoretical and ethical concerns? Answering this question affirmatively would surely preclude consulting work for counterinsurgency projects.

The potential consequences of anthropologists engaging in counterinsurgency work could be wide-ranging, with multiple impacts on military personnel and those living under occupation. But when such work is performed clandestinely this undermines and endangers the work of social scientists more generally, not to mention their families and informants, potentially putting them at risk. As anthropologist Hugh Gusterson notes, "once Thai peasants or Somali clansmen learn that some anthropologists are secretly working for the US government, they begin to suspect all other anthropologists. Anthropologists have a professional obligation to one another not to conduct slash-and-burn fieldwork."[29]

Those serving the short-term interests of military and intelligence agencies and contractors will end up harming the entire discipline in the long run, particularly in an era of rapid global communication. Such collaboration leads down a slippery slope that may ultimately prove disastrous for anthropologists and, more importantly, the research participants with whom we work. If the discipline moves towards open cooperation with counterinsurgency efforts today, what is to keep it from moving towards more covert cooperation tomorrow—or, eventually, towards a mercenary anthropology in which cultural knowledge itself is used as a weapon? The words of anthropologist Neil Whitehead serve to remind us that over time, counterinsurgents tend to mirror their enemies:

> As we look at counterinsurgency campaigns, those counterinsurgency campaigns tend to proceed by exactly the same kinds of military ploys that are being used by their terrorist enemies. So the selective assassination of individuals, the planting of particular kinds of bomb, or the mining of particular kinds of places which are heavily used by civilians even if they are at the same time being used by terrorists—these are all ways in which the military activity of the state, as it engages with a terrorist enemy, itself becomes more like terrorism.[30]

Counterinsurgency campaigns in which the state has resorted to terroristic "military ploys" include those in Guatemala, Vietnam, Algeria, Northern Ireland, East Timor, Chile, and Argentina, to name but a few examples over the last half century.

It is with such concerns in mind that a colleague and I submitted two resolutions to members of the American Anthropological Association at its November 2006 annual meeting. One condemned torture and the use of anthropological knowledge as an element of torture, while the other condemned the US occupation of Iraq.[31] Nearly 300 anthropologists—the largest number in decades—packed the conference auditorium and adopted both resolutions, which were then submitted to the Association's full membership by postal ballot. Several months later, the resolutions were passed overwhelmingly, sending an unambiguous message to the military and intelligence agencies seeking to recruit anthropologists (as well as to anthropologists working on their behalf), namely that members of the Association staunchly oppose wars of aggression and will stand united against activities that might breach our professional ethics.

Although academic resolutions are not likely to transform US government policies (much less the practices of contractors to the military), they do articulate a set of values and ethical concerns shared by many anthropologists. They could potentially extend and amplify dialogue among social scientists around issues of torture, collaboration with the military, and the potential abuse of social science in the so-called war on terror. Anthropologists may well inspire others to confront directly—and resist—the militarization of their disciplines at this critical moment in the history of the social sciences.

Notes

1. George Packer, "Knowing the Enemy," *New Yorker*, December 18, 2006, http://www.newyorker.com/archive/2006/12/18/061218fa_fact2. Though Packer erroneously described Kilcullen as holding a "doctorate in political anthropology," Kilcullen did submit a PhD dissertation to the School of Politics, University College, University of New South Wales, in affiliation with the Australian Defence Force Academy. It is based upon research in West Java and East Timor. In the dissertation, Kilcullen makes reference to using multi-disciplinary research techniques including anthropological methods and analysis. See David Kilcullen, "Political Consequences of Military Operations in Indonesia 1945–2000: A Fieldwork Analysis of the Political Power-Diffusion Effects of Guerrilla Conflict," (PhD dissertation, School of Politics, University of New South Wales, 2000).

2. Militarized anthropology can be defined as anthropology *for* military institutions, not *of* military institutions. Though some claim that it is possible to "anthropologize" the military—that is, to incorporate anthropological perspectives into military decision-making and consequently transform the military from within—the historical record is full of instances in which military officials ignored anthropologists' insights when they ran counter to pre-established missions, and adopted them when they were aligned with these missions. In militarized settings, anthropologists have tended to function as cogs in large bureaucracies with pre-determined goals—not surprising, given the vast difference in power between US military institutions and American anthropology over the past century. There has been no significant difference between militarized anthropology and an "anthropologized" military.

3. US Army, *Counterinsurgency: Field Manual 3-24* (Washington DC: Government Printing Office, 2006), 1/15.

4. Ibid., 3/2.

5. Ibid., 3/6.

6. Ibid., 3/8.

7. Ibid., 5/10. Anthropologists have sometimes participated in wartime propaganda campaigns. For example, Gregory Bateson designed and executed "black propaganda" campaigns in Burma, Thailand, India, China and Ceylon. For discussion of the ethical complications accompanying such work see David Price, "Gregory Bateson and the OSS," *Human Organization* 57, no. 4 (1998): 379–384.

8. David Price, "Pilfered Scholarship Devastates General Petraeus's Counterinsurgency Manual," *CounterPunch*, October 30, 2007, http://www.counterpunch.org/price10302007.html (accessed May 20, 2010).

9. US Army, *Counterinsurgency*, 3/6–3/7.

10. See David Kilcullen, "Twenty–Eight Articles: Fundamentals of Company-Level Counterinsurgency," *Military Review*, May–June 2006, http://usacac.army.mil/cac2/COIN/repository/28_Articles_of_COIN-Kilcullen(Mar06).pdf (accessed May 20, 2010). See also T.E. Lawrence, "Twenty-Seven Articles," *Arab Bulletin*, August 20, 1917.

11. US Army, *Counterinsurgency*, A/1.

12. Ibid., A/5.

13. Ibid., A/7.

14. Ibid.

15. Ibid., A/3.

16. Ibid., A/6.

17. Ibid., A/7.

18. Ibid.

19. Thomas Ricks, "Officers with PhDs Advising War Effort," *Washington Post*, February 5, 2007. Over the years, numerous scholars have outlined how military institutions and peacekeeping forces can benefit from a deeper understanding of "culture." See, for example, Ken Booth, *Strategy and Ethnocentrism* (London: Croom Helm, 1979); Robert A. Rubinstein, *Peacekeeping under Fire: Culture and Intervention* (New York: Paradigm Publishers, 2008).

20. David Kilcullen, "Counterinsurgency Redux," *Survival* 48, no. 4 (2006): 104, 105, 107.

21. US Army, *Counterinsurgency*, 1.

22. Joe Klein, "Good General, Bad Mission," *Time*, January 12, 2007.

23. Many articles in these journals are poorly written and inaccurate. When anthropological works are cited, arguments regarding ethical and theoretical issues are sometimes omitted. For example, a *Military Review* article makes the unsupported claim that "anthropologists en masse, bound by their own ethical code and sunk in a mire of postmodernism, are unlikely to contribute

much of value to reshaping national security policy or practice"—even though dozens of anthropologists are contributing to national security by directly informing citizens about US foreign policy issues. See Montgomery McFate, "Anthropology and Counterinsurgency: The Strange Story of Their Curious Relationship," *Military Review,* March–April 2005, 37.

24. Robert H. Scales, "Army Transformation: Implications for the Future," (testimony before the US House Armed Services Committee), July 15, 2004, http://www.au.af.mil/au/awc/awcgate/congress/04-07-15scales.pdf (accessed May 20, 2010).

25. Ibid.

26. Montgomery McFate and Andrea Jackson, "An Organizational Solution for DOD's Cultural Knowledge Needs," *Military Review,* July–August 2005, 21.

27. Montgomery McFate, "The Military Utility of Understanding Adversary Culture," *Joint Force Quarterly* 38 (2005): 43.

28. Anthropologist Dale Eickelman provides insight by noting that al-Qaeda sympathizers are not stuck in the past or deeply moored in history, but rather are thoroughly modern. He argues that the network is a "flexible multinational organization" that uses "new communications technologies" to disseminate its ideologies. His analysis leads to the following proposal: "The best long-term way to mitigate the continuing threat of terrorism is to encourage Middle Eastern states to be more responsive to their populations' demands for participation." See Dale Eickelman, "First, Know the Enemy, Then Act," *Los Angeles Times,* December 9, 2001.

29. Hugh Gusterson, "Anthropology and the Military—1968, 2003, and Beyond?" *Anthropology Today* 19, no. 3 (2003): 25. By "slash-and-burn fieldwork," Gusterson is referring to clandestine fieldwork that would undermine the ability of other scientists to conduct future research. While it is true that people in many parts of the world (including many Native Americans) have suspected anthropologists of conducting secret research for the CIA, other US government agencies, or non-governmental organizations, the professional ethics codes of the American Anthropological Association and the Society for Applied Anthropology have provided researchers (and their research participants) with a framework for understanding the responsibilities and ethical obligations of the anthropologist since 1971 and 1949, respectively.

30. Neil Whitehead, quoted in *War Is Sell,* DVD directed by Brian Standing, (Madison, WI: Prolefeed Studios, 2004).

31. The anti-torture resolution notes that "the American Anthropological Association unequivocally condemns the use of anthropological knowledge as an element of physical and psychological torture; condemns the use of physical and psychological torture by US Military and Intelligence personnel, subcontractors, and proxies; and urges the US Congress and President George W. Bush to…comply fully with national and international anti-torture laws, including the Geneva Conventions and protocols, the UN Convention Against Torture, the 1996 US War Crimes Act, and US Criminal Code, Sections

2340–2340A." See American Anthropological Association, "Statement on Torture," June 2007, http://aaanet.org/issues/policy-advocacy/Statement-on-Torture.cfm (accessed June 1, 2010). The Iraq resolution states that "the American Anthropological Association condemns the US-led invasion and occupation of Iraq and urges the US Congress and President George W. Bush to…immediately withdraw all US military personnel, intelligence agents, and subcontrators from Iraq; and cease all US military operations and vacate all U.S. military bases in Iraq" among other things. See American Anthropological Association, "Statement on the US Occupation of Iraq," June 2007, http://aaanet.org/issues/policy-advocacy/Statement-on-the-US-Occupation-of-Iraq.cfm (accessed June 1, 2010).

Chapter 4
The Arab Mind and Abu Ghraib

For more than five years, many questions have been raised about how Israeli anthropologist Raphael Patai's book *The Arab Mind* might have been implicated in the torture of Iraqi prisoners at the Abu Ghraib prison compound. Veteran journalist Seymour Hersh described the significance of Patai's book in a widely read article published in the *New Yorker* magazine on May 25, 2004.[1] His report, which described the genesis and development of a secret Pentagon program for harsh interrogation of suspected al-Qaeda operatives, appeared four weeks after the television broadcast of grisly photos depicting torture and abuses committed by US troops at Abu Ghraib.[2]

Many social scientists were particularly shocked by the following sections of Hersh's article:

> The notion that Arabs are particularly vulnerable to sexual humiliation became a talking point among pro-war Washington conservatives in the months before the March 2003 invasion of Iraq. One book that was frequently cited was *The Arab Mind*, a study of Arab culture and psychology, first published in 1973, by Raphael Patai, a cultural anthropologist who taught at, among other universities, Columbia and Princeton, and who died in 1996. The book includes a 25-page chapter on Arabs and sex, depicting sex as a taboo vested with shame and repression. "The segregation of the sexes, the veiling of the women...and all the other minute rules that govern and restrict contact between men and women, have the effect of making sex a prime mental preoccupation in the Arab world," Patai wrote. Homosexual activity, "or any indication of homosexual leanings, as with all other expressions of sexuality, is never given any publicity. These are private affairs and remain in private." The Patai book, an academic told me, was "the bible of the neocons on Arab behavior." In their discussions, he said, two themes emerged—"one, that Arabs only understand force and, two, that the biggest weakness of Arabs is shame and humiliation."[3]

According to Hersh, the Abu Ghraib photos may have been part of an effort to create informants by exploiting "shame and humiliation"—themes that were a central part of Patai's book:

> The government consultant said that there may have been a serious goal, in the beginning, behind the sexual humiliation and the posed photographs. It was thought that some prisoners would do anything—including spying on their associates—to avoid dissemination of the shameful photos to family and friends. The government consultant said, "I was told that the purpose of the photographs was to create an army of informants, people you could insert back in the population."[4]

Intense reactions followed the publication of Hersh's article. In September 2004, *Anthropology News* (the American Anthropological Association's official newsletter) published several commentaries examining torture in the context of Abu Ghraib, including one that focused exclusively on *The Arab Mind*.[5]

The subsequent controversy raised the troubling question of how knowledge about other cultures might be easily misused by policy makers. Many social scientists in particular were disturbed by the mere possibility that Patai's work might have been culled by neoconservative policy makers seeking propaganda sources for their objectives. Had he still been alive, what would Patai have made of the way his book had reportedly become essential reading for officers in the US military?[6]

This chapter begins with a sample of anthropological responses to Hersh's allegations. Then, it examines new revelations pointing more precisely to the role that *The Arab Mind* played (and continues to play) in military and intelligence circles, particularly its tendency to dehumanize the Arab "other" in the minds of many US military personnel deploying to the Middle East. It concludes by analyzing a range of implications surrounding the Patai controversy in the context of "attack[s] on cultural sensitivity, particularly Arab male sensitivity" in the so-called war on terror.[7] Here I will be concerned not so much with reviewing the content of Patai's book (which others have covered extensively) as with the possible reasons for, and consequences of, the selection of *The Arab Mind* by US military and intelligence personnel.

Anthropological Responses to the *New Yorker* Article

Various anthropologists responded to Hersh's report after its appearance. Writing in *The Nation*, Amitav Ghosh reflected upon US interrogators and their British counterparts during the era of empire:[8]

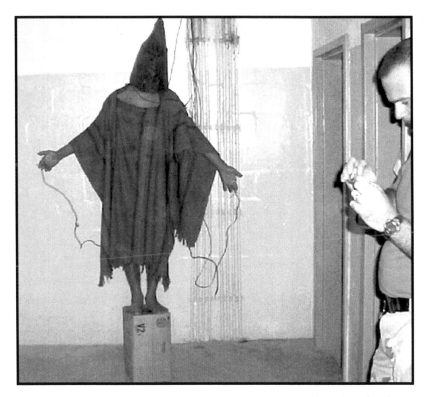

Figure 4.1: Iraqi prisoner tortured by US military personnel at Abu Ghraib, November 2003. (Photo in the public domain.)

The methods employed in Abu Ghraib and Guantánamo Bay are said to have been informed by the ideas of anthropologists like Raphael Patai, who, in his notorious 1973 work *The Arab Mind*, wrote at length about Arab conceptions of sexuality, honor, and masculinity. British prison officials in India were also careful to target what they thought were deep-rooted fears and taboos. They believed, for instance, that Indians dreaded sea voyages more than death itself: This was, in their eyes, one of the great advantages of island prisons.[9]

Montgomery McFate also mentioned *The Arab Mind*, noting that Patai's book was a case of "bad anthropology" leading to "bad strategy." She added that "the alleged use of Patai's book as the basis of the psychological torment at Abu Ghraib, devoid of any understanding of the broader context of Iraqi culture, demonstrates the folly of using decontextualized culture as the basis of policy."[10]

Later, I raised the possibility that interrogators might have used Patai's book "to provide culturally specific material for developing torture techniques"[11]—not an implausible scenario, given the fact that the commanding officer in Iraq, US Army Lieutenant General Ricardo Sánchez, issued a secret memo in late 2003 approving the use of canines to "exploit Arab fear of dogs."[12] Exploitation of phobias is clearly outlined in the US Army's *Field Manual 34-52—Intelligence Interrogation* which notes that "it is critical the interrogator distinguish what the source fears in order to exploit that fear."[13] Subsequent reports, however, indicate that "reverse engineering" of SERE (Survival, Evasion, Resistance, Escape)—a US military program which trains soldiers to endure capture—played a leading role in the design of aggressive interrogation techniques including torture. Two psychologists, James Elmer Mitchell and Bruce Jessen, reportedly played a key role in this process.[14]

Alfred McCoy's research into the ways in which US spy agencies began incorporating behavioral science research a half-century ago provides historical context. In his book *A Question of Torture*, McCoy describes how brutal torture methods were augmented in the 1950s and 1960s by the work of American and Canadian psychologists who discovered that sensory deprivation, disorientation, and self-inflicted pain could break down the human psyche more effectively than physical assaults. These scientists unwittingly paved the way for what McCoy calls "a distinctively American form of torture," relying on psychological assaults, used extensively by the CIA and its proxies during the latter half of the twentieth century. According to McCoy, these techniques were further refined beginning in 2002 when US agents at Guantánamo Bay under General Geoffrey Miller's leadership created a "de facto behavioral research laboratory" for attacking perceived Arab male vulnerabilities related to sexual identity. Miller was assigned to Iraq in 2003, where he was charged with transferring interrogation techniques from Guantánamo Bay to Iraqi prisons. Although anthropological knowledge was not implicated in the CIA's culturally specific interrogation techniques until the late 1970s, McCoy's work implies that such processes are now well under way.[15]

Some anthropologists, such as David Price, cautioned against giving too much credence to a direct link between Patai's book and Abu Ghraib, while recalling the CIA's "pilfering" of anthropology during the Cold War:

The CIA has long recognized that anthropology, with its broadly traveled and culturally and linguistically competent practitioners, has highly useful skill sets. And while we should not read too much into published reports that the CIA-directed torture techniques at Abu

CHAPTER 4

Ghraib were fine-tuned for high levels of culturally specific humiliation by the reading of anthropologist Raphael Patai's book *The Arab Mind* (Patai's scholarship is stained with Orientalist stereotypes and it doesn't take an insider's knowledge that Arabs generally abhor dogs and sexual humiliation to presume that tormenting bound naked men with vicious dogs would be an effective means of torture), anthropologists have long had their work pilfered by American intelligence agencies.[16]

Laura McNamara—an anthropologist employed by Sandia National Laboratories—was even more reluctant about making a connection between Patai's book and the Abu Ghraib scandal. For example, at the March 2009 meetings of the Society for Applied Anthropology, McNamara remarked that "the more you read them [Seymour Hersh's words], the more you realize that Hersh's allegations about *The Arab Mind* and Abu Ghraib comprise no more than a loose collection of associations—it's a lot of words without a whole lot of direct fact."[17] According to McNamara, when she questioned Seymour Hersh about the *New Yorker* article, he adamantly denied making any claims about a direct link between Patai's book and the methods employed by US interrogators at Abu Ghraib.

Fear Up Harsh: Creating a "Culture of Abuse"

Although it now seems unlikely that Patai's book is directly related to specific interrogation practices employed by US personnel at Abu Ghraib or Guantánamo Bay, new information—notably, the account of Tony Lagouranis, a former US Army interrogator—brings into sharper focus the ways in which *The Arab Mind* has been incorporated into the training of US military intelligence personnel and officers.

In January 2004, Lagouranis first arrived in Iraq and was assigned to Abu Ghraib. He then joined a special intelligence gathering team that conducted interrogations at various detention centers throughout Iraq until January 2005. Lagouranis's book, *Fear Up Harsh*, paints a frightening picture of the downward spiral leading ordinary men and women to brutalize prisoners.[18]

The book's second chapter highlights how military intelligence personnel were frequently exposed to negative stereotypes about Arabs. Lagouranis's initial experiences at Abu Ghraib included a lecture titled "The Arab Mind" presented by a US Army psychiatrist:

Major Morgan started his lecture by admitting that he didn't know any Arabs, and had little contact with them. He assured us, however, that he had read a few books on the subject.... It was odd that someone stationed in the middle of Iraq and charged with lecturing on the Arab mind had not taken the time to get to know a few Arabs. [19]

According to Lagouranis, the lecture began with a description of taboos and, eventually, crude stereotypes of Arabs:

We kicked things off with a few items of cultural sensitivity. *Don't show an Arab the sole of your foot. Don't humiliate a man in public. Men should not touch Arab women—and female soldiers should avoid touching Arab men. Arabs like to exchange pleasantries before getting down to business—ask about their families.* I considered the absurdity of doing this in an interrogation, as our lecturer moved ever more deeply into the Arab mind. *Arabs*, apparently, *can't create a timeline. They don't think linearly or rationally. They have a different relationship with the truth than we do. They prefer the beautiful to the true. They rely on metaphor instead of facts. They think through association, not logic or reason.... Lying is not taboo or dishonorable to Arabs.* This seemed to relate to that different relationship with truth they have. *So you can't trap them in a contradiction or force them to admit they're lying. They'll consider you impolite and uncultured.* I rolled my eyes and looked around the room to share my dismay with others. But most were nodding in understanding and agreement. Very few of us recognized this as racist bullshit.[20]

Lagouranis then connects the lecture to Patai's book:

Our instructor wasn't relying on a very large body of research to produce these "facts." He essentially borrowed everything he said from a single book, *The Arab Mind*.... The central problem with *The Arab Mind*, and with the lecture we got, was with the way they both set up the Arabs as distant from and alien to the "Western mind." Nothing about the Arab mind, it seems, can be understood unless it is compared to the Western mind. We reason—they tell stories. We use facts—they use metaphors. And so on. There was no attempt to understand Arabs on their own terms. It was strictly us versus them. And so, while the intention of this lecture was to help us appreciate this alien culture and work with it, the effect it had was to reinforce prejudice and give many soldiers an excuse to give up on ever understanding or improving Iraqi society. *That's just the way they are. Nothing we can do about it.... These people can't do anything for themselves.*[21]

Later, Lagouranis notes: "The [prison] guards and I talked often, about their cynical view of the war. *The problems here go back thousands of years.*

The Arabs understand only force. We're too nice to work in this part of the world. Standard stuff."[22]

In 2005, the investigative TV news program *Frontline* conducted an interview with Lagouranis in which he was asked about how stereotypes affected interrogators:

Frontline: What was the effect of that kind of information on [US interrogators]?

Lagouranis: They believed it, and they continued throughout the whole year that we were there with that idea about Arabs, that they're liars and they don't make sense; they're not rational.

Frontline: And so what happens in an environment...where that becomes the way you feel about the people in your control?

Lagouranis: Well, partly that lends to the frustration. Because they're blaming their lack of ability to get intelligence on the fact that a logical argument presented to somebody, or whatever psychological way that you're going to back them into a corner isn't going to work on an Arab.... I think it added to the frustration and probably contributed to this culture of abuse.[23]

In June 2007, I contacted Lagouranis, who received an honorable discharge from the military in 2005 and now resides in Chicago. He confirmed that knowledge about Patai's book was widespread among intelligence agents, and it was frequently included on recommended reading lists. Lagouranis's description of life in Iraqi detention centers reveals a world in which the "culture of abuse" developed and spread infectiously. Pressure from superiors to obtain intelligence, persistent attacks from insurgents launching grenades and mortars, overcrowded prisons, ambiguous rules of engagement, the constant circulation of DVDs with Hollywood movies and TV shows glorifying torture—not to mention dehumanizing stereotypes about the "Arab mind" that were taught to military personnel in both formal and informal settings—together contributed to a toxic atmosphere in which brutal interrogations became commonplace. In the end, Iraqi prisoners often provided little more than false confessions.

Twenty-First-Century Orientalism

In his book Lagouranis reveals that *The Arab Mind* played a vital role in helping to create an environment conducive to abuse of Iraqi detainees by exoticizing and dehumanizing Arab people. The book fits squarely within a tradition of European (and American) discourses portraying the people of the Middle East as primitive, exotic, sensuous, and dangerous—a series of discourses analyzed by Edward Said in the book *Orientalism*. Said argued that this style of thought was inextricably connected with the political, economic and cultural project of empire—not only as a rationalization of European (and later US) imperial rule over the Middle East, but as a precursor that appeared to justify it, making it natural, desirable, and good: "Orientalism can be discussed and analyzed as the corporate institution for dealing with the Orient—dealing with it by making statements about it, authorizing views of it, describing it, by teaching it, settling it, ruling over it: in short, Orientalism as a Western style for dominating, restructuring, and having authority over the Orient."[24] Said's work is often interpreted as a critique of British and French orientalists of the nineteenth and early twentieth centuries, yet his critique also targets contemporary orientalists, including Patai.[25]

Why would US military officials and intelligence agents (and neoconservative policy makers, according to Hersh) use a book portraying Arabs as fatalistic, disorganized, ineffective dissimulators? Some might argue that *The Arab Mind* was the most accessible ethnography available to English language readers, since it can be purchased quickly and inexpensively.

Figure 4.2: Orientalist paintings such as "The Snake Charmer" by Jean-Léon Gérôme portrayed Middle Eastern people as exotic, primitive, and dangerous. (Image in the public domain.)

CHAPTER 4

However, other easily accessible ethnographies are much richer, more culturally nuanced and not orientalist. For example, Elizabeth Fernea's book *Guests of the Sheik*, set in a Shia village in southern Iraq, is used in many introductory anthropology classes. Lila Abu-Lughod's *Veiled Sentiments* is another fine-grained ethnography that portrays the lives of Egyptian Bedouins in a sensitive and humanizing way.[26] How might Lagouranis and other interrogators have treated Iraqi prisoners if they had read these books rather than Patai's? Would it have made any difference? Or were there simply too many military and intelligence personnel interested in learning about and exploiting the supposed weaknesses of the "Arab mind"?

It seems all but inevitable that Patai's book (or something similar) would become a key text for those planning and executing the invasion and occupation of Iraq. After all, occupying armies are not in the business of understanding the humanity of the occupied; they are charged with the task of policing them, controlling them, and interrogating them. Said's *Orientalism* provides a framework for understanding the intellectual influences behind the US-led invasion of Iraq and its terrible aftermath, including the Abu Ghraib abuses.[27] In the final weeks of his life, Said wrote:

> It is surely one of the intellectual catastrophes of history that an imperialist war confected by a small group of unelected US officials was waged against a devastated third world dictatorship on thoroughly ideological grounds.... The major influences on George W. Bush's Pentagon and National Security Council were men such as Bernard Lewis and Fouad Ajami, experts on the Arab and Islamic world who helped the American hawks to think about such preposterous phenomena as the Arab mind and the centuries-old Islamic decline which only American power could reverse. Today bookstores in the US are filled with shabby screeds bearing screaming headlines about Islam and terror, the Arab threat and the Muslim menace, all of them written by political polemicists pretending to knowledge imparted by experts who have supposedly penetrated to the heart of these strange oriental peoples. CNN and Fox, plus myriad evangelical and right wing radio hosts, innumerable tabloids and even middle-brow journals, have recycled the same unverifiable fictions.... Without a well-organized sense that the people over there were not like "us" and didn't appreciate "our" values—the very core of traditional orientalist dogma—there would have been no war.[28]

Patai's caricature of the depraved Arab, amplified by latter-day orientalists on cable news programs, easily accompanied and justified the twenty-first-century phase of an imperial pattern more than two centuries old.

Justifying Military Occupation in the Middle East

"It should be clear to anthropologists that anything we say can and will be used in ways outside our control," cautioned Gregory Starrett in an article about Abu Ghraib.[29] Perhaps the most constructive thing that might yet come of *The Arab Mind* controversy is a clearer understanding of the ways in which military and intelligence agents might use anthropological knowledge against the people with whom we work, in the Middle East, in Southeast Asia, in Latin America, and beyond.

Reviewing the available data, the following points can tentatively be made: (1) there is no direct evidence indicating that military and intelligence personnel at Abu Ghraib systematically used *The Arab Mind* as a torture "handbook"—in other words, interrogators do not appear to have studied the book in order to find creative ways of tormenting detainees;[30] (2) military and intelligence personnel learned about *The Arab Mind* before and after deploying to the Middle East, and many came away with dehumanizing stereotypes portraying Arabs as fatalistic, preoccupied with sex and prone to lying—thereby setting the stage for a "culture of abuse"; and (3) neoconservative policy makers were familiar with *The Arab Mind* and other contemporary orientalist texts and used the media to widely disseminate ideas about the alleged depravity of Arab and Muslim societies to state the case for a US-led invasion of Iraq.

Against this backdrop, it might be worthwhile to consider the implications of the actual and potential uses of such "cultural knowledge" by military and intelligence agencies. In theoretical terms, Patai's book illustrates the potential consequences of using a narrow range of ideas—in this case the "national character study" based upon a particular branch of psychological anthropology. A more recent example comes from the work of some military anthropologists who rely exclusively upon structural functional approaches lacking historical or political context, entirely removing the US military from the frame of analysis, as if "adversary culture" could be isolated (see chapter 3 of this book).[31] One-dimensional analyses of personality, kinship or social structure can easily lead to distorted, dehumanizing portrayals, and we should constantly be aware of this tendency in order to avoid it.[32] A more complete set of conceptual approaches might foster more humanizing (and scientifically adequate) ethnography.

The entire episode surrounding Patai's *The Arab Mind* raises the question: How can we develop methods of ethnographic writing that minimize the possibility of the CIA "harvesting" cultural knowledge, or that might reduce the chances of it being turned against the people with whom we work? Is this possible without descending into an obscurantism that further removes anthropological writing from the reach of general audiences, or self-censoring materials that expose supposed cultural vulnerabilities easily exploited by interrogators? Perhaps a more effective strategy might emerge if more US anthropologists followed the example of colleagues from Mexico, Brazil, and France (to name but a few), where many anthropologists shape public understanding by critically engaging *general* audiences rather than military, political, or economic elites.

In ethical terms, we must continue questioning the terms of engagement between anthropologists and military and intelligence agencies. If Pentagon officials, intelligence agents, and commanders have been studying *The Arab Mind*, should anthropologists try to dissuade them from such outdated ethnography? Should anthropologists seek to recommend better (non-orientalist) ethnographies to military officials?[33] It seems unlikely that non-orientalist ethnographies about Arabs or Muslims would change anything, since the broader context is one of military occupation, of conquest: the US military is deeply entrenched across the Middle East and beyond. This context presents a serious challenge to those seeking to "anthropologize" the military. Perhaps what is more desperately needed is critical ethnographies of the United States (particularly from the point of view of non-US anthropologists) in order to better understand the dynamics of what historian Niall Ferguson calls "an empire in denial." Such work might help concerned Americans find ways to more effectively mobilize their fellow citizens against the occupations of Iraq and Afghanistan. After all, according to public opinion polls, a majority of the American public has opposed the Iraq War for more than five years, and the Afghan War for more than three years.[34] What is missing is organization.

Finally, despite recent concerns over the credibility of anthropologists in the eyes of military and intelligence agencies, it is important to consider how bizarre statements by a small number of US military anthropologists can undermine our credibility from the perspectives of those with whom we work. Imagine what a Yemeni herdsman or an Indonesian farmer might think about a visiting anthropologist if he or she takes seriously the dubious notion that anthropology was born as a "warfighting discipline."[35]

Though anthropological concerns over the uses and misuses of ethnography are important, they pale in comparison to the potential effects upon people in the Middle East, North Africa, and Central Asia as US military and intelligence agencies relentlessly seek "cultural knowledge" about these regions. If *The Arab Mind* "is the book everyone is talking about" in the Pentagon, it is not as a result of its scientific value, nor its ethnographic richness, nor the originality of its arguments. Patai's "essential" book makes sense as a "first read" for Colonel DeAtkine and other officers (not to mention the Iraq war architects) because its dehumanizing portrayal of a deficient Arab mind neatly justifies the invasion and occupation of Iraq, unflinching support for the Israeli occupation of Palestinian territories, and a substantial US military presence across the Middle East and beyond. In short, it serves as an intellectual buttress for the extension of US military power. As an orientalist text, the book has been used to facilitate control of the "other" by placing the other in a subordinate position—with the full range of torturous consequences, from dehumanization to occupation and conquest. Social scientists can and should offer something more than a tool kit for empire.

Notes

1. Seymour Hersh, "The Gray Zone," *New Yorker*, May 25, 2004, http://www. newyorker.com/fact/content/?040524fa_fact. See also Raphael Patai, *The Arab Mind* (New York: Scribner, 1973). Hersh rose to international prominence following his report on the 1968 massacre at My Lai, Vietnam, (in which US soldiers killed hundreds of civilians) and the subsequent cover-up.

2. Aspects of the secret interrogation program were introduced in Iraq by US Army Major General Geoffrey Miller beginning in 2003. See George R. Fay, *Article 15-6 Investigation of the Abu Ghraib Facility and 205th Military Intelligence Brigade* (2004), 10, 24–25, 57–62. See also Antonio Taguba, *Article 15-6 Investigation of the 800th Military Police Brigade* (2004), 7–9.

3. Hersh, "The Gray Zone."

4. Ibid. The "government consultant" described by Hersh "spent much of his career directly involved with special-access programs...subject to the Defense Department's most stringent level of security."

5. Gregory Starrett, "Culture Never Dies: Anthropology at Abu Ghraib," *Anthropology News* 45, no. 6 (2005): 10–11. See also Stacy Lathrop, "Human Nature, Rights, and Ethics," *Anthropology News* 45, no. 6 (2005): 8.

6. Colonel Norvell B. DeAtkine—a Middle East studies instructor at the US Army John F. Kennedy Special Warfare School—wrote a foreword to the 2002 edition of Patai's book describing it as "essential reading," noting that it "forms the basis of my cultural instruction." See Norvell B. DeAtkine, "Foreword," in Raphael Patai, *The Arab Mind* (New York: Hatherleigh Press, 2002), x–xviii.

It is recommended as a "first read" for majors and lieutenant colonels head-ed to Iraq, according to the US Army's Command and General Staff College Deploying Officer Reading List. It is also listed in the US Marine Corps Professional Reading List.

7. Alfred McCoy, quoted in "Professor McCoy Exposes the History of CIA Inter-rogation," *Democracy Now!* (syndicated by Pacifia Radio), February 17, 2006, http://www.democracynow.org/2006/2/17/professor_mccoy_exposes_the_ history_of (accessed November 12, 2007).

8. Amitav Ghosh, "Theater of Cruelty: Reflections on the Anniversary of Abu Ghraib," *The Nation*, July 18–25, 2005, 31–32.

9. Ibid., 31.

10. Montgomery McFate, "Anthropology and Counterinsurgency: The Strange Story of their Curious Relationship," *Military Review*, March–April 2005, 37.

11. Roberto J. González, "Standing Up against Torture and War," *Anthropology News* 48, no. 3 (2007): 5.

12. Ricardo Sánchez, "CJTF-7 Interrogation and Counter-Resistance Policy," October 2003, http://www.aclu.org/safefree/general/175611g120050329.html (accessed January 29, 2010). The idea that Arabs are inordinately fearful of dogs is apparently not unusual among some high-ranking military officers, though such a phobia is nowhere mentioned in Patai's book. On May 26, 2006, at the court martial hearing for US Army Sergeant Santos Cardona (an Abu Ghraib dog handler), Major General Geoffrey Miller, who had been in charge of Guantanamo prison before being transferred to Iraq, testified that he was aware of an alleged "cultural fear of dogs in Arab culture"—though he denied recommending dogs for use in Iraqi prisons—see Hina Shamsi, "General Miller Takes the Stand," *Human Rights First*, May 2005, http://www. humanrightsfirst.org/blog/cardona/2006/05/general-miller-takes-stand.aspx (accessed January 29, 2010). Sánchez, Miller, and others may have assumed that statements attributed to the Prophet Muhammad about the impure and evil nature of dogs (found in numerous *hadith*) are interpreted literally by Arab Muslims today, though clearly any shackled person exposed to snarling German shepherds would be terrified.

13. US Army, *Intelligence Interrogation: Field Manual 34-52* (Washington DC: Government Printing Office, 1992), 3/16.

14. Katherine Eban, "Rorschach and Awe," *Vanity Fair*, July 17, 2007, http:// www.vanityfair.com/politics/features/2007/07/torture200707 (accessed January 29, 2010).

15. See Alfred McCoy, *A Question of Torture* (New York, Metropolitan Books, 2006).

16. David Price, "The CIA's Campus Spies," *CounterPunch*, March 12, 2005, http:// www.counterpunch.org/price03122005.html (accessed January 30, 2010).

17. Laura McNamara, "Culture, Torture, Interrogation, and the Global War on Terrorism," (presentation, annual meetings of the Society for Applied

Anthropology, Santa Fe, NM, March 17–21, 2009), http://sfaapodcasts. net/2009/05/10/scholars-security-and-citizenship-part-i-sar-plenary/ (accessed February 15, 2010).

18. Tony Lagouranis and Allen Mikaelian, *Fear Up Harsh: An Army Interrogator's Dark Journey through Iraq* (New York: NAL Caliber, 2007). "Fear up harsh" refers to an interrogation approach in which (according to US Army *Field Manual 34-52*) "the interrogator behaves in an overpowering manner with a loud and threatening voice. The interrogator may even feel the need to throw objects across the room to heighten the source's implanted feelings of fear." See *US Army Field Manual 34-52*, 3/16.

19. Lagouranis and Mikaelian, *Fear Up Harsh*, 17.

20. Ibid.

21. Ibid., 18–19.

22. Ibid., 115. Among Patai's most widely cited assertions about Arabs is their supposed tendency to extreme fatalism (see Patai, *The Arab Mind*, 156–160). US intelligence agencies' interest in the psychology of Arabs predates Patai's book. In the early 1960s, the CIA published a classified article on the subject (see Paul A. Naffsinger, "'Face' among the Arabs," *CIA Studies in Intelligence* 8, no. 3 [1964]: 43–54). It describes Arabs as prone to lying, obsessed with honor, and "almost paranoiac…entertaining delusions of grandeur, claiming to be persecuted, magnifying faults in others" (ibid., 49). It also claims that Arabs suffer from "all-is-from-Allah fatalism" (ibid., 48).

23. Tony Lagouranis, quoted in "The Torture Question," *PBS Frontline*, October 18, 2005, http://www.pbs.org/wgbh/pages/frontline/torture/interviews/ lagouranis.html#4 (accessed August 20, 2007).

24. Edward Said, *Orientalism.* (New York: Vintage, 1978), 3.

25. Patai, an Israeli anthropologist, wrote *The Arab Mind* in the years following the 1967 Six Day War, which clearly made his work relevant to the Israeli military. Said's critique of contemporary orientalists includes Bernard Lewis, Harold Glidden, Sania Hamady, and others. Patai's book was foreshadowed by sociologist Sania Hamady's *Temperament and Character of the Arabs* (New York: Twayne Publishers, 1960).

26. Elizabeth Fernea, *Guests of the Sheik: An Ethnography of an Iraqi Village,* (Garden City, NY: Doubleday, 1965). See also Lila Abu-Lughod, *Veiled Sentiments: Honor and Poetry in a Bedouin Society* (Cairo: American University in Cairo Press, 1987).

27. Nadia Abu El-Haj, "Edward Said and the Political Present," *American Ethnologist* 32, no. 4 (2005): 538–555. See also Emram Qureshi, "Misreading *The Arab Mind,*" *Boston Globe,* May 30, 2004.

28. Edward Said, "A Window on the World," *The Guardian,* August 2, 2003, http:// www.guardian.co.uk/books/2003/aug/02/alqaida.highereducation (accessed July 4, 2004).

29. Gregory Starrett, "Culture Never Dies: Anthropology at Abu Ghraib," *Anthropology News* 45, no. 6 (2004): 10–11.

30. However, an account written by a US Army interrogator who served in Kandahar describes how his team members combined fear up harsh with "new layers of technique. They conducted exhaustive research, designed exploitation plans based on nationality, then picked off prisoners in their mug shot book by turning one against another." See Chris Mackey and Greg Miller, *The Interrogators: Task Force 500 and America's Secret War against Al Qaeda,* (New York: Back Bay Books, 2004), 286. Many of the specific torture techniques employed at Guantánamo and Abu Ghraib were "reverse engineered" by US military personnel who had undergone Survival, Evasion, Resistance, and Escape training. See US Department of Defense, Office of the Inspector General, *Review of DoD-Directed Investigations of Detainee Abuse* (August 2006), 23–30, http://www.fas.org/irp/agency/dod/abuse.pdf (accessed March 4, 2010). See also Eban, "Rorschach and Awe."

31. Montgomery McFate, "The Military Utility of Understanding Adversary Culture," *Joint Force Quarterly* 38 (2005): 42–48.

32. It is this tendency that led some to lambaste US anthropologists for dehumanized portrayals of Native Americans. See Vine Deloria, Jr., *Custer Died for Your Sins* (New York: Macmillan, 1969).

33. Anthropologist Brian Selmeski has described undertaking such a task in 2006, when he was invited to Ft. Leavenworth, Kansas (the site of a US Army educational center) to assist with an officer course. Upon seeing *The Arab Mind* as assigned reading, Selmeski questioned the director about the book's selection. The director replied, "This is the book everyone is talking about." According to Selmeski, "I pointed out that even if lots of people were talking about it, this was not the book his students *should* be reading if it was the primary way they were going to learn about Arab culture (and certainly not about Islam or Iraq)." Selmeski recommended other titles "to either counter-balance or replace the book," and notes that "as a result of my active engagement and critique, the course is now being revised. I am involved in some of this process, but have no way of knowing yet what the final outcome will be, especially not about one particular book" (personal communication with the author, August 11, 2007).

34. Dana Milbank and Claudia Deane, "Poll Finds Dimmer View of Iraq War, 52% Say U.S. Has Not Become Safer," *Washington Post*, June 8, 2005, http://www.washingtonpost.com/wp-dyn/cotent/article/2005/06/07/AR2005060700296 (accessed May 15, 2010). See also "For the First Time, Americans Oppose Afghan War," *Angus Reid Global Monitor*, January 25, 2007, http://www.angus-reid.com/polls/view/14497 (accessed May 15, 2010).

35. McFate, "Military Utility," 24.

Chapter 5
Human Terrain

Between July 2005 and August 2006, the US Army assembled an experimental counterinsurgency program called the Human Terrain System (HTS).[1] The program's building blocks are five-person teams ("human terrain teams" or HTTs) assigned to brigade combat team headquarters in Iraq and Afghanistan, comprising regional studies experts and social scientists, some of whom are armed.[2]

This program, which emerged as the result of the military's alleged interest in culture, has been uncritically portrayed in the media as saving lives, thanks to what appears to be an orchestrated Pentagon public relations campaign.[3] Yet the way in which HTS has been packaged—as a kinder, gentler counterinsurgency—is completely unsupported by evidence. Despite HTS supporters' frequent claims that the program has drastically reduced US "kinetic operations" (military attacks) in Afghanistan, Pentagon officials have not provided independent confirmation of these assertions. Indeed, there is no verifiable evidence that HTTs have saved a single life—American, Afghan, Iraqi, or otherwise. According to Zenia Helbig (a former HTT member), an internal evaluation team that recently produced a positive report on HTS included evaluators with a vested interest in the program.[4] It appears that HTS has two faces: one designed to rally public support for an unpopular war, and the other to collect intelligence to help salvage a failing occupation.

It is likely that HTS was created as an intelligence program. As the army launched HTS, some military analysts described it as "a CORDS for the twenty-first century," in reference to Civil Operations Revolutionary Development Support, a Vietnam War-era counterinsurgency effort.[5] CORDS gave birth to the infamous Phoenix Program, in which South Vietnamese officials allied with US agents gathered intelligence data to help target tens of thousands of people for "neutralization" (incarceration or assassination), including many civilians.[6] At the time, CORDS was publicly hailed as a humanitarian project for winning "hearts and minds," while Phoenix simultaneously (and secretly) functioned as its paramilitary arm.

Figure 5.1: Human terrain team member US Army Major Robert Holbert speaks with school officials during a cordon and search operation in Noni, Afghanistan, June 2007. (Photo courtesy of US Army.)

This dubious history provides a critical reference point for understanding the potential uses of HTS. With a budget of approximately $250 million, this may be the most expensive social science project in history, and it appears to be growing quickly.[7] The program deserves close scrutiny and critique, since HTS social scientists have discussed aspects of it in ways that do not square with military journals, job announcements, and journalists' accounts. For example, some anthropologists involved in HTS have maintained that social scientists do not conceal their identities in Afghanistan, yet journalists have contradicted this claim.[8] In addition, HTS leaders have claimed that the data collected by HTS personnel is open and unclassified, yet James K. Greer (deputy director of HTS), has been quoted as saying: "When a brigade plans and executes its operations, that planning and execution is, from an operational-security standpoint, classified. And so your ability to talk about it, or write an article about it, is restricted in certain ways."[9]

Such issues motivated a group of anthropologists—the Network of Concerned Anthropologists—to oppose involvement in counterinsurgency work and in direct combat support. (Disclosure: ten colleagues and I founded the Network in the summer of 2007.) In light of the ethical concerns and potential conflicts, the American Anthropological Association

(AAA) Executive Board issued a statement in November 2007 express-
ing disapproval of the program. At the 2007 AAA conference, members
also adopted a non-binding resolution opposing certain kinds of secrecy in anthropological work—a resolution motivated by concerns about
HTS. In December 2009, the AAA went even further when it publicly
released a report conducted by its ad hoc Commission on the Engagement
of Anthropology with US Security and Intelligence Communities
(CEAUSSIC), stating that "when ethnographic investigation is determined
by military missions, not subject to external review, where data collection
occurs in the context of war, integrated into the goals of counterinsurgency, and in a potentially coercive environment—all characteristic factors
of the HTS concept and its application—it can no longer be considered a
legitimate professional exercise of anthropology."[10]

The Origins of Human Terrain

Recently defined as "the social, ethnographic, cultural, economic, and
political elements of the people among whom a force is operating...defined
and characterized by sociocultural, anthropologic, and ethnographic data,"
the concept of human terrain has become popular in US military circles.[11]
Military analysts often contrast human terrain with geophysical terrain—
a familiar concept for senior officers trained for conventional warfare
against the Soviets. It implies that twenty-first-century warriors will fight
"population-centric" wars; therefore, the key to successful warfare is the
control of *people*. This is more than a "hearts and minds" approach, for
the emphasis lies primarily on exploitation of tribal, political, religious,
and psychological dynamics: "in Iraq, US and coalition forces must recognize and exploit the underlying tribal structure of the country; the power
wielded by traditional authority figures; the use of Islam as a political ideology; the competing interests of the Shia, the Sunni, and the Kurds; the
psychological effects of totalitarianism; and the divide between urban and
rural," writes a military anthropologist.[12]

Human terrain is not a new concept. Its reactionary roots stretch
back forty years, when it appeared in a report by the infamous US House
Un-American Activities Committee about the perceived threat of Black
Panthers and other militant groups. From the beginning, human terrain
was linked to population control:

> Traditional guerrilla warfare...[is] carried out by irregular forces,
> which just about always dispose of inferior weapons and logistical

Figure 5.2: In the late 1960s, the US House Un-American Activities Committee used the term "human terrain" in reference to domestic counterinsurgency campaigns against the Black Panther Party (a member of whom is shown in this photo circa 1970) and other militant groups. (Photo courtesy of US Library of Congress.)

support in general, but which possess the ability to seize and retain the initiative through a superior control of the human terrain. This control may be the result of sheer nation-wide support for the guerrillas against a colonial or other occupying power of foreign origin; it may be the result of the ability of the guerrillas to inflict reprisals upon the population; and it can be because the guerrillas promise more to the population.[13]

Human terrain appeared again in the 1972 book *The War for the Cities* by Robert Moss, a right-wing journalist who in the 1970s edited *Foreign Report*, a journal affiliated with the *Economist*. Like HUAC, Moss examined the threat of diverse "urban guerrillas," including the Black Panthers, Students for Democratic Society, and Latin American insurgents. Human terrain appeared in reference to the latter: "The failure of the rural guerrillas to enlist large scale peasant backing in most areas also showed up in their distorted view of the political potential of the peasantry and their failure to study the human terrain.... Che Guevara's ill-conceived Bolivian campaign was the supreme example of these deficiencies."[14]

Contemporary human terrain studies date back ten years, when retired US Army Lieutenant Colonel Ralph Peters published "The Human Terrain of Urban Operations." Peters has written more than twenty books, yet is more widely known as a neoconservative pundit.[15] For years, Peters has espoused a bloody version of Huntington's "clash of civilizations" thesis. He has argued that the US military will have to inflict "a fair amount of killing" to promote economic interests and a "cultural assault" aimed at recalcitrant populations:

> There will be no peace.... The de facto role of the US armed forces will be to keep the world safe for our economy and open to our cultural assault. To those ends, we will do a fair amount of killing. We are building an information-based military to do that killing.... Much of our military art will consist in knowing more about the enemy than he knows about himself, manipulating data for effectiveness and efficiency, and denying similar advantages to our opponents.[16]

Peters has also argued that it is the "human architecture" of a city, its "human terrain...the people, armed and dangerous, watching for exploitable opportunities, or begging to be protected, who will determine the success or failure of the intervention." He describes a typology of cities ("hierarchical," "multicultural," and "tribal") and the challenges that each presents to military forces operating there: "The center of gravity in urban operations is never a presidential palace or a television studio or a bridge or a barracks. It is always human."[17]

As the ideas Peters espoused began circulating among military analysts, others gradually adopted human terrain. Lieutenant Colonel Michael Morris noted that the "purpose of [al-Qaeda's] covert infrastructure [or 'shadow government'] is to operationalize control of human terrain." A year later, Lieutenant Colonel Richard McConnell and colleagues suggested that US "military transition teams" training Iraqi troops needed a better understanding of "human terrain": "You are not here to make this into an American unit—you are here to help this unit become the best Iraqi unit it can be." Lieutenant Colonel Fred Renzi made the case for "ethnographic intelligence" to help understand "*terra incognia*...the *terra* in this case is the human terrain."[18]

Some CIA agents also appropriated the term. Henry Crumpton, leader of the CIA's Afghan campaign post-9/11, has written about agents working there during that period, including one "who spoke Farsi/Dari,

[and] was a cultural anthropologist intimately familiar with the tribes of the region.... These CIA officers needed to map the human terrain of their patch in Afghanistan, while understanding and contributing to the larger strategy." In spite of Crumpton's use of the term, so far there is no indication of CIA involvement with HTS.[19]

Pundits and think tanks have enthusiastically embraced human terrain. Conservative columnist Max Boot wrote a commentary entitled "Navigating the 'Human Terrain,'" in which he referred to the need for "Americans who are familiar with foreign languages and cultures and proficient in such disciplines as intelligence collection and interrogation." The RAND Corporation commissioned two counterinsurgency monographs advocating the importance of "understanding the human terrain," though the emphasis is on information technologies and cognitive mapping rather than ethnographic expertise.[20]

Before examining the genesis of HTS, it is worth thinking about how the very term "human terrain" might influence the thought—and consequently actions—of its users by objectifying and dehumanizing people. Consider the words of US Army Lieutenant Colonel Edward Villacres, who leads an HTT in Iraq: the team's objective is to "help the brigade leadership understand the human dimension of the environment that they are working in, just like a map analyst would try to help them understand the bridges, and the rivers, and things like that."[21] The unusual juxtaposition of words portrays people as geographic space to be conquered—human beings as territory to be captured, as flesh-and-blood *terra nullius*. Much more serious is the way the term (like "collateral damage" and "enhanced interrogation") vividly illustrates George Orwell's notion of "political language...designed to make lies sound truthful and murder respectable."[22]

The Birth of HTS

How did "human terrain" become a system? By 2006, desperation about mismanagement of the wars had set in among many military and intelligence officials. US casualties were mounting, Iraqi insurgent groups were becoming stronger, and Taliban fighters were regrouping. Some war planners began seeking gentler counterinsurgency tactics, according to an uncritical account prepared for the US Army War College's Strategic Studies Institute by anthropologist Sheila Miyoshi Jager:

> In sharp contrast to former Secretary of Defense Donald Rumsfeld's heavy-handed approach to counterinsurgency which emphasized

aggressive military tactics, the post-Rumsfeld Pentagon has advocated a "gentler" approach, emphasizing cultural knowledge and ethnographic intelligence...This "cultural turn" within DoD highlights efforts to understand adversary societies and to recruit "practitioners" of culture, notably anthropologists, to help in the war effort in both Iraq and Afghanistan.[23]

An early advocate was Major General Robert Scales, who told the US House Armed Services Committee that "the British Army created a habit of 'seconding' bright officers to various corners of the world so as to immerse them in the cultures of the Empire.... At the heart of a cultural-centric approach to future war would be a cadre of global scouts.... They should attend graduate schools in disciplines necessary to understand human behavior and cultural anthropology."[24] Backed up by Scales's ringing endorsement of imperialist strategy, the political groundwork was set for anthropological participation in cultural-centric warfare.

Scales would not need to wait long. In 2005, Montgomery McFate and Andrea Jackson published a pilot proposal for a Pentagon "Office of Operational Cultural Knowledge" focused on human terrain and consisting of social scientists with "strong connections to the services and combatant commands."[25] They would provide:

1. "on-the-ground ethnographic research (interviews and participant observation)" on the Middle East, Central Asia, etc.;

2. "predeployment and advanced cultural training...[and] computer-based training on society and culture";

3. "sociocultural studies of areas of interest (such as North Korean culture and society, Iranian military culture, and so on)";

4. "cultural advisers for planning and operations to commanders on request" and "lectures at military institutions";

5. "experimental sociocultural programs, such as the cultural preparation of the environment—a comprehensive and constantly updated database tool for use by operational commanders and planners."[26]

Initial costs for the first year were estimated at $6.5 million. The proposal was consistent with one of the authors' earlier provocative (if historically dubious) suggestions: "The national security structure needs to be infused with anthropology, a discipline invented to support warfighting in the tribal zone."[27]

Soon after, Jacob Kipp and colleagues from the army's Foreign Military Studies Office at Fort Leavenworth, Kansas, outlined the "Human Terrain

System" to "understand the people among whom our forces operate as well as the cultural characteristics and propensities of the enemies we now fight." Captain Don Smith headed the implementation of HTS from July 2005 to August 2006, and the program was housed in the Training and Doctrine Command at Fort Leavenworth.[28] Each team would comprise an HTT leader (major or lieutenant colonel), a cultural analyst (civilian MA/PhD cultural anthropologist or sociologist), a regional studies analyst (civilian MA/PhD in area studies with area language fluency), an HT research manager (military intelligence background), and an HT analyst (military intelligence background).

In early 2007, BAE Systems began posting HTS job announcements on its company website; it was joined later by Wexford Group (CACI) and MTC Technologies. Before deployment, HTT members received military and weapons training, and in February 2007 the first team arrived in Afghanistan. The others deployed to Iraq in summer 2007.

Proponents insist that HTTs "are extremely helpful in terms of giving commanders on the ground an understanding of the cultural patterns of interaction, the nuances of how to interact with those cultural groups on the ground"—a dubious claim, since none of the PhD-qualified anthropologists working in HTTs had prior regional knowledge at the time that Montgomery McFate made this claim.[29] However, HTTs are designed to collect regionally specific data on political leadership, kinship groups, economic systems, and agricultural production. The data is to be sent to a central database accessible to other US government agencies: the CIA would be particularly interested. Furthermore, "databases will eventually be turned over to the new governments of Iraq and Afghanistan to enable them to more fully exercise sovereignty over their territory."[30] (It is worth remembering that CORDS officials hoped to ensure the South Vietnamese government's political stability through the Phoenix Program, but it was used as a mechanism for eliminating political opponents.)

HTTs will supply brigade commanders with "deliverables" including a "user-friendly ethnographic and sociocultural database of the area of operations that can provide the commander data maps showing specific ethnographic or cultural features." HTTs use Mapping Human Terrain (MAP-HT) software, "an automated database and presentation tool that allows teams to gather, store, manipulate, and provide cultural data from hundreds of categories."[31] According to the Secretary of Defense's budget, the goal is:

> to reduce IED [improvised explosive device] incidents via improved situational awareness of the human terrain by using "green layer

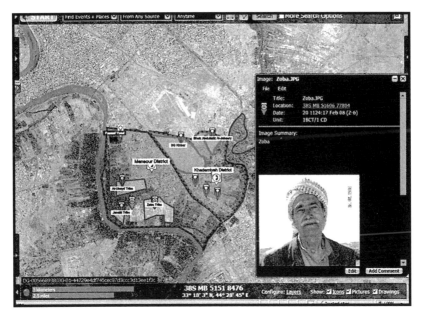

Figure 5.3: Mapping the human terrain in Baghdad, Iraq, using the MAP-HT computer program. (Photo courtesy of US Department of Defense.)

data/unclassified" information to understand key population points to win the "will and legitimacy" fights and surface the insurgent IED networks.... Capability must be further developed to provide a means for commanders and their supporting operations sections to collect data on human terrain, create, store, and disseminate information from this data, and use the resulting information as an element of combat power.[32]

In unvarnished language, a fuller picture emerges: the goal of HTS data is to help "win the 'will and legitimacy' fights" (perhaps through propaganda), to "surface the insurgent IED networks" (presumably for targeting), and to serve "as an element of combat power" (i.e. as a weapon). HTS supporters have equivocated when confronted with the question of whether such a database might be used to target Iraqis or Afghans. In a radio interview, an HTS architect stated: "The intent of the program is not to identify who the bad actors are out there. The military has an entire intelligence apparatus geared and designed to provide that information to them. That is not the information that they need from social scientists." She claimed that HTT social scientists have "a certain amount of discretion" with data, while providing no evidence that safeguards exist to prevent others from using it against informants. When asked about lack of independent oversight, she answered: "We would like to set up a board of advisors. At the moment, however, this program is proof of concept.... It's not a permanent program. It's an experiment."[33]

"Human Terrain" as Technological Fantasy

Pentagon budgets reflect a strong commitment to so-called cultural knowledge acquisition. Consequently, engineers, mathematicians, and computer scientists have demonstrated acute interest in human terrain for modelling, simulation, and gaming programs. Among them is Barry Silverman, a University of Pennsylvania engineering professor, who bluntly asks: "Human Terrain Data: What Should We Do with It?"[34] Silverman has been at the forefront of efforts to develop computerized behavior modelling programs designed to provide insight into the motivations of terrorists and their networks, and he hopes to integrate HTS data into these programs. According to one report, "a Silverman simulation is an astoundingly sophisticated amalgamation of more than one hundred models and theories from anthropology, psychology, and political science, combined with empirical data taken from medical and social science field research, surveys, and experiments." The goal is to predict how various actors—"a terrorist, a soldier, or an ordinary citizen"—might react to "a gun pointed in the face, a piece of chocolate offered by a soldier.... [Silverman] is now simulating a small society of about 15,000 leader and follower agents organized into tribes, which squabble over resources."[35]

At the heart of Silverman's simulations are "performance moderator functions" representing "physical stressors such as ambient temperature, hunger, and drug use; resources such as time, money, and skills; attitudes such as moral outlook, religious feelings, and political affiliations; and personality dispositions such as response to time pressure, workload, and anxiety."[36]

Silverman makes grand claims about the potential utility of HTS data for human social profiling, though he has apparently not yet obtained any of it: "the HT datasets are an invaluable resource that will permit us in the human behavior M&S [modelling and simulation] field to more realistically profile factions, and their leaders and followers."[37]

Similarly, a Dartmouth research team has created the Laboratory for Human Terrain, "focused on the foundational science and technology for modelling, representing, inferring, and analyzing individual and organizational behaviors."[38] It includes an engineer, a mathematician, and a computer scientist who specialize in "adversarial intent modeling, simulation, and prediction," "dynamic social network analysis," and "discovery of hidden relationships and organizations." The Pentagon awarded a $250,000 grant to Eugene Santos to develop a "Dynamic Adversarial Gaming Algorithm" (DAGA) for "predicting how individuals or groups...react to social, cultural, political, and economic interactions.... DAGA can evaluate how rhetoric from religious leaders combined with recent allied killing of radical military leaders, and perceptions of potential economic growth can cause shifts in support from moderate or radical leadership."[39] The Dartmouth group uses the "Adversary Intent Inferencing" (AII) model, a prototype of which was tested using scenarios replicating Gulf War battles.[40]

These programs are a small part of "Human Social Culture Behavior Modeling," in which the goal is to "build computer models...[by] combining recent [insurgent] activity with cultural, political, and economic data about the region collected by DOD-funded anthropologists"—perhaps HTT personnel. *Wired* magazine's blog reports a boom in wartime simulation projects, including Purdue University's "Synthetic Environment for Analysis and Simulation" which can "gobble up breaking news, census data, economic indicators, and climactic events in the real word, along with proprietary information such as military intelligence. Iraq and Afghanistan computer models are the most highly developed and complex. Each has about five million individual nodes that represent entities such as hospitals, mosques, pipelines, and people."[41] HTS data could conceivably be incorporated into this computer model.

The Air Force Research Lab has requested proposals for modelling programs, and suggests that "researchers should investigate cultural, motivational, historical, political, and economic data to determine if there are mathematical and statistical models that can be used to predict the formation of terrorist activities.... [The] goal is to determine sets of actions that can influence the root cause behaviors and cultivate a culture that does not support the development of criminal activity."[42]

These programs focus upon modelling and simulation, but it is not difficult to imagine that in the near future, agents might use cultural profiles for pre-emptive targeting of statistically probable (rather than actual) insurgents or extremists in Iraq, Afghanistan, Pakistan or other countries deemed to be terrorist havens.

Some Pentagon officials have already begun contemplating such applications. In February 2007, a dazzlingly illustrated PowerPoint presentation was released, which unambiguously stated that a "need to 'Map the Human Terrain' across the kill chain—enables the entire kill chain for the

GWOT [Global War on Terror]."[43] The presentation (by Assistant Deputy Undersecretary of Defense James Wilcox) notes that "sometimes we ID the enemy but...do not have an adequate/appropriate Strike Solution in time," indicating that at least one senior Pentagon official sees such information as a potentially useful weapon.[44]

Despite HTS proponents' claims that the program will save lives, Pentagon officials are likely to use data in line with their own war fighting plans.

The High Cost of HTS

On May 7, 2008, Michael Bhatia—a political scientist and HTS member—was tragically killed in a roadside bomb attack in Afghanistan, making him the program's first casualty of war.[45] On June 24, 2008, another HTS member, political science graduate student Nicole Suveges, was killed in a bomb attack in Sadr City, Baghdad. On November 4, 2008, yet another HTS team member, Paula Loyd, was doused with kerosene and set alight by an Afghan man who was then executed by another member of Loyd's team. She died from her wounds on January 7, 2009.[46]

These deaths underscore the high human cost of the Human Terrain System. Given these tragic events, we might ask: What motivates social scientists to participate in HTS? Though relatively few have written about their experiences, it is worth listening to what they have to say. Corporate anthropologist Mark Dawson, in a blog entry submitted days after the tragic death of Nicole Suveges, explained how a void in his career attracted him to the program:

> I have been a corporate person for many years.... Few of us have ever considered that there is a chance of getting killed during the fieldwork. So why am I doing this? God knows, the program has its warts.... It's not the money...life would be safer (and my base pay was higher) in Silicon Valley.... For me, I feel like after all my time in the corporate world, I have something to give back.... Surely I can turn that skill to something more meaningful, and a longer lasting effect? So that's why I am doing it. I need to put my money where my mouth is. Do I believe in the power of cultural understanding to prevent violence or not? I do.... Will this all blow up in my face? Maybe.[47]

Archaeology professor David Matsuda joined HTS with the objective of helping end the war: "I'm a Californian. I'm a liberal. I'm a Democrat. My impetus is to come here and help end this thing," he declared in a news article. "I came here to save lives, to make friends out of enemies."[48]

On the other hand, Marcus Griffin, a cultural anthropologist who blogged about his HTS work for nearly a year before suddenly removing all his past posts from the Web without any explanation, was driven partly by a sense of patriotism, occasionally signing off with such catchphrases as "freedom is never free." He perceived himself to be a military man—an anthropologist who was "going native" by embedding:

> Going "native" in anthropology is a fairly common strategy to gain a better understanding of the people with whom one is working. I am about a month away from deploying to Baghdad as part of the US Army's new Human Terrain System and have almost gone completely native. How am I doing this? First, I am working out regularly with Lt. Gato. He is showing me how to develop greater strength and endurance.... Thanks to him I am gaining greater strength and larger muscles. Second, I cut my hair in a high and tight style and look like a drill sergeant.... Third, I shot very well with the M9 and M4 last week at the range.... Shooting well is important if you are a soldier regardless of whether or not your job requires you to carry a weapon. Fourth, I am trying to learn military language with all the acronyms and idioms.... Today among soldiers, I am looking and more often acting just like them.... That is what going native is all about: walking in someone else's shoes in order to know what their life is like and therefore why they do what they do.[49]

Marcus Griffin omits any mention of Iraqis in his description of cultural understanding. For him, "going native" has nothing to do with Iraqis. It means looking, speaking, and acting just like a soldier. Griffin ultimately left his academic position at Christopher Newport University to become a full-time senior social science advisor to the Pentagon.

Zenia Helbig reportedly joined the program for financial reasons: *Chronicle of Higher Education* staff writer David Glenn noted that Helbig inherited an "immigrant need for financial stability" from her Ukrainian parents. (In a phone conversation, she later told me that her parents imbued her with a sense of patriotic duty towards the country that had received them.)[50]

Others have demonstrated a much greater level of empathy for those living under the yoke of occupation. After I had published several articles on the topic of human terrain, a former HTS employee (whom I will refer to by the pseudonym "Terry") contacted me. For more than a year, we maintained email and telephone communication. Terry's warmth, intelligence, and sincerity made a lasting impression. At times, Terry's words reflected an ambivalent and even contradictory position:

One of the main reasons I was able to build strong rapport and gain more trust from the Iraqis than anyone around me is because I listened to them, learned from them, and at a very deep level respected and admired them. Their lives were as important to me as anyone else's, including my own.... More often than not, I was told by Iraqis that I "have a very good heart." They were human to me, and I looked out for their interests as much as I was obligated to work with the military through this program.

Many of those who have chosen to participate in HTS appear to have done so for humanitarian reasons—in order to "do good," or at least to prevent a horrible situation from getting even worse. But in the end, the program places human terrain team members in an untenable situation: they face conflicting obligations to their employer (BAE Systems), to US Army commanders, and to Iraqi and Afghan research participants. Such dilemmas raise a serious question: Do the immense human and material costs of HTS—costs borne by US taxpayers, American social scientists and military personnel, and most importantly, the people of Iraq and Afghanistan—justify its continuation?

Human Terrain: Possible Futures

Examination of the information available, summarized above, reveals that HTS—and HTS data—may perform various functions simultaneously. Images of a gentler counterinsurgency might serve as propaganda for US audiences opposed to military operations in Iraq and Afghanistan: propaganda that offers the apparently wonderful compromise of fighting a war that makes us feel good about ourselves. Public relations campaigns portraying HTT personnel as life-saving heroes might attract young scholars who want to do good, like the embedded administrators who served colonial interests. Information collected by HTTs might feed into a database accessible to the CIA, the Iraqi police, or the Afghan military for strategic or tactical intelligence, or for use in targeting suspected insurgents for abduction or assassination. Agents might employ HTS data to design propaganda campaigns that exploit Iraqi or Afghan fears and vulnerabilities, or to co-opt local leaders into a system of indirect rule. Finally, HTS data might help create simulation and modelling programs which could conceivably be used for profiling imagined enemies by means of statistical probability. It is vital that we discuss ethical issues covering the range of possibilities.

As I noted in my introduction, some military analysts draw explicit connections between HTS and CORDS/Phoenix, which used local information to help target suspects for incarceration, interrogation, or assassination.[51] Phoenix featured a computerized database:

Phoenix was enhanced with the advent of the Viet Cong Infrastructure Information System.... [In January 1967] the Combined Intelligence Staff fed the names of 3000 VCI [Viet Cong "infrastructure," including communist cadres and National Liberation Front members among others] (assembled by hand at area coverage desks) into the IBM 1401 computer at the Combined Intelligence Center's political order of battle section. At that point the era of the computerized blacklist began.... VCIIS became the first of a series of computer programs designed to absolve the war effort of human error and war managers of individual responsibility.[52]

Phoenix Program personnel collected a wealth of intelligence information, which they then passed on to analysts:

VCIIS compiled information...on VCI boundaries, locations, structures, strengths, personalities, and activities.... [It] included summary data on each recorded VCI in the following categories: name and aliases; whether or not he or she was "at large"; sex, birth date, and place of birth; area of operations; party position; source of information; arrest date; how neutralized; term of sentence; where detained; release date; and other biographical and statistical information, including photographs and fingerprints, if available.... Phoenix analysts [were able] instantly to access and cross-reference data, then decide who was to be erased.[53]

As a result, between 1967 and 1972 South Vietnamese officials, US advisors and mercenaries "erased" more than 26,000 suspected members of the so-called Viet Cong "infrastructure," including civilians—acts that amounted to war crimes. Nowhere is this mentioned in Kipp's depiction of HTS as "a CORDS for the twenty-first century," yet the historical record points to the potential dangers of computerized counterinsurgency databases.

The future of HTS is unclear. Some are already calling for change. Credible accounts have emerged about difficulties plaguing HTS, including "recruitment shortfalls," "haphazard and often pointless" training, and a program "nearly paralyzed by organizational problems."[54] Former HTT member Zenia Helbig has publicly criticized the program, claiming that during four months of training, there was no discussion about informed consent or the potential harm that might befall Iraqis or Afghans. Furthermore, Helbig claims that "HTS's greatest problem is its own desperation. The program is desperate to hire anyone or anything that remotely falls into the category of 'academic,' 'social science,' 'regional expert,' or 'PhD,' which has often resulted in gross incompetence."[55] If such desperation persists, it is conceivable that HTS might eventually wither, though there are indications that BAE Systems and other contractors will soon target students of political science and international relations for recruitment. In the long run, HTS, HTTs, "reachback research centers" and MAP-HT may turn out to be technological fantasies that were crushed soon after embedded social scientists' boots hit the ground. On the other hand, the Pentagon's creation of AFRICOM—the African Command, which will establish permanent US military bases on that continent—has given HTS's managers a new potential market for the program's expansion. According to one report, HTS director Steve Fondacaro "has visited AFRICOM as a preliminary step towards setting up human terrain teams there."[56]

In the future, historians may question why a small number of anthropologists—whose progressive twentieth-century predecessors created the modern culture concept, critiqued Western ethnocentrism in its various guises, and invented the teach-in—decided to enlist as embedded specialists in an open-ended war of dubious legality.[57] They might wonder why these anthropologists began harvesting data on Iraqis and Afghans as a preferred method of practical "real-world" engagement. They might ask why, at a time when majorities in the United States, Iraq and Afghanistan called for the withdrawal of US troops, this group of anthropologists supported an occupation resulting in hundreds of thousands of civilian deaths. Economic incentives (approximately $250,000 for a year)—and the results of decades of veneration of the military and those who support it—go some way toward explaining these phenomena. Scholars are not immune to nationalist and imperialist appeals in a highly militarized context.

Future historians might also be puzzled about some social scientists' failure to learn lessons from an earlier era: "When we strip away the terminology of the behavioral sciences, we see revealed, in work such as this, the mentality of the colonial civil servant, persuaded of the benevolence of the mother country and the correctness of its vision of world order, and convinced that he understands the true interests of those backward peoples whose welfare he is to administer."[58]

The fact that some social scientists have received HTS warmly reveals historical amnesia and a profound lack of imagination. To the extent that HTS uses "cultural knowledge" to create propaganda campaigns to win "'will and legitimacy' fights," it deserves condemnation. To the extent

CHAPTER 5

that HTS peddles anthropological techniques and concepts in support of conquest and indirect rule, it deserves rejection. To the extent that HTS might be employed to collect intelligence or target suspected enemies for assassination, the program deserves elimination—and a period of sober reflection about the situation of American social science today.

Notes

1. According to an article in the journal *Military Review*, "the concept for the current Human Terrain System was suggested by Montgomery McFate Ph.D., J.D., and Andrea Jackson as described in their article, 'An Organizational Solution for DoD's Cultural Knowledge Needs." See Jacob Kipp et al., "The Human Terrain System: A CORDS for the 21st Century," *Military Review*, September–October 2006, 15.

2. There are approximately twenty-five HTTs in Iraq and Afghanistan. It is not clear whether other US government agencies have been involved in the design or implementation of the program.

3. For example, see David Rohde, "Army Enlists Anthropology in War Zones," *New York Times*, October 5, 2007; Scott Peterson, "US Army's Strategy in Afghanistan: Better Anthropology," *Christian Science Monitor*, September 7, 2007; Anne Mulrine, "Culture Warriors," *US News and World Report*, December 10, 2007.

4. Zenia Helbig, personal communication with the author on December 6, 2007.

5. Kipp et al., "The Human Terrain System."

6. Douglas Valentine, *The Phoenix Program* (New York: Morrow, 1990).

7. According to one report, HTS is now a $250 million program. See David Axe, "After Setbacks, Human Terrain System Rebuilds," *World Politics Review*, November 25, 2009, http://www.worldpoliticsreview.com/article.aspx?id=4697 (accessed March 3, 2010). The American Anthropological Association's ad hoc Commission on the Engagement of Anthropology with US Security and Intelligence Communities (CEAUSSIC) recently noted that "despite ongoing controversy it was recently reported that the HTS program is slated for at least a $40 million expansion." See American Anthropological Association CEASSIUC, *Final Report on The Army's Human Terrain System Proof of Concept Program*, October 14, 2009, http://www.aaanet.org/cmtes/commissions/CEAUSSIC/upload/CEAUSSIC_HTS_Final_Report.pdf (accessed December 10, 2009).

8. David Rohde quoted in "Anthropology and War," *The Diane Rehm Show* (American University Radio), October 10, 2007, http://thedianerehmshow.org/shows/2007-10-10/anthropologists-and-war (accessed October 15, 2007).

9. David Glenn, "Anthropologists Vote to Clamp Down on Secret Scholarship," *Chronicle of Higher Education News Blog*, December 1, 2007, http://chronicle.com/news/article/3532/anthropologists-vote-toclamp-down-on-secretscholarship (accessed December 4, 2007).

10. American Anthropological Association Executive Board. "Statement on the Human Terrain System Project." October 31, 2007. http://www.aaanet.org/pdf/EB_Resolution_110807.pdf (accessed December 17, 2007). See also AAA Commission on the Engagement of Anthropology with US Security and Intelligence Communities, *Final Report on The Army's Human Terrain System Proof of Concept Program*, October 14, 2009, http://www.aaanet.org/cmtes/commissions/CEAUSSIC/upload/CEAUSSIC_HTS_Final_Report.pdf (accessed December 13, 2009).

11. Kipp et al., "Human Terrain System," 9, 15.

12. Montgomery McFate, "Anthropology and Counterinsurgency: The Strange Story of Their Curious Relationship," *Military Review*, February 2005, 37.

13. US House Un-American Activities Committee, *Guerrilla Warfare Advocates in the United States* (Washington DC: Government Printing Office, 1968), 62. HUAC suggested that urban unrest might require that the president declare an "internal security emergency" which would enable a 1950 law authorizing detention of suspected spies or saboteurs. Much of the law was repealed in the 1970s, but some elements were restored in the 2001 USA Patriot Act.

14. Robert Moss, *The War for the Cities* (New York: Coward, McCann, and Geoghegan, 1972), 154. One of Moss's books was reportedly funded by the CIA as pro-Pinochet propaganda in the 1970s. See Frank Landis, "Moscow Rules Moss's Mind," *Covert Action Information Bulletin* 24, no. 14 (1985): 36–38.

15. Ralph Peters, "The Human Terrain of Urban Operations," *Proceedings* 30, no. 1 (2000): 4–12. Peters has also suggested radically redrawing Middle East borders: Iraq would be partitioned into an "Arab Shia state," "Sunni Iraq" and "free Kurdistan" (including eastern Turkey); "free Baluchistan" would be carved from southeastern Iran and southwestern Pakistan; Afghanistan would absorb much of northwestern Pakistan; half of Saudi Arabia's territory would be distributed to Yemen, "Greater Jordan" and a new "Islamic sacred state." See Ralph Peters, "Blood Borders," *Armed Forces Journal*, June 2006, http://www.afji.com/2006/06/1833899/.

16. Ralph Peters, "Constant Conflict," *Parameters*, Summer 1997, 14.

17. Peters, "Human Terrain," 4, 12.

18. Michael Morris, "Al Qaeda as Insurgency," *Joint Force Quarterly* 39 (2005): 46; Richard McConnell, Christopher Matson, and Brent Clemmer, "MiTT and Its 'Human Terrain,'" *Field Artillery*, January–February 2007, 11; Fred Renzi, "Terra Incognita and the Case for Ethnographic Intelligence," *Military Review*, May 2006, 16.

19. Henry Crumpton, "Intelligence and Homeland Defense," in *Transforming US Intelligence*, ed. Jennifer Sims and Burton Gerber (Washington DC: Georgetown University Press, 2005), 170.

20. Max Boot, "Navigating the 'Human Terrain,'" *Los Angeles Times*, December 7, 2006; Martin Libicki et al., *Byting Back: Regaining Information Superiority against 21st Century Insurgents* (Santa Monica, CA: RAND Corporation, 2007); David Gompert, *Heads We Win: Improving Cognitive Effectiveness in Counterinsurgency* (Santa Monica, CA: RAND Corporation, 2007).

21. John Agoglia, quoted in "Anthropology and War."

22. George Orwell, "Politics and the English Language," in *A Collection of Essays* (New York: Harcourt Brace Jovanovich, 1953), 171.

23. Sheila Miyoshi Jager, *On the Uses of Cultural Knowledge* (Washington DC: Strategic Studies Institute, 2007).

24. Robert Scales, "Army Transformation: Implications for the Future," (testimony before US House Armed Services Committee, July 15, 2004), http://www.au.af.mil/au/awc/awcgate/congress/04-07-15scales.pdf (accessed January 30, 2007).

25. Montgomery McFate and Andrea Jackson, "An Organizational Solution to DOD's Cultural Knowledge Needs," *Military Review*, April 2005, 20.

26. Ibid., 20–21.

27. Montgomery McFate, "The Military Utility of Understanding Adversary Culture," *Joint Force Quarterly* 38 (2005): 43.

28. Kipp et al., "Human Terrain System," 8, 15.

29. Montgomery McFate quoted in "Anthropology and War." See also Helbig, Zenia, "Personal Perspective on the Human Terrain System" (presentation, annual meetings of the American Anthropological Association, Washington DC, November 29, 2007), http://blog.wired.com/defense/files/aaa_helbig_hts.pdf (accessed January 22, 2008).

30. Kipp et al., "Human Terrain System," 14.

31. Ibid., 13.

32. "Green layer" data refers to information related to civilian populations (as opposed to "blue layer" [US forces] or "red layer" [insurgents]) in occupied Iraq and Afghanistan. These neat categories defy the messy reality of counterinsurgency wars. The Defense Secretary allocated $500,000 in 2007, $2.7 million in 2008, and $1.3 million in 2009 for MAP-HT. See US Office of Secretary of Defense, *OSD RDT&E Budget Item Justification* (Washington DC: Department of Defense, 2007), http://www.dtic.mil/descriptivesum/Y2008/OSD/0603648D8Z.pdf (accessed January 7, 2009).

33. Montgomery McFate quoted in "Anthropology and War."

34. Barry Silverman, "Human Terrain Data: What Should We Do with It?" in *Proceedings of 2007 Winter Simulation Conference*, ed. S. G. Henderson (2007), http://repository.upenn.edu/cgi/viewcontent.cgi?article=1330&context=ese_papersilv (accessed January 7, 2009).

35. Harry Goldstein, "Modeling Terrorists," *IEEE Spectrum*, September 2006, 30.

36. Ibid.

37. Silverman, "Human Terrain Data."

38. Dartmouth College Laboratory for Human Terrain, *Laboratory for Human Terrain,* http://www.dartmouth.edu/~humanterrain/ (accessed January 7, 2009).

39. Dartmouth College Laboratory for Human Terrain, "Approach," *Laboratory for Human Terrain,* http://www.dartmouth.edu/%7Ehumanterrain/ Approach.html (accessed January 7, 2009).

40. Eugene Santos and Qunhua Zhao, "Adversarial Models for Opponent Intent Inferencing," in *Adversarial Reasoning,* ed. Alexander Kott and William McEneaney (Boca Raton, FL: Chapman and Hall, 2006), 13.

41. See Yudhijit Bhattacharjee, "Pentagon Asks Academics for Help in Understanding Enemies," *Science* 316 (2007): 534–535. See also Noah Shachtman, "'Sim Iraq' Sent to Battle Zone," *Danger Room (Wired Blog),* November 19, 2007, http://blog.wired.com/defense/2007/11/mathematical-mo.html (accessed December 22, 2007).

42. US Air Force, "Mitigate IED Threat by Leveraging an Effect-Based Approach," *SITIS Archives,* http://www.dodsbir.net/sitis/archives_display_topic. asp?Bookmark=32088 (accessed July 5, 2008).

43. John Wilcox, *Precision Engagement—Strategic Context for the Long* War, (presentation, US Department of Defense Precision Strike Winter Roundtable, February 1, 2007), http://www.dtic.mil/ndia/2007psa_winter/wilcox.pdf (accessed July 5, 2008).

44. For a similar depiction of how "focusing on the 'human terrain'" can help "exploit vulnerabilities," see Greg Jannarone, *Behavioral Influences Analysis: Mission and Methodology Overview* (presentation, US Air Force Behavioral Influences Analysis Center, Maxwell Air Force Base, Alabama), http://www. au.af.mil/bia/slides/bia_msn_bfg.pdf (accessed January 23, 2008).

45. Bhatia was a prolific scholar who published one book and edited two others. See Michael V. Bhatia, *War and Intervention: Issues for Contemporary Peace Operations* (Sterling, VA: Kumarian, 2003); Michael V. Bhatia ed., *Terrorism and the Politics of Naming* (New York: Routledge, 2007); Michael V. Bhatia et al. eds., *Afghanistan, Arms, and Conflict* (New York: Routledge, 2008).

46. David Glenn, "Social Scientist in Army's 'Human Terrain' Program Dies in Afghanistan," *Chronicle of Higher Education,* May 9, 2008; Joe Sterling, "American Grad Student Dies in Iraq," *CNN News,* June 26, 2008; Farah Stockman, "Anthropologist's War Death Reverberates," *Boston Globe,* February 12, 2009.

47. Mark Dawson, "Some Thoughts As My Additions to Ethnography.com Wind Down," *Ethnography.com,* June 2008, http://www.ethnography.com/2008/07/ some-thoughts-as-i-head-overseas/ (accessed August 12, 2008).

48. David Matsuda, quoted in Peter Graf, "US Deploys Latest Tactic in Iraq: Anthropology," Reuters News Service, January 9, 2008, http://www.alertnet. org/thenews/newsdesk/L06475304.htm (accessed January 20, 2008).

CHAPTER 5

49. Marcus Griffin, "Going Native," *From an Anthropological Perspective,* July 10, 2007, http://web.archive.org/web/20071021082810/marcusgriffin.com/blog/2007/07/going_native.html#more (accessed May 15, 2008).

50. Zenia Helbig quoted in David Glenn, "Former Human Terrain System Participant Describes Program in Disarray," *Chronicle of Higher Education,* December 5, 2007, 8.

51. Kipp et al., "Human Terrain System."

52. Valentine, *The Phoenix Program,* 258–259.

53. Ibid., 259.

54. Glenn, "Former Human Terrain System Participant," 8.

55. Zenia Helbig, personal communication with the author, December 6, 2007. In the same communication, Helbig also told me that BAE Systems, responsible for HTT recruitment and training, was exceedingly inept and more concerned with maximizing profits than with meeting program objectives. According to Helbig, BAE Systems was awarded the HTS contract through an "omnibus" provision giving preferential consideration to existing contractors. If true, this would fit a decades old pattern of a privatized Pentagon characterized by mismanagement, waste, and war profiteering.

56. Nathan Hodge, "Help Wanted: 'Human Terrain' Teams for Africa," *Danger Room (Wired Blog),* January 12, 2009, http://www.wired.com/dangerroom/2009/01/help-wanted-hum/ (accessed January 20, 2009).

57. In other parts of this book, I show a darker and less progressive side of anthropology's history. The discipline has had a complicated history of both progressive and imperialist tendencies, and its practitioners have engaged in substantial self-critique (including critiques of imperialism). In spite of this, anthropologists who have participated in HTS seem to be unaware of, or are unimpressed with, the critiques.

58. Noam Chomsky, *American Power and the New Mandarins* (New York: Pantheon, 1969), 41.

Part III
Controlling Behavior

Chapter 6
Counterinsurgency in the Colonies

After a long hiatus, the term "counterinsurgency" has reappeared in the lexicon of American English. But what does it mean?

In its broadest sense, counterinsurgency refers to the methods by which a dominant power imposes its will upon a subordinate population. Specifically, it refers to the elimination of an uprising against a government.

Insurgency, insurgent, surge, and *insurrection* all share the same etymological roots—they entered the English language from the Latin word *surgere,* to rise up, approximately 500 years ago. However, counterinsurgency has a much more recent history. Its origins date back to 1960, when the US Department of Defense issued a classified Special Forces manual entitled *Counterinsurgency Operations.*

Even though the term counterinsurgency is relatively new, armies have long been involved in such work in North America. A historian notes that the Carlisle Barracks (site of the US Army War College) was originally constructed in the mid-1700s "for the purpose of instructing British and Provincial troops in counterinsurgency, which back then meant fighting Indians."[1] Much later, counterinsurgency became a label for a system of social control that had existed for centuries. It has gone by many names including "imperial policing," "counter-guerrilla" or "counter-revolutionary" operations, "small wars," and (more recently) "low- intensity" conflict and "stability operations."

The goal of counterinsurgents, imperial police, counter-guerrillas, and counter-revolutionaries was (and is) suppression or annihilation of revolutionary movements or struggles for independence in occupied territories.

Because counterinsurgency is a locally-based method of social control, it relies heavily upon intimate knowledge about local people. Civil and military officials representing modern colonial states have therefore taken great interest in the social, economic, political, and religious lives of their subjects.[2] Over the years, military planners and colonial administrators have sought the counsel of anthropologists who might provide them with simple analytical tools to help accomplish short-term objectives: to put down an uprising, to manufacture propaganda, to conduct psychological warfare, or to divide one ethnic group or religious sect from another.

It is worth examining some of the forgotten chapters in the history of colonial anthropology because they can provoke normative questions that are of great contemporary relevance: What should be the aim of social scientific work? What are the bounds—ethical, theoretical, methodological—of sociocultural research, and how should these bounds be determined? And how should anthropologists respond when the Pentagon recruits them for counterinsurgency programs today? This chapter will focus on the uses of American, French, Japanese, and British social science in the Philippines, Indochina, Taiwan, and the Middle East (respectively) for the purpose of exploring these questions in greater detail. My primary focus is the American colonial state in the Philippines.

Winning Hearts and Minds in the Philippines—A Century Ago

At the turn of the nineteenth century, US officials faced the novel challenge of administering the country's first overseas colonies. America's imperial acquisitions—in Hawaii, Puerto Rico, Cuba, Guam, and the Philippine Islands—effectively transformed ten million people into colonial subjects by the end of the 1890s.[3]

Men like Senator Henry Cabot Lodge, Presidents William McKinley and Theodore Roosevelt, and Captain Alfred Thayer Mayhan aggressively promoted US expansionism in spite of immense opposition at home. The quest for new markets and access to natural resources drove the country's imperial adventures at a time when European countries and Japan were extending their power globally. "Spreading democracy, Christianizing heathen nations, building a strong navy, establishing military bases around the world, and bringing foreign governments under American control were never ends in themselves," but were rather the ideological, military, and political manifestations of an expanding corporate economy.[4]

Of all the territories absorbed by the United States after the Spanish-American War of 1898, the Philippines undoubtedly presented the greatest difficulties of any colony for American administrators. Its population included more than seven million people, speaking more than 150 different languages, living across an archipelago of a dozen major islands and thousands of smaller ones. As if these demographic, linguistic, and geographical complexities were not enough, thousands of people had revolted against the US military occupation of the islands following the war's end. Philippine independence from Spain did not mean Filipino sovereignty

Figure 6.1:
Filipino insur-
gents detained
by US forces in
Manila, circa
1901. (Photo
courtesy of
US Library of
Congress.)

to President William McKinley, much less to his successor Theodore Roosevelt. American troops brutally suppressed the insurgents by 1902, but not before they killed an estimated 20,000 Filipino combatants. As many as 200,000 more died as a direct result of the war, mostly civilians. The US Army's counterinsurgency war in the Philippines—which led to as many as 10,000 American casualties—smoldered for nearly another decade before "pacification" was complete.

The US colonial administration—the so-called Philippine Commission—employed social scientists to help accomplish their objectives once the fighting diminished. Among the most influential was Albert E. Jenks, who served as Chief of the Ethnological Survey of the Philippine Islands (originally created as the "Bureau of Non-Christian Tribes") from October 1903 until June 1905.[5] Jenks received a doctorate in economics from the University of Wisconsin in 1899, but his graduate research on the "primitive economics" of the Ojibwa, the Dakota, the Menomini, and other Native American groups was both ethnographic and anthropological. After his work in the Philippines, he settled into an academic position at the University of Minnesota, where in 1907 he became a professor of anthropology. Several years later, he founded that university's anthropology department which he chaired until he retired in 1938. Today, Jenks is perhaps best known for his role in organizing the Philippines exhibit of the 1904 St. Louis World's Fair, which displayed nearly 1,200 living Filipinos in mock villages as curiosities for the enjoyment of the viewing public.

Jenks was an enthusiastic imperialist, like many of his contemporaries. In reflecting upon his experience in "building a province" in the Philippines, he noted that "Europe would have taken up the problem of the Philippines without fear or hesitancy...[but] America had neither practice nor theory of Oriental colonization."[6] Jenks viewed this task as an intellectual challenge, a patriotic duty, and a calling. His words vividly illustrate the ideology of the "white man's burden," while emphasizing the need to protect life and property from "insurrectos":

> But the great Philippine problem is not in the cities; it is in the provinces. Here is the home of the savage and the barbarian.... They bred the historic insurrectos, and today they give us the ladrones. How can life and property be protected through a reasonable certainty of peace? How can slavery be best blotted out? How can the native be taught to labor continuously for wages? How can we make a people, who know taxation only as pillage and robbery, willing to pay taxes because taxpaying builds much in making manhood? How can we improve tropical agriculture?[7]

Jenks was most interested in telling the story of Bontoc province—a mountainous region in the central part of northern Luzon—and its inhabitants, particularly the Igorot. His narrative recounted the process by which the Igorot (who, Jenks tells us, "barely escapes being a savage,") benefited from "the best Americanism."[8] Jenks's lurid description of the "natural instincts" of the Igorot—particularly headhunting—was followed by a revealing passage: "An American feels that such things do not make for civilization; but the Spaniards did some good in Bontoc province. They taught the Igorot the important lesson of obedience to a conquering and superior people."[9] Such language illustrates the social evolutionism characteristic of most anthropological (and imperialist) work at the turn of the century.

In his account, Jenks contrasted both the brutal methods of Spanish rule and the "savage" ways of the Igorot with enlightened American administration. By implementing what would today be called a "hearts and minds" strategy—medical care, standardized schooling, etc.—US administrators and soldiers were able to pacify the Bontoc region, according to Jenks. Even more remarkable for Jenks was the fact that the US colonial government was able to create an armed constabulary force—essentially an imperial police force—made up of Igorot men:

> The soldiers have a fine military bearing, and are the best-trained native soldiers I have seen in the provinces.... They were "caught" only during the past two years. They were then naked, long-haired, wild men. Under the coat of most of them is the tattoo proclaiming its wearer a true headhunter. Today they are proud to be soldiers for America. Nowhere else in the archipelago is there so striking an illustration of the fact that the primitive man can be made to serve himself and America, if he is taken before he is weakened by the vices of "civilization."[10]

Jenks's words portrayed the Igorot as noble savages transformed into loyal subjects—a position consistent with a long-standing Western "romantic view of 'military tribes' (or 'races') that pictured former valiant enemies as respected soldiers of the colonial armies."[11] (An earlier example of this tendency was evident in British efforts to recruit "Gurkhas" for the British Indian army after 1857.)[12]

Figure 6.2: The US colonial administration in the Philippines organized native men into constabulary forces, as in the case of this group from Pampanga province on the island of Luzon, circa 1909. (Photo courtesy of the US Library of Congress.)

Before delving more deeply into the broader significance of Jenks's work, it is worth mentioning that he was by no means the only American social scientist working for the Philippine Commission at the turn of the century. In fact, at least two other men with anthropological training and experience—David P. Barrows and Merton L. Miller—also helped organize the Bureau of Non-Christian Tribes and, later, the Ethnological Survey, thereby helping to lay the foundation for US administration of the Philippine highlands. Barrows (who later became a professor and then president of the University of California) played a particularly influential role in forging US policies. Originally trained in political science, he had this to say about the role of ethnology in the Philippines:

> [The burden] is equally great for the ethnologist and the statesman, and nowhere, it may be asserted, must the constructive work of administration be so dependent for information and guidance upon the researches of the expert student.... The success of this effort, so full of possibilities for the future of life and intercourse in the Far East, will depend in a large measure on our correct understanding and scientific grasp of the peoples whose problems we are facing.[13]

Anthropologist Fred Eggan has noted that these men—all of whom worked closely with Dean Worcester, a zoologist and ethnologist who served as Secretary of the Interior in the islands from 1901 to 1913—may be considered to be "the first applied anthropologists, in the sense of persons with anthropological training who were faced with practical problems."[14] This is especially significant in light of the fact that Jenks, Barrows, and Miller were doing their work decades before applied anthropology was recognized as such in the United States. From another perspective, their projects can be interpreted as a textbook example of colonial anthropology.

Looking back on the efforts of the anthropologists of the Philippine Ethnological Survey, it is clear that its scientists took an extraordinarily paternalistic view of the indigenous mountain villagers of the archipelago. They tended to see the Philippine Islands' majority population—Filipinos who lived in the plains and coastal cities—as a potential threat to the Igorot and others living in the highland regions. In this respect, US officials acted in a similar fashion to their Japanese colonial counterparts, who employed paternalistic policies towards Taiwan's aboriginal population (also mountain dwelling peoples) immediately after the island was acquired from China at the end of the Sino-Japanese War in 1895. Japanese officials' stated objective was to protect these groups from the Chinese population, but it is clear that they had political and economic motives as well, particularly the development of camphor plantations.[15] Colonial officials developed a comparable pattern a few years later in French Indochina, where they adopted measures to protect indigenous mountain villagers (Montagnards) from encroachment by the Vietnamese as well as from the predations of French plantation owners.[16]

These three cases from southeast Asia share various characteristics: a scientifically-based approach to colonial administration that employed ethnologists to collect ethnographic data; extensive mapping of indigenous regions and the "ethnicization" of native peoples; the forging of alliances with aboriginal headmen; paternalistic policies designed to gradually "civilize" hill or mountain societies while integrating them into the colonial apparatus and shielding them from lowlanders; and close cooperation between civilian administrators and military officers. Colonial administration was reduced to a problem of rational scientific management. In most instances, the colonizers used what would today be called humanitarian aid (economic development programs, health care, education, etc.) to create bonds with the colonized aborigines.

What is more, in each of these cases, the cultural relativism of the ethnologists—that is, their efforts at understanding the Bontoc Igorot, the aboriginal hill peoples of Taiwan, and the Montagnards—also potentially served military objectives. They might be interpreted as cases of warfare by ethnographic means, for applied colonial anthropology was easily appropriated by administrators seeking to divide and conquer their new subjects by pitting aboriginal people against their Filipino, Chinese, and Vietnamese counterparts who inhabited the low-lying areas. For example, according to historian Paul Barclay, Dean Worcester "saw the highlands and its residents as a possible bulwark against lowland insurrection."[17] Barclay has also described such efforts in Taiwan as "emblematic of early Japanese hopes for an alliance of aborigines and the colonial government against resentful and rebellious Chinese lowlanders" who were the principal source of resistance to Japanese rule: "The Japanese considered its counterinsurgency to be a war against Han Taiwanese. In the early years, top Japanese officials envisioned a future of mutually beneficial relations, and possibly an alliance, with the aborigines."[18]

Anthropologist Oscar Salemink notes that in French Indochina, "the French and later the Americans sought the support of the Montagnards against the nationalist movements of the Vietnamese," a fact borne out by the creation of the "Battaillons Montagnards" as early at the 1940s.[19] (By the early 1960s the US military was emulating the French example, and even used a pirated translation of Georges Condominas's ethnography

Nous Avons Manget la Foret for its counterinsurgency war.) In the end, seemingly liberal attempts to introduce humanitarian aid and the benefits of civilization became means of more effectively exercising political and military control over the colonies.

These efforts bear a striking resemblance to techniques implemented during an earlier period of world history. French commander and colonial administrator Joseph Galliéni (1849–1916) was an architect of pacification policies in Indochina, French Sudan, and Madagascar in the late 1800s. In a classic statement, he described how ethnographic intelligence could facilitate a divide-and-conquer strategy:

> It is the study of the races who inhabit a region which determines the political organization to be imposed and the means to be employed for its pacification. An officer who succeeds in drawing a sufficiently exact ethnographic map of the territory he commands, has almost reached its complete pacification, soon followed by the organization which suits him best.... If there are habits and customs to respect, there are also rivalries which we have to untangle and utilize to our profit, by opposing the ones to the others, and by basing ourselves on the ones in order to defeat the others.[20]

Social science can easily become a martial art under these conditions.

Indirect Rule in British Mesopotamia and East Africa

American and French ethnologists were not alone in their support of colonial projects. Two archaeologists helped establish a de facto system of British colonial rule in Iraq (then called Mesopotamia) after World War I. Although the roles they played differed in some respects from those played by Jenks, Barrows, and Miller in the Philippines, they were guided by many of the same assumptions: an enthusiasm for applying the tools of cultural familiarity for more effective social control; the unquestioned assumption that Western powers were exceptionally able at managing non-Western peoples; and a belief in the fundamental correctness of imperialism.

T. E. Lawrence—immortalized as Lawrence of Arabia by the US media—is best known for helping to coordinate the so-called Arab Revolt against the Ottoman Turks beginning in 1916. But Lawrence was first drawn to the Middle East when he was given the opportunity to do archeology work in northern Syria under the tutelage of David George Hogarth. When World War I erupted, Lawrence eagerly lent his geographic expertise and familiarity with Arabic language and culture to the

Figure 6.3: T. E. Lawrence (immortalized by the US media as "Lawrence of Arabia"), who was trained as an archaeologist, helped the British establish a de facto system of colonial rule in Mesopotamia after World War I. (Photo courtesy of US Library of Congress.)

war effort. He was assigned to the British army in Cairo and soon began supplying money and weapons to Arab fighters led by Prince Feisal. (Feisal was the son of King Hussein, who ruled over the Hejaz—the lands surrounding the holy cities of Mecca and Medina.) Using guerrilla tactics such as dynamiting the vital Hejaz Railway, Lawrence's Arab allies disrupted Turkish supply lines throughout the Middle East. In 1917, they won a key victory at Aqaba, the site of a Turkish fort, and their efforts eventually helped British troops take Jerusalem and Damascus. By 1918, the British occupied all of modern-day Iraq.

Feisal's Arab fighters cooperated with the British after many assurances that they would be rewarded with political autonomy. For years, Lawrence and others sought to convince British government officials that a peculiar form of Arab independence would be beneficial. In a 1916 intelligence report, he noted that the Arab Revolt was:

> beneficial to us, because it marches with our immediate aims, the break up of the Islamic "bloc" and the defeat and disruption of the Ottoman Empire, and because *the states [Sharif Hussein] would set up to succeed the Turks would be...harmless to ourselves.... The Arabs are even less stable than the Turks. If properly handled they would remain in a state of political mosaic, a tissue of small jealous principalities incapable of cohesion.*[21]

Writer and archaeologist Gertrude Bell, who had gained much respect among British commanders for her analyses of intelligence information about Arab groups who might be encouraged to join the revolt against Turks, was another supporter of Iraqi independence—of an odd sort. Bell attempted to persuade British officials that the facade of an administration could be created with competent local men—in other words, she proposed creating a controlled system of indirect rule.

Even so, she doubted that influential Shia clergy were up to the task, since they were "sitting in an atmosphere which reeks of antiquity and is so thick with the dust of ages that you can't see through it—nor can they."[22] She feared the prospect of Shia leaders in a majority Shiite region; indeed, in 1920 she wrote: ."The object of every government here has always been to keep the Shia divines from taking charge of public affairs." Perhaps it is for this reason that she declared: "Mesopotamia is not a civilized state."[23]

The proposals offered by Lawrence and Bell did not convince British government officials to grant Arabs autonomy after the League of Nations awarded Britain a mandate over Mesopotamia in 1920. Sunni and Shia understandably viewed the mandate as a form of colonialism since the British immediately imposed direct rule on the region under the leadership of High Commissioner Sir Percy Cox. They quickly put aside their differences and rose up against their British masters. In the end, hundreds of British troops were killed in the uprising. The government eventually resorted to aerial bombing and the use of white phosphorus (a chemical that produces severe burns as well as liver, heart, and kidney damage) to put down the rebellion, killing nearly 10,000 Arabs in the process.

By 1921, Winston Churchill (then British secretary of state for the Colonies) consulted with Lawrence and Bell in Cairo, where they were vindicated: to save costs, the British established "a mixture of direct and indirect rule" based on the model of colonial India.[24] They installed Feisal as the colony's monarch, which effectively created a puppet regime dependent on Great Britain politically and economically.

After Feisal was made king, Bell was assigned to the British High Commission advisory group in Baghdad. There she and Sir Percy Cox forged a series of divide-and-conquer policies that survived beyond the twentieth century, including the use of Kurdish territory as a buffer against Turkey and Russia; the promotion of Sunni Muslims over the Shia majority; repression or expulsion of Shia clergymen in Najaf, Kerbala, and Kazimain; the buying off of big landowners and tribal elders; fraudulent elections; and deployment of air power for political control.[25]

After 1932, when Iraq gained its nominal independence, British commanders were still given the right to maintain military bases in, and move troops through, Iraq. (By this point, the country was of great economic importance to the British because of its oil resources.) The Iraqi monarchy lasted as a client regime with little change until 1958, when it was toppled by a military coup.

Although both Lawrence and Bell were probably considered "liberal" in the 1920s from a British perspective—after all, they advocated indirect rather than direct rule—the end result was not substantively different, from the Iraqi point of view. After King Feisal assumed power, British advisers in Baghdad still made key political and economic decisions, thousands of British troops remained in the region for decades, and the British-owned Iraqi Petroleum Company was granted full concessions over Iraqi oil. Both Lawrence and Bell maintained a paternalistic view that took for granted the necessity of European intervention in the affairs of people deemed less than civilized.

A few years later, in another British colony, administrators called upon the services of a social anthropologist. Late in 1929, thousands of indigenous Igbo women spontaneously rioted in southeastern Nigeria, then a part of the British Empire. The women blocked roads, set fire to buildings, assaulted chiefs, and challenged troops sent by the government to restore order. The uprising ended after a few weeks, but not before colonial forces killed fifty people.[26]

The "Women's Riots" have been explained as the result of an increasingly oppressive tax system and a steep drop in the price of palm products, the key source of income for local people. (For years, British companies had relied upon palm oil exported from Nigeria, Malaya, and other colonies to lubricate industrial machinery throughout the empire.) But Igbo women also rebelled against the despised Native Administration which the British had installed in the region, a political system which established Native Courts managed by corrupt chiefs—local men who effectively served as powerful lackeys. The idea behind this system of indirect rule was to minimize the costs of maintaining political and economic control by co-opting local leaders who would collect taxes, resolve local conflicts, and manage affairs on behalf of the British.

Once the women's rebellion was smothered, the British government began investigating its causes and possible ways to prevent such occurrences in the future. They sought the assistance of C. K. Meek, a social anthropologist with more than eighteen years of experience in northern

Nigeria. According to Meek, he "was to deal with the Intelligence reports from the point of view of applied anthropology."[27]

In his analysis, Meek argued that the chiefs and courts installed by the British were radically different from village-councils and other decentralized political arrangements that had existed in southeastern Nigeria during the pre-colonial period. He suggested that more nuanced and culturally appropriate forms of Native Administration might lead to a more stable situation in which "the Ibo advances along the path of political progress."[28]

As in the case of T. E. Lawrence and Gertrude Bell, Meek's peers undoubtedly saw him as a liberal, since he advocated indirect (as opposed to direct) rule of Britain's African colonies. Furthermore, his sensitive description of "the vigour and intelligence of the Ibo people, which have made them one of the largest and most progressive tribes in Africa," must have appeared remarkably sympathetic in the eyes of many Britons.[29] Yet in the end, Meek was unable to envision Igbo life beyond the British empire. He was fully aware that the government's attitude towards anthropology was that it should serve as the "handmaiden to administration" by providing data that would help the government "make the fullest use of Native institutions as instruments of local administration."[30] Meek's work paternalistically denied from the outset the possibility of Ibo self-determination. Underlying his work was the notion that Africans were unable to adapt to the modern world without British protection.

Meek, Lawrence, and Bell were hardly alone in seeing colonialism's inevitability, or indirect rule as the best option for European control of African colonies. S. F. Nadel, a leading figure in social anthropology, was also a strong proponent. When, in the late 1930s, British government officials recruited Nadel to help control Nuba peoples in what was then the Anglo-Egyptian Sudan, he eagerly accepted. According to Nadel, his study "was primarily planned to be of practical value to administrators and others." He noted that the government considered the Nuba to be

> powerfully affected by the authority of the Government, the forces of economics and the influence of science.... Their lives were still largely conditioned by superstitions and customs imperfectly known to the administration.... Keen officials, especially technical officials, were apt to override native customs rather than make use of them.[31]

For Nadel, making use of Nuba customs included establishing "Native Courts" with "Government-sponsored Chieftainships"—that is, indirect rule. (Two years later, problems with the courts led government troops to drive the Jebel Tullushi indigenous group out of their mountain homes.)[32]

Nadel was incapable of envisioning Africa beyond colonialism, or to see the role of the social scientist as anything other than "of practical value to administrators" seeking to control native peoples. Such perspectives reveal these anthropologists' complicity in the colonial enterprise. Although Meek saw his role as a benevolent one, and Nadel argued that "the blunders of the anthropologists will be 'better' blunders," neither Meek, nor Nadel, nor dozens of other anthropologists challenged the assumption that colonizers had the right—and the obligation—to decide what was best for the natives.[33]

While some might condemn these anthropologists for their work, it is important to understand the time in which they lived. Few of their peers dared to envision a world beyond colonialism—after all, they believed that Europeans were bringing the hallmarks of civilization to the colonies: schools, health clinics, modern science, and technology. In short, it is easier to understand their actions if we consider the totalistic ideology of empire.

Towards an Anti-Imperial Anthropology

These and many other examples illustrate the different ways in which anthropologists (and ethnographic data) were used by colonial governments in Africa, Asia, Latin America, the Middle East, and Oceania. But not everyone agreed with the inevitability of American, British, French, or Japanese imperialisms—nor with the idea of anthropological participation in such enterprises. The father of American anthropology, Franz Boas, publicly expressed his dismay at changes he had witnessed following his emigration to the United States in the 1880s. In a letter to the *New York Times* published in 1916, he wrote:

> At the time of my arrival here more than thirty years ago, I was filled with admiration of American political ideals.... I thought of it as a country that would not tolerate interference with its own interests, but that would also refrain from active interference in the affairs of others, and would never become guilty of the oppression of unwilling subjects. Events like the great movement westward, and the Mexican war, appeared rather as digressions from the self-imposed path of self-restraint. A rude awakening came in 1898, when the aggressive imperialism of that period showed that the ideal had been a dream. Well I remember the heated discussions which I had that year with my German friends when I maintained that the control of colonies was opposed to the fundamental ideas of right held by the American

people, and the profound disappointment that I felt when, at the end of the Spanish war, these ideals lay shattered. The America that had stood for right, and right only, seemed dead; and in its place stood a young giant, eager to grow at the expense of others, and dominated by the same desire of aggrandizement that sways the narrowly confined European states.... I have always been of the opinion that we have no right to impose our ideals upon other nations, no matter how strange it may seem to us that they enjoy the kind of life they lead, how slow they may be in utilizing the resources of their countries, or how much opposed their ideals may be to ours.[34]

Boas's courageous statement came at a time when nativist (and racist) sentiment was running high in the US. But he steadfastly believed in the social responsibility of scientists: the idea that anthropologists (and other scientists) had an obligation to share the results of their objective research with the public and with policy makers, even when the science produced truths that threatened powerful interests. It is likely that Boas was opposed to the idea of American imperialism because it was premised upon the flawed (and scientifically disproved) notion of the racial and cultural superiority of the United States vis-a-vis other societies.

History tells us that anthropology has occasionally played an essential role in resisting imperialism. For example, in the 1930s a young Kikuyu man named Jomo Kenyatta from British East Africa (today Kenya) arrived in London and attended seminars led by the renowned anthropologist Bronislaw Malinowski. In 1938 Kenyatta published a stirring ethnography of Kikuyu life, *Facing Mount Kenya*, which inspired many people by examining the painful consequences of British colonialism from an insider's perspective.[35] He used anthropology as a tool for challenging—not supporting—colonial rule. He also had the ability to question assumptions that few of his European colleagues were able to articulate, including the notion that Africans were incapable of self-rule. Kenyatta became a revolutionary leader and eventually the first Prime Minister and President of independent Kenya in the 1960s.[36] His experience reveals that human science is as capable of challenging power as it is of serving it.

In the twenty-first century, social scientists once again find that their knowledge has become revelant to the needs of occupation forces and neocolonial administrators seeking to implement "stability operations" and counterinsurgency programs abroad (see chapters 3 and 5 of this book). Efforts to militarize anthropology depart dramatically from the idea that scholars are obligated "to humanity as a whole and that, in a conflict of duties, our obligations to humanity are of higher value than those toward the nation.... Patriotism must be subordinated to humanism."[37] When the lines separating the professional social scientist, the colonial administrator, and the counterinsurgency technician are blurred, social science itself becomes something that can be sold to the highest bidder.

Others—perhaps traumatized by the Cold War, or a lingering memory of it—have become "epistemological radicals" obsessed with trivia, mere "flights from facts of power which expressed denial of domestic repression and US imperialism abroad."[38] Journalist Robert Fisk, in a searing critique of "poisonous academics and their claptrap of exclusion," observed that phrases such as "dialogic apologetics," "persecutorial othering," "remythification," and "hermeneutic possibility" serve as distancing mechanisms. "It is part of the secret language of academe—especially of anthropology," he noted. "University teachers—especially in the States—are great at networking...but hopeless at communicating with most of the rest of the world."[39] These trends have indeed served to "reinvent armchair anthropology, and intentionally or not, legitimated a retreat from responsibility."[40]

Many anthropologists are resisting the retreat from social responsibility by enlightening public debate, including recent debates on US-led wars of occupation. Robert Fernea, who first conducted research in Iraq more than a half century ago, warned that a prolonged United States occupation there would likely lead to civil war.[41] Hugh Gusterson has spoken out in public forums about the impossibility of winning a war in Afghanistan.[42] Barbara Nimri Aziz and Nadje Al-Ali have done much to humanize Iraqis often dehumanized by the corporate media.[43] Their activist work (Aziz produces a popular radio program in New York; Al-Ali is a founding member of Act Together—Women's Action for Iraq) has greatly stimulated public discussion.

The dilemmas posed by counterinsurgency in colonial settings stand as object lessons for "persons with anthropological training who [are] faced with practical problems," that is, for applied anthropologists.[44] In particular, the experiences of Albert Jenks, David Barrows, T. E. Lawrence and others illustrate how technical problem-solving for powerful sponsors can easily lead those sponsors to implement grandiose attempts at social engineering ultimately doomed to failure. This is a pattern that has repeated itself many times over in authoritarian modernization initiatives, such as hydroelectric dam projects and forced agricultural collectivization schemes.[45] Before attempting to apply the social sciences, it is important to ask: For whom? To what end? And with what consequences?

The human sciences hold great promise for those seeking a more just world, but its practitioners are more likely to be effective when they maintain roles outside of the military, its contract firms, and other authoritarian organizations, and when they communicate widely and publicly. It is by enlightening the public that we might spark progressive change in democratic societies.

Notes

1. Thomas A. Bass, "Counterinsurgency and Torture," *American Quarterly* 60, no. 2 (2008): 233.

2. Some have made a useful distinction between "modern" colonial states (that employed a rational scientific approach to conquest) and "pre-modern" colonial states (that did not). See Paul Barclay, "'They Have for the Coast Dwellers a Traditional Hatred': Governing Igorots in Northern Luzon and Central Taiwan, 1895–1915," in *The American Colonial State in the Philippines*, ed. Julian Go and Anne L. Foster (Durham, NC: Duke University Press, 2003), 217–255.

3. Julian Go and Anne L. Foster, *The American Colonial State in the Philippines* (Durham: Duke University Press, 2003).

4. Stephen Kinzer, *Overthrow: America's Century of Regime Change from Hawaii to Iraq* (New York: Times Books), 34.

5. Alexander F. Chamberlain, "Review of *The Bontoc Igorot* by Alfred E. Jenks," *American Anthropologist* 7 (1905): 696–701.

6. Alfred E. Jenks, "Building a Province," *The Outlook*, May 21, 1904, 170.

7. Ibid., 170–171.

8. Ibid., 171.

9. Ibid., 173.

10. Ibid., 175.

11. Oscar Salemink, "Ethnography as Martial Art: Ethnicizing Vietnam's Montagnards, 1930–1954," in *Colonial Subjects: Essays on the Practical History of Anthropology*, ed. Peter Pels and Oscar Salemink (Ann Arbor: University of Michigan Press, 1999), 283.

12. Peter Pels, "The Rise and Fall of the Indian Aborigines: Orientalism, Anglicism, and the Emergence of an Ethnography of India, 1833–1869," in *Colonial Subjects: Essays on the Practical History of Anthropology*, ed. Peter Pels and Oscar Salemink (Ann Arbor: University of Michigan Press, 1999), 94.

13. David P. Barrows, *Report of the Bureau of Non-Christian Tribes of the Philippine Islands for the Year Ended August 31, 1902* (Washington DC: Report of the Philippine Commission, Bureau of Insular Affairs, War Department), Appendix Q, 681.

14. Fred Eggan, "Applied Anthropology in the Mountain Province, Philippines," *Social Organization and the Applications of Anthropology: Essays in Honor of Lauriston Sharp*, edited by Robert J. Smith (Ithaca, NY: Cornell University Press, 1974), 196–197.

15. Barclay, "Coast Dwellers."

16. Salemink, "Ethnography as Martial Art," 286.

17. Barclay, "Coast Dwellers," 236.

18. Ibid., 227–228.

19. Salemink, "Ethnography as Martial Art," 292, 315–316

20. Joseph Galliéni, quoted in ibid., 282–283. The idea of ethnography as "martial art" was articulated by Oscar Salemink (op. cit., 282).

21. T. E. Lawrence, quoted in Robert Dreyfuss, *Devil's Game: How the United States Helped Unleash Fundamentalist Islam* (New York: Metropolitan Books, 2005), 41.

22. Gertrude Bell, quoted in James Buchan, "Miss Bell's Lines in the Sand," *The Guardian*, March 12, 2003, http://www.guardian.co.uk/world/2003/mar/12/iraq.jamesbuchan (accessed May 19, 2008).

23. Gerturde Bell, quoted in Rachel Aspden, "Read and Digest, Mr. Blair," *The Guardian*, September 3, 2006, http://www.guardian.co.uk/books/2006/sep/03/biography.features (accessed May 19, 2008); see also Buchan, "Miss Bell's Lines."

24. Charles Tripp, "Iraq: The Imperial Precedent," *Le Monde Diplomatique* (English edition), January 3, 2003, http://mondediplo.com/2003/01/02empire (accessed May 20, 2008).

25. William O. Beeman, "The US-Shi'ite Relationship in a New Iraq: Better than the British?" *Strategic Insights*, May 2004, http://www.ccc.nps.navy.mil/si/2004/may/beemanMay04.asp (accessed May 20, 2008).

26. C.K. Meek, *Law and Authority in a Nigerian Tribe: A Study in Indirect Rule* (Oxford, UK: Oxford University Press, 1937).

27. Ibid., xi.

28. Ibid., ix, x, 354.

29. Ibid., 355.

30. Ibid., xv.

31. S. F. Nadel, *The Nuba* (London: Oxford University Press, 1947), xi.

32. James Faris, "Pax Britannica and the Sudan: S. F. Nadel," in *Anthropology and the Colonial Encounter*, ed. Talal Asad (New York: Humanity Books, 1973), 157.

33. S. F. Nadel, *The Foundations of Social Anthropology* (London: Cohen & West, 1951), 55.

34. Franz Boas, "Letter to the Editor," *New York Times*, January 7, 1916.

35. Jomo Kenyatta, *Facing Mount Kenya* (London: Secker and Warburg, 1938).

36. Lamentably, Kenyatta's rule did not usher in a political utopia. He led the country for more than fifteen years and established a highly centralized regime increasingly intolerant of opponents. The executive branch of government overshadowed other institutions, and under such a system Kenyatta's cronies were able to plunder Kenya and repress organized opposition for nearly a decade (from 1969 to 1978).

37. Franz Boas, quoted in David Price, *Anthropological Intelligence: The Deployment and Neglect of Anthropology in the Second World War* (Durham, NC: Duke University Press, 2008), 2.

38. Laura Nader, "The Phantom Factor: Impact of the Cold War on Anthropology," in *The Cold War and the University*, ed. Andre Schiffrin (New York: The New Press, 1997), 140.

39. Robert Fisk, "Let Us Rebel Against Poisonous Academics and Their Preposterous Claptrap of Exclusion," *The Independent*, May 14, 2005, http://www.independent.co.uk/opinion/commentators/fisk/robert-fisk-let-us-rebel-against-poisonous-academics-and-their-preposterous-claptrap-of-exclusion-490624.html (accessed June 13, 2008).

40. Nader, "Phantom Factor," 134.

41. Robert Fernea, "Why If We Don't Leave Iraq Now We May Bring on a Civil War," *History News Network* (January 10, 2005). http://hnn.us/articles/9517.html (accessed January 5, 2010).

42. Hugh Gusterson, "Why the War in Afghanistan Cannot Be Won," *Bulletin of the Atomic Scientists* (September 21, 2009). http://www.thebulletin.org/web-edition/columnists/hugh-gusterson/why-the-war-afghanistan-cannot-be-won (accessed September 27, 2009).

43. Barbara Nimri Aziz, *Swimming Up the Tigris* (Gainesville, FL: University Press of Florida, 2007); Nadje Al-Ali and Nicola Pratt, *What Kind of Liberation? Women and the Occupation of Iraq* (Berkeley: University of California Press, 2009).

44. Eggan, "Applied Anthropology," 196–197.

45. See, for example, James C. Scott, *Seeing Like a State* (New Haven, CT, and London: Yale University Press, 1998).

Chapter 7
Going "Tribal"

Few anthropologists today would consider using the term "tribe" as an analytical category, or even as a concept for practical application. Years ago, Morton Fried observed that "many anthropologists have attempted to avoid the word, or deliberately isolate it in inverted commas" because of its persistent ambiguities.[1] In common usage, it has tended to acquire two interrelated meanings. Historians, political scientists, and the public have used "tribe" to describe archaic, "savage," or non-literate peoples; for example, ancient Germanic tribes. At the same time, government officials have frequently adopted it as an administrative category for classifying colonized groups across Africa, Asia, and North America. In the United States, the concept of tribe was employed during the nineteenth century to refer to Native American groups in both senses: as uncivilized savages and as subjects to be relocated and administered by the War Department's Office of Indian Affairs—an early example of American cultural militarization that suggests a pattern of continuity spanning much of our country's history. Often, the "tribe" was not so much a model *of* reality as it was a model *for* reality—for an imagined future that was eventually realized by military means.

Perhaps it is for these reasons that more than a half-century ago, anthropologist E. R. Leach cautioned:

> It is largely an academic fiction to suppose that in a "normal" ethnographic situation one ordinarily finds distinct "tribes" distributed about the map in an orderly fashion with clear-cut boundaries between them…. My own view is that the ethnographer has often only managed to discern the existence of "*a* tribe" because he took it as axiomatic that this kind of cultural entity must exist.[2]

Yet as military planners have recast the wars in Afghanistan and Iraq as "non-lethal" counterinsurgency struggles to win hearts and minds, the tribe has become both an analytical tool and a focal point for the wars' architects. Many influential voices have called for the mobilization of tribes in Afghanistan and Iraq. In December 2007, British prime minister Gordon

Figure 7.1: A US Army captain and Human Terrain Team members sit on a rug and talk with a local village elder in Afghanistan, August 2009. Similar images were common in nineteenth century Orientalist art. (Photo courtesy of US Department of Defense.)

Brown emphatically declared the need to strengthen "traditional Afghan *arbakai* [village militias]" and noted that British forces must "understand the tribal dynamics" in order to accomplish this objective.[3] Several months later, US Army General David Petraeus reported from Bagram Air Base in Afghanistan: "This is a country in which support of the tribes, of the local communities, for the overall effort is essential.... It is a country that has not had a tradition of central government extending into the far reaches of its provinces."[4] US Defense Secretary Robert Gates agreed in November 2008: "At the end of the day the only solution in Afghanistan is to work with the tribes and provincial leaders in terms of trying to create a backlash... against the Taliban."[5] And in March 2009, President Barack Obama told the *New York Times* that in Afghanistan, "You have a less governed region, a history of fierce independence among tribes. Those tribes are multiple and sometimes operate at cross purposes, and so figuring all that out is going to be much more of a challenge."[6]

Recent interest in Afghanistan's "tribes" appears to stem from a desperate political situation. Neither the central government nor more than 120,000 US and NATO troops have been able to stop a resurgent Taliban, who according to credible reports have established checkpoints as close

Figure 7.2: US and Afghan officials consult with tribal elders and Islamic clergy in Khost, Afghanistan, September 2006. (Photo courtesy of the US Navy.)

as fifteen miles from Kabul. Tribal engagement strategies also appear to be inspired by events in the western Iraqi province of al-Anbar, where US forces have been paying off Sunni strongmen who began opposing al-Qaeda in Iraq—an ongoing process of bribing "tribesmen" that was reportedly inspired by the work of social scientists.[7]

In Afghanistan and Iraq, proponents of such strategies include military men, employees of private military companies, and think tank researchers. They have frequently cited the work of anthropologists and other social scientists. For example, an article headed "Iraq Tribal Engagement: Lessons Learned" by Lieutenant Colonel Michael Eisenstadt—a US Army Reserves Middle East foreign area officer with an MA in Arab Studies—includes a section entitled "Anthropology 101: What Is a Tribe?" In it, the author makes brief references to the work of Marshall Sahlins, Robert Fernea, Dale Eickelman, Charles Lindholm, Louise Sweet and other scholars. Most of these references date back to the 1960s, yet Eisenstadt gives no indication of how the term has become problematic among anthropologists.[8]

A closer reading of such work reveals several underlying assumptions. For example, when military planners discuss the "tribe," they refer to a ranked society with a "chief" (or "sheik") positioned firmly at the top of the hierarchy. (This is not the relatively egalitarian tribe that undergraduate students learn about in introductory classes.) They also suggest—in orientalist fashion—that tribesmen are traditional or pre-modern people unfamiliar with Western ways.[9]

It is worth noting that other expressions—such as "ethnicity" and "ethnic"—also appear in military discourses, but the semantic contexts of such terms differ significantly. A review of speeches, briefings, and documents posted at the US Defense Department's official website (http://www.defenselink.mil) and articles from leading military journals (such as *Military Review*) reveals that military planners apply the "ethnic" concept to a wide range of regions and countries, including the Middle East, Central and South Asia, Africa, China, Kosovo, and other Balkan regions and the former Soviet republics (for example, Georgia and Moldova). They also apply it when discussing the composition of the US armed forces. By contrast, military planners apply the tribal concept almost exclusively to Iraq and other Middle Eastern countries, Afghanistan, Pakistan, and (increasingly) Africa.

Why would an outdated anthropological concept become such a vital idea? David Kilcullen, who holds a PhD in politics from the University of New South Wales and served as an advisor to Petraeus in Iraq, gives a partial explanation of why some consider it useful: "Since the new threats are not state-based, the basis for our approach should not be international relations (the study of how nation-states interact in elite state-based frameworks) but anthropology (the study of social roles, groups, status, institutions and relations within human population groups in nonelite, nonstate-based frameworks)."[10] What is largely obsolete to contemporary anthropologists apparently has a crucial place among twenty-first-century counterinsurgency theorists.

As in the case of US government tribal policies during the nineteenth century, the concept of tribe has surfaced at a particular historical moment: a moment in which an expansionist state with occupation forces implements "pacification" programs to quell insurrectionists. This was clearly the case with the Indian Removal Act of 1830 and the brutal Indian Wars that followed it, and it appears to be the case in Iraq and Afghanistan, as counterinsurgency specialists portray tribal-based strategies as necessary and effective tools for military application. It is telling that today many soldiers and military planners refer to al-Anbar as "the Wild West" and Iraq as "Indian Country."[11]

CHAPTER 7

PowerPoint, "Tribal Engagement," and the "Surge"

On September 10, 2007, Petraeus—who has a PhD in international relations from Princeton University (see chapter 3 of this book)—appeared before the US Congress to provide testimony regarding the results of the so-called "surge" in Iraq (an increase of 30,000 US combat troops which was initiated in February 2007).[12] As he approached the climax of his presentation, Petraeus used PowerPoint images to display graphs representing declining numbers of insurgent attacks and US and Iraqi casualties in al-Anbar, and pointed to Sunni tribes as a prime source of progress:

> The most significant development in the past six months likely has been the increasing emergence of tribes and local citizens rejecting al-Qaeda and other extremists. This has, of course, been most visible in Anbar Province. A year ago the province was assessed as 'lost' politically. Today, it is a model of what happens when local leaders and citizens decide to oppose al-Qaeda and reject its Taliban-like ideology.... We have, in coordination with the Iraqi government's National Reconciliation Committee, been engaging these tribes and groups of local citizens who want to oppose extremists.[13]

It was a milestone moment for a general enamored with public relations, but only a day before his presentation, the *Washington Post* provided

Figure 7.3: General David Petraeus appears before Congress to testify on the situation in Iraq, September 11, 2007. At the time, Petraeus was the top US military commander in Iraq. (Photo courtesy of US Department of Defense.)

a detailed account of how Bush administration insiders had used top military commanders to help sell the surge throughout the summer. The article referred to a White House "rapid-response PR unit hard-wired into Petraeus' shop," as well as a coordinated advertising strategy:

> Ed Gillespie, the new presidential counselor, organized daily conference calls at 7:45 am and again late in the afternoon between the White House, the Pentagon, the State Department, and the US Embassy and military in Baghdad to map out ways of selling the surge.... From the start of the Bush plan, the White House communications office had been blitzing an e-mail list of as many as 5,000 journalists, lawmakers, lobbyists, conservative bloggers, military groups, and others with talking points or rebuttals of criticism.[14]

The report highlighted Petraeus's role in the process:

> Petraeus was doing his part in Baghdad, hosting dozens of lawmakers and military scholars for PowerPoint presentations on why the Bush strategy had made gains. Many Republicans and even Democrats came home impressed, and suddenly even critics were agreeing that Petraeus had made some progress in security even though the Iraqi political situation remained a mess. Petraeus also persuaded intelligence officials to revise some key judgments of a new National Intelligence Estimate on Iraq to reflect security gains. Some visitors suspected a skewed picture. "We only saw things that reinforced their message that the surge was working," said [US House] Representative Jan Schakowsky.[15]

Petraeus's Congressional testimony implied that the surge had enabled the US military to provide support to "tribes" which had in turn reduced violence by driving al-Qaeda in Iraq out of power. In essence it implied that correlation proved causation. The commercial media overwhelmingly supported and echoed the general's interpretation while barely exploring alternative explanations for reduced violence, such as the ceasefire declared by Shia cleric Moqtada al-Sadr or the thorough ethnic cleansing of Iraqi cities—a process that led to thousands of deaths, the creation of millions of refugees, and the country's Balkanization.

Petraeus got his way. By the spring of 2008, the general's tribal engagement strategy—which reportedly paid out more than one billion dollars to mostly Sunni groups—was in full swing.

Dividing and Conquering in Iraq

For Iraqis, the strategy is likely to be reckless and potentially disastrous over the long run. Documentary filmmaker Rick Rowley was embedded with US troops in 2007, and described how tribal engagement works:

> Through a combination of threats and enticements like releasing their kids from prison, the US military has gotten [Sunni] groups to join a coalition. They're paid money for small construction projects, and they're eventually incorporated into the Iraqi police force, where they're armed and paid, given a gun, a badge and the power to arrest.... I didn't see anyone give an M16 to anyone. But I did see a US captain hand wads of cash to militiamen who were guarding checkpoints.[16]

Support for the tribes evidently meant supporting some of Iraq's worst war criminals:

> In the town of Fallahat, where there used to be a lot of Shia, there are now no Shia.... [We] found them living on the outskirts of Baghdad in a refugee camp.... There are no services, no doctors, no hospitals, no schools, no running water, no work, no sanitation.... The refugees we talked to knew the names of the people who have kicked them out and bombed their houses. And they are exactly the same tribes the Americans are working with.... Maliki's head of negotiations with Sunni groups told us the groups the Americans are working with include some of the country's worst war criminals.[17]

Why would US forces pursue this strategy? According to Rowley: "The US is funding sectarian militias fighting in a civil war in order to momentarily decrease attacks on Americans.... It's an easy way to produce immediate statistical successes on the ground, a decrease in attacks on American soldiers."[18]

A showdown appears imminent. In August 2008, observers reported that Iraq's government (dominated by Shiites) arrested hundreds of the US's Sunni allies. In a front-page *New York Times* article on tensions between the US-supported Sunnis and the Iraqi government, Iraq Army Brigadier General Nasser al-Hiti commented on the movement's leaders: "These people are like cancer, and we must remove them." According to the report, the Iraqi crackdown "is causing a rift with the American military, which contends that any significant diminution of the Awakening could result in renewed violence.... 'If this is not handled properly, we could have a security issue,' said Brigadier General David Perkins, the senior military spokesman in Iraq. 'You don't want to give anybody a reason to turn back to al-Qaeda.'"[19]

Independent correspondent Nir Rosen predicted this scenario months in advance. Rosen, who has conducted years of unembedded journalism in Iraq, noted in an expose that the US strategy "seems simple: to buy off every Iraqi in sight.... The US is now backing more than 600,000 Iraqi men in the security sector—more than half the number Saddam had at the height of his power." He also warned that "unless the new Iraqi state continues to operate as a vast bribing machine, the insurgent Sunnis who have joined the new militias will likely revert to fighting the ruling Shiites, who still refuse to share power."[20] In a separate interview, Rosen reported that in Baghdad, "each neighborhood is walled off. You have a warlord or militiaman in charge of it.... Iraq has really become Somalia: different warlords controlling different areas.... There is no government in Iraq. It's a collection of different militias, who as we see, even fight among themselves."[21]

Others warn that over the long term, US support for groups of local citizens is likely to aggravate armed conflict between and among Sunni and Shia groups, creating a situation comparable to the Lebanese civil war of the 1970s and 1980s.[22] Like the Syrians, who invaded and kept tens of thousands of troops in Lebanon through years of sectarian conflict (while pitting Lebanese factions against each other), the United States seems unable or unwilling to end the Iraqi civil war. From this perspective, tribal engagement in Iraq resembles a high-stakes strategy of divide-and-conquer that will potentially lead to more tragedy in the years ahead. If there appears to be a relative calm in Iraq, it is because the presence of more US troops has temporarily frozen sectarian violence. The similarities to colonial-era tactics employed in Northern Ireland, India, Rwanda, Vietnam, and Lebanon should give pause to those concerned about Iraq's future.

In the meantime, *Newsweek* magazine reported without a trace of irony that "Petraeus says he instructs his young officers, 'Go watch *The Sopranos* in order to understand the power dynamics at work in Iraq.'"[23]

Of Bribes and Tribes

Some commentators at Washington DC-based think tanks and military contract firms had been advocating the pursuit of tribal-based strategies for years, but their ideas were largely ignored by Pentagon planners who preferred a strong central government in post-Saddam Iraq. For example, Israeli historian Amatzia Baram argued that tribes would be essential for a US victory. In an op-ed piece for the *New York Times* written only months after the US-led invasion, he argued that reducing violence in Iraq depended on reaching out to tribesmen in the "Sunni Triangle":

The easiest [method] would simply be to hire the sheiks and their tribesmen—putting them on salaries and allowing them to spread the wealth among their people.... If a sheik refused to cooperate, not only could his perks be withheld, they could be given to a neighboring sheik. This would eventually pit the uncooperative sheik against his own tribesmen.... If this weren't enough to get the sheik into line, it wouldn't be too difficult for the coalition to enact "regime change" on a small scale.[24]

Others began reaching similar conclusions. Global Resources Group—a private intelligence firm created by W. Patrick Lang (a retired US Special Forces officer who holds an MA in Middle East studies and anthropology) and Lin Todd (a former military intelligence officer)—assembled a 390-page report entitled *Iraq Tribal Study: al-Anbar Governorate* which frankly and unapologetically discussed the benefits of renting tribes.[25] Its list of contributors includes R. Alan King, who is a retired US Army civil affairs and psychological operations officer; Andrea Jackson, who is a former research director for the Lincoln Group (a Washington DC-based public relations firm); and Ahmed Hashim, a US Army officer with a PhD in international relations. *Iraq Tribal Study* was reportedly circulated in the US Army Command and General Staff College at Fort Leavenworth, Kansas, which was led by Petraeus at the time. It is not clear to what extent he was influenced by the document, but there was clearly much talk about tribal strategies at Leavenworth during his tenure there.

The document focuses on three relatively small groups: Albu Fahd, Albu Mahal, and Albu Issa. The authors apparently selected them because of the prominent role their leaders played in challenging al-Qaeda operatives in Ramadi, Qaim, and Fallujah respectively. The objectives of *Iraq Tribal Study* are clearly stated in several chapter titles, particularly "Emerging Insights on Influencing the Tribes of al-Anbar" and "Influencing the Three Target Tribes." Subheadings read like a how-to manual: there are instructions for how to "Leverage Traditional Authority," "Use a Compelling Ideology," "Use Appropriate Coercive Force," and "Use Economic Incentives and Disincentives." In addition, the authors provide views on "How to Persuade the Tribes to Stop Supporting Insurgency," "How to Persuade the Tribes to Support the Coalition," and "How to Work and Live with Tribesmen."

Such sections spell out techniques for pressing local power brokers into the service of US occupation forces. When the authors of *Iraq Tribal Study* suggest leveraging "traditional authority," they mean co-opting local leaders; when they recommend creating a "compelling ideology," they mean conducting psychological warfare; when they call for "appropriate coercive force," they mean controlling and focusing attacks upon suspected insurgents; and when they mention "economic incentives and disincentives," they mean rewarding Iraqis who cooperate with US demands and punishing those who do not. These are the basic techniques of imperial policing—a blend of persuasive and coercive strategies as old as the idea of empire.

Among other things, *Iraq Tribal Study* reviews the periods of Ottoman rule (1534–1918) and the British Mandate (1920–1932) in Mesopotamia for clues on adapting imperial techniques to the twenty-first century. A section entitled "Engaging the Shaikhs: British Successes, Failures, and Lessons" states:

> Convincing the sheiks that the British were the dominant force...had a powerful effect.... Subsidies and land grants bought loyalty.... It may be useful to examine the tribal landscape for modern parallels.... Development funds immediately come to mind.... The key lies in putting into the sheik's hands the ability to improve their people's livelihoods, and thereby the sheik's own status.[26]

In the next paragraph, the authors describe how the British handled recalcitrant sheiks: "Punitive assaults, both by infantry column and with air strikes, on the villages of shaikhs judged uncooperative brought about short-term cooperation and long-term enmity. Enabled largely by airpower, the British were able to stay in Iraq—with minimal resources—through its independence in 1932 and beyond."[27]

Given such a crude understanding of tribes, perhaps it is not surprising that some influential planners view the US military as the "strongest tribe" (in the words of former Assistant Secretary of Defense Bing West) in a region whose people they portray as incapable of respect for democratic principles—despite evidence to the contrary.[28]

At another point in *Iraq Tribal Study*, the authors noted how Saddam Hussein's social control methods might be emulated:

> The Baath regime fostered competition between tribes in a "divide and rule" campaign. This method was, and remains, effective because it exploits tribal honor and competition over limited resources. Competition between tribes can be a compelling way to secure the cooperation of one tribe at the expense of the other. A tribe is likely to cooperate to keep another tribe from getting the benefits.[29]

By the end of the study, the authors are more forthright about manipulating Iraqis, and outline strategies for "influencing three target tribes" through bribes: "Iraq's tribal values are ripe for exploitation. According to an old Iraqi saying, 'You cannot buy a tribe, but you can certainly rent one'.... Shaikhs have responded well to financial incentives."[30] The authors offer specific suggestions for using development funds to win support, and recommend involving sheiks in the distribution of resources, including health care services, dietary supplements, water and sewage treatment plants, telephone and electrical service, and farm equipment.

Iraq Tribal Study is at times schizophrenic. Occasionally the authors include passages espousing cultural relativism. On the one hand, they note that "RESPECT (*Ihtiram* in Arabic) is the key to working with tribesmen anywhere in the world," and suggest that readers " not assume that they want to be like you" and " not reject their ways as primitive or backward."[31] On the other hand, they often portray Arabs and Islam in unflattering (and sometimes stereotypical) terms: they solemnly comment on "the fatalistic outlook that pervades Iraqi and Arab society," state that "Iraqi Arabs are generally submissive and obedient to their superiors," and suggest that Islam is characterized by a "medieval mind set...in which change is neither beneficial nor virtuous."[32]

Eventually, members of the Pentagon's technical intelligentsia expressed enthusiasm for tribal strategies. Montgomery McFate, who has a PhD in cultural anthropology and is currently senior social science advisor to the $250 million US Army Human Terrain System (see chapter 5 of this book), discussed divide-and-conquer tactics in an essay published by the US Naval War College. McFate (who also has years of experience in secret intelligence-gathering)[33] noted that the British "discovered that the divide-and-conquer strategy was the most expedient means of governing a society dominated by tribes.... The British goal was to 'keep the monarchy stronger than any one tribe but weaker than a coalition of tribes,' thereby giving British administrators decisive authority in arbitrating disputes." She suggested that "tribal use of force follows predictable patterns that, if understood, offer opportunities to states engaged in conflict with tribes," and outlined what she considered to be the essence of the "tribal ethos": the "blood feud," "raiding," "collective self-defense," and "restoration of honor."[34] The article was saturated with over-generalizations. She concluded: "Only by understanding how tribes are mobilized for war against the state, and by understanding the unwritten (but highly formalized) norms by which they fight, US forces can adapt their own warfighting to that of their adversary."[35]

Not all advocates of tribal engagement argued in such unqualified terms. In a widely cited piece published online, David Kilcullen argued: "Our dilemma in Iraq is, and always has been, finding a way to create a sustainable security architecture.... [It] requires balancing competing armed interest groups, at the national and local level.... This might represent a step toward an intra-communal 'balance of power' that could potentially be quite stable over time." Kilcullen's essay is optimistic, but it also warns of risks:

> The process may create armed groups outside [central] Government control, which might engage in human rights violations.... Some Iraqi Army commanders have expressed concern about the potential for regional warlordism.... There is an outside chance that tribes which have 'flipped' from supporting AQI [al-Qaeda in Iraq] could simply flip back—especially if they believe the government is not effectively supporting them or taking their interests into account."[36]

The New Machiavellians

There are problems with going tribal. To begin with, there is good reason to believe that tribal strategies will lead to more violence in Iraq. Steven Simon, a senior fellow at the Council on Foreign Relations and a RAND Corporation analyst, states that the strategy "is not linked to any sustainable plan for building a viable Iraqi state" but instead "is stoking the revanchist fantasies of Sunni Arab tribes and pitting them against the central government and against one another...recent short-term gains have come at the expense of the long-term goal" of a stable Iraq. He argues that "tribalism, warlordism and sectarianism" are being unleashed in the country, with what threaten to be catastrophic consequences in the long run.[37]

US Army Lieutenant Colonel Gian Gentile, who commanded an armored reconnaissance squadron in Baghdad, is another prominent critic of the counterinsurgency tactics advocated by architects of the surge. Gentile takes issue with the idea (popular among Petraeus's followers) that the Vietnam War could have been won if counterinsurgency tactics had been implemented earlier: "The false chronicle of the surge in Iraq not only camouflages realities on the ground; it is recklessly ahistorical. It twists the history of the Iraq War *and* the Vietnam War and, in doing so, perpetuates illusions with very real consequences." He continues:

> Never mind the strange assumption that what was effective, or was guessed to have been effective, in Vietnam will be effective once more in Iraq. Never mind the rather telling differences between the South Vietnamese armed forces and the Iraqi armed forces. The United States lost the war in Vietnam. And we lost it for reasons having less to

Figure 7.4: US soldiers install a concrete separation barrier in the Iraqi town of Shula, June 2008. (Photo courtesy of US Air Force.)

do with tactics than with the will, perseverance, cohesion, indigenous support, and sheer determination of the other side, coupled with the absence of any of those things on the American side. Now there is a similarity worth pondering.[38]

There is yet another assumption worth examining. As I noted above, war planners generally assume that US military personnel are dealing with tribal leaders embedded within clearly ranked hierarchical political systems in which sheiks are in firm control of their subjects. This is a disastrous assumption because it excludes the ordinary tribesman from the decision-making process and erroneously suggests that the sheiks are entirely responsible for the actions of "their" people. Consequently, the money for Sunni "Awakening" and "Sons of Iraq" groups is channelled exclusively through these leaders, reinforcing the tribal model imposed upon them from above. In short, the hierarchical tribe with highly concentrated leadership may well become a self-fulfilling prophecy.

This does not mean that Iraqis are passively receiving the tribal model. On the contrary, there are clear indications that some have embraced it in order to gain access to more power in relation to outside forces and also within their own societies. For example, Abdul Sattar Abu Risha—typically described in the media as a dashing Sunni sheik—gained international fame in September 2007, when then President Bush met him and other "Awakening" leaders in al-Anbar. US officials hailed Abu Risha as a staunch ally in the fight against al-Qaeda. But many other Iraqis viewed him as a usurper, an embezzler, and "a con man who has received millions of dollars in construction contracts from the Americans who have tried to turn him into a symbol of their success."[39] Ten days after meeting with Bush, Abu Risha was assassinated, possibly by al-Qaeda operatives or by rival Sunnis angered by what they saw as his betrayal.

The fact that Petraeus and other entrepreneurial social technicians are now seeking to employ tribal strategies in Afghanistan should give pause to those concerned about the country's long-term stability. Proposals call for providing not only cash but also weapons to local leaders who agree to oppose the Taliban. As Petraeus's boosters march in lockstep with these plans, and as US president Barack Obama initiates a surge there, almost no one is mentioning that a system of tribal militias was attempted more than two years ago in Afghanistan. The 10,000-member Auxiliary Police Force was an utter disaster. Its participants stole weapons, stopped reporting for work, and effectively became private militias. In 2008, NATO quietly scrapped the program.

And what are we to make of the peculiar use of the outdated tribe concept by militarized social scientists? It appears that these technicians are not concerned about the ambiguity of tribes because they are in the business (literally) of providing tools to help military commanders achieve immediate objectives. Short-term mission success trumps all other considerations.

Anthropologist Richard Tapper provides an excellent critical analysis of the historical functions of the tribe concept, and its current manifestation—in the context of US-led occupations in Iraq and Afghanistan—is entirely consistent with past usage:

> The nature of indigenous concepts of tribe...has too often been obscured by the apparent desire of investigators (anthropologists, historians, and administrators) to establish a consistent and stable terminology for political groups.... Unfortunately, Middle Eastern indigenous categories...are no more specific than are English terms such as "family" or "group".... The ambiguity of the terms and the flexibility of the system are of the essence in everyday negotiations.... Most of the terms that have been translated as "tribe" contain such ambiguities, and attempts to give them—or tribe—precision as to either level, function, or essence are misdirected.[40]

In the current context, US military forces have been asked to carry out a quintessentially imperial mission—pacification of Iraq and Afghanistan, and the technicians have been quick to provide the necessary instruments, from tribal maps to hints for dividing and conquering.

Some might ask: if not tribes, then what? A starting point might be to acknowledge that rapidly shifting configurations of power—not latent tribalism—are characteristic of both Iraq and Afghanistan. (The idea that the United States, NATO, or NGOs can "balance" the demands of "armed interest groups" implies that the groups are relatively stable, a flawed notion.) Some researchers have begun systematically delineating the wide variety of local power configurations in Afghanistan—from "feudal war-lordism" (often connected with opium production) in Kandahar province, to "fragmented warlordism" (characterized by a staggering array of "mini-fiefdoms" and "a complete lack of religious [or] ethnic-tribal" institutions) across Kunduz province, to decentralized egalitarian "tribalism" in parts of Paktia province.[41] Advocates of a US-led "surge" in Afghanistan might be troubled by their conclusion: "The international presence does not always have a taming influence on the structures of violence. Ultimately, it was the establishing and equipping of Afghan warlords and their militias by the US army in its 'war on terrorism' which caused the temporary emergence of warlordism with Bacha Khan in Paktia and continues to determine secu-rity structures in Kandahar to this day."[42]

Assumptions underpinning the work of counterinsurgency techni-cians include a fundamental acceptance of modern warfare in general and the ongoing US-led occupations in particular. They subscribe to the false notion that counterinsurgency is more antiseptic, more humane, less dam-aging than conventional warfare, and they adhere strictly to Machiavellian principles: do not question the prince or his war, but instead use the most efficient means to achieve his aims. Within this schema, the new Machiavellians calmly discuss the relative merits of dividing and conquer-ing populations versus supporting their puppet governments, of bribing stubborn tribals versus threatening them with force, of ethnic cleansing versus the construction of apartheid-style "separation barriers." It is hard to know whether to be more shocked by the reckless proposals offered by these planners in the name of "stability operations" (read pacification) or by the cool equanimity with which they discuss these suggestions.

A recent episode, which took place at the University of California, Berkeley, provides some insight into the peculiar mentality of counterin-surgency's technicians. Mongomery McFate and Steve Fondacaro of the

Human Terrain System (see chapter 5 of this book) gave a PowerPoint presentation to an audience of approximately fifteen people (including me), most of whom were graduate students in political science and geography. During the question-and-answer session, a graduate student asked whether tribal strategies might lead to political instability and violence in the long run. McFate jokingly replied: "That's above my pay grade," implying that only those at higher levels of the Pentagon bureaucracy should be concerned about such consequences. While some might be surprised at such a cavalier response to a serious question about the possibility of long-term violence in Iraq, the incident says a great deal about why such work is incompatible with ethical anthropology.

It also prompts a broader and more disturbing question: by what processes are social scientists—ostensibly trained to reflect critically upon their work—able easily to transform a landscape of homes reduced to rubble, of refugee camps, of charred flesh, and mass graves into a grid of color-coded tribal maps, flow charts, Venn diagrams and bar graphs, ready to be inserted into PowerPoint format? The surreal transformation of war's violence—its sublimation by statistical means—is perhaps the inevitable product of "security-speak elites with an interest in perpetuating war rather than finding solutions" to it.[43]

The experiences of Latin American anthropologists offer a cautionary tale. Gustavo Lins Ribeiro notes that counterinsurgency consulting

> would be unthinkable to anthropologists in Brazil, where the most delicate ethical issues concern the activities of a handful of anthropologists aligned with developmentalist initiatives that are contested by native populations. Covert ethnography or an anthropologist working as a spy for the military would amount to an earthquake.... Anthropologists in Brazil still bear in mind the memory of a time, the 1964–1985 military dictatorship, when Brazilians had to learn how to live with powerful and repressive national security agencies.[44]

Anthropologists might yet play a role in humanizing the human sciences. There are other choices for those seeking a more just, more peaceful world besides colluding with administrators and military institutions.[45]

Social science holds tremendous potential for challenging persistent and damaging assumptions, often taking the form of propaganda perpetuated by the most powerful members of society: the idea that counterinsurgency is a gentler form of warfare, the notion that Iraqis and Afghans are incapable of self-government (or even civilized behavior); a belief in the inevitability of a clash of civilizations between the West and the rest, and the pernicious, stubborn ideology of American exceptionalism—the corrosive idea that the United States is fundamentally different from and better than other societies. We have a historic opportunity to contribute critical thought, reflection, and action in a way that helps realize a more just and humane future.

Notes

1. Morton Fried, *The Notion of Tribe* (Menlo Park, CA: Cummings, 1975), 1. It is worth mentioning that the term tribe is still used in many introductory anthropology texts. In spite of the most recent anthropological critiques of this concept, it is still circulates within parts of the discipline.

2. E. R. Leach, *Political Systems of Highland Burma* (Cambridge, MA: Harvard University Press, 1954), 290. I do not wish to overstate the case—a carefully defined notion of Pushtun "tribal" society can illuminate underlying political dynamics. See, for example, David B. Edwards, *Before Taliban: Genealogies of the Afghan Jihad* (Berkeley: University of California Press, 2002).

3. "In the Dark," *Economist*, February 2, 2009, 49.

4. "Petraeus Says Afghan Tribes Could Help Fight Militants," *International Herald Tribune*, November 6, 2008, http://www.iht.com/articles/ap/2008/11/06/asia/AS-Afghanistan-Petraeus.php (accessed January 25, 2009).

5. Greg Bruno, "A Tribal Strategy for Afghanistan," *Washington Post*, November 11, 2008.

6. Helene Cooper and Sheryl Gay Stolberg, "Obama Ponders Outreach to Elements of Taliban," *New York Times*, March 7, 2009.

7. The strategy of paying off opponents may have originated in British counterinsurgency efforts in Malaysia during the 1950s. Field Marshal Sir Gerald Templar arranged for insurgents to receive rewards for surrendering.

8. Michael Eisenstadt, "Tribal Engagement: Lessons Learned," *Military Review*, May 2007, 16–31.

9. Official Defense Department photos depict US soldiers sitting on cushions and drinking tea with tribal leaders, as if participating in such a ritual is enough to earn their trust and co-operation. Such images are reminiscent of orientalist paintings from the late nineteenth and early twentieth centuries.

10. David Kilcullen, "Anatomy of a Tribal Revolt," *Small Wars Journal Blog*, August 29, 2007, http://smallwarsjournal.com/blog/2007/07/coin-in-a-tribal-society-1/ (accessed March 20, 2008).

11. Stephen Silliman, "The 'Old West' in the Middle East: US Military Metaphors in Real and Imagined Indian Country," *American Anthropologist* 110, no. 2 (2008): 237–247.

12. Although Petraeus has successfully cultivated his image as an enlightened warrior-scholar, he had no combat experience prior to 2003.

13. Peter Baker et al., "Among Top Officials, 'Surge' Has Sparked Dissent, Infighting," *Washington Post*, September 9, 2007.

14. Ibid.

15. Rick Rowley quoted in Katie Halper, "US is Paying Off Iraq's Worst War Criminals," *Alternet*, September 18, 2007, http://www.alternet.org/world/62827/ (accessed November 2, 2008).

16. Ibid.

17. Ibid.

18. Richard A. Oppel, "Iraq Takes Aim at US-tied Sunni Groups' Leaders," *New York Times*, August 22, 2008.

19. Nir Rosen, "The Myth of the Surge," *Rolling Stone*, March 6, 2008.

20. Nir Rosen, quoted in interview is available at "Iraq Has Really Become Somalia," *Democracy Now!* (syndicated by Pacifica Radio), April 1, 2008, http://www.democracynow.org/2008/4/1/iraq_has_become_somaliaa_collection_of (accessed April 3, 2008).

21. Juan Cole, "Petraeus, Iraq and the Lebanon Analogy," *Informed Comment*, April 9, 2008, http://www.juancole.com/2008/04/petraeus-iraq-and-lebanon-analogy.html (accessed April 20, 2008).

22. Babak Dehghanpisheh and Evan Thomas, "Scions of the Surge," *Newsweek*, March 14, 2008.

23. Amatzia Baram, "Victory in Iraq, One Tribe at a Time," *New York Times*, October 28, 2003.

24. Lin Todd et al., *Iraq Tribal Study: al-Anbar Governorate* (unpublished manuscript, 2006), http://turcopolier.typepad.com/the_athenaeum/files/iraq_tribal_study_070907.pdf (accessed October 28, 2008).

25. Ibid., 5/23.

26. Ibid.

27. For discussion of democratic projects in the Middle East see Laura Nader, "Iraq and Democracy," *Anthropological Quarterly* 76 no. 3 (2003): 479–483.

28. Todd et al., *Iraq Tribal Study*, ES/4.

29. Ibid., 7A/12.

30. Ibid., A1/1.

31. Ibid., 2/31, A2/2.

32. McFate reportedly worked in her mother-in-law's private intelligence firm during the 1990s, often under the pseudonym Montgomery Sapone. Her 1999 CV included the following description of her responsibilities: "Collect and analyze intelligence on European activities of major international

environmental organization for a company specializing in domestic and international opposition research, special investigations, issues management and threat assessment. Write weekly intelligence update on European animal rights and eco-terrorist activity." See James Ridgeway, Daniel Schulman, and David Corn, "There's Something about Mary," *Mother Jones*, July 30, 2008, http://www.motherjones.com/news/feature/2008/07/mary-mcfate-sapone-gun-lobby-nra-spy.html (accessed August 15, 2008).

33. Montgomery McFate, "The 'Memory of War': Tribes and the Legitimate Use of Force in Iraq," in *Armed Groups*, ed. Jeffrey H. Norwitz (Newport, RI: US Naval War College, 2008), 296–297.

34. Ibid., 302. Such rampant overgeneralizations have been a persistent feature of anthropology, and history tells us that they are easily employed for military purposes. Proposals for "writing against culture"—that is, *against* typifications of culture and society by focusing upon individual lives, internal variation, and social complexity—offer one means of addressing fundamental issues of domination. See Lila Abu-Lughod, "Writing against Culture," in *Recapturing Anthropology: Working in the Present*, ed. Robin Fox (Santa Fe, NM: School of American Research Press, 1991), 137–162.

35. Kilcullen, "Anatomy of a Tribal Revolt."

36. Steven Simon, "The Price of the Surge," *Foreign Affairs*, May–June 2008, 57–76.

37. Gian P. Gentile, "A (Slightly) Better War: A Narrative and Its Defects," *World Affairs Journal* 171, no. 1 (2008): 61–62.

38. Rick Rowley, quoted in "Exclusive Report from Iraq." *Democracy Now!* (syndicated by Pacifica Radio), September 11, 2007, http://www.democracynow.org/2007/9/11/exclusive_report_from_iraq_u_s (accessed September 15, 2007).

39. Richard Tapper, "Anthropologists, Historians, and Tribespeople," in *Tribes and State Formation in the Middle East*, ed. Philip S. Khoury and Joseph Kostiner, (Berkeley: University of California Press, 1990), 50.

40. Conrad Schetter, Rainer Glassner, and Masood Karokhail, "Beyond Warlordism: The Local Security Architecture in Afghanistan," *Internationale Politik und Gesellschaft* 2 (2007): 136–152.

41. Ibid., 150. Other critiques of the US military's simplistic notions of tribe have appeared in recent months. For example, an unclassified report by US Army Human Terrain System researchers demonstrates a more nuanced approach to social structural analysis—among other things, it warns that US strategies are premised upon a faulty understanding of the tribal concept. That such a critique has emerged does not change the fact that it has occurred within the context of a US-led military occupation. See US Army Human Terrain System Reachback Research Center, "My Cousin's Enemy Is My Friend: A Study of Pushtun 'Tribes' in Afghanistan," September 2009, http://easterncampaign.files.wordpress.com/2009/11/my-cousins-enemy-is-my-friend-a-study-of-pashtun-tribes.pdf (accessed December 27, 2009).

42. Antonius C. G. M. Robben, "Anthropology and the Iraq War: An Uncomfortable Engagement," *Anthropology Today* 25, no. 1 (2009): 3. It may not be surprising that many Pentagon social science advisors haven't adopted more anthropologically-informed perspectives, but it is essential to challenge their work, for a highly influential clique within the military establishment has consistently used its academic credentials as a basis for claims to authority.

43. Gustavo Lins Ribeiro, "Security for Whom? Anthropologists and Repressive State Elites," *Focaal* 50 (2007): 148.

44. For example, anthropologist Ashraf Ghani served as Afghanistan's finance minister from July 2002 to December 2004, and was a nominee for the 2009 Afghan presidential elections. The work of other Afghan-born anthropologists (M. Jamil Hanifi, Sayed Askar Mousavi, Nazif Shahrani) indicates that anthropologists' involvement in the country is indeed complex.

Afterword
Decommisioning Culture

On the surface, the possibility of demilitarizing American society—of decommissioning culture—seems remote. As these words are being written, more than 120,000 US troops remain in occupied Iraq, accompanied by approximately the same number of civilian contractors working for firms like Blackwater and Halliburton. By the summer of 2010, approximately 100,000 US troops will be stationed in Afghanistan, and more than 100,000 Defense Department contractors are there today.[1] President Barack Obama's defense budget for 2010 authorizes $550 billion for the Pentagon and an additional $130 billion in spending for the wars in Iraq and Afghanistan—an amount greater than that spent on defense by former President George W. Bush during his last year in office. Furthermore, over 2,400 civilians were killed in Afghanistan during President Obama's first year in office (many of them killed in drone attacks), making it the deadliest year since the US-led invasion of the country began in 2001. In the meantime, the US Defense Department recently reported success in meeting its recruitment goals, probably due to the fact that many people are unable to find work as recession plagues the global economy.[2]

The bigger picture is more disturbing still. The United States accounts for nearly *half* of the world's military expenditures. To put it another way, our government spends more on its military than *the next fourteen countries combined.*

Given these grim realities, what are the prospects for those concerned about our militarizing culture? What hope can be offered to young Americans when a president promising change prolongs military occupations abroad and increases the Pentagon's budget at home?

Disconnections

The end result of a militarized society is a greater propensity for war and its consequences: death, disfigurement, disease, depression, destruction.

Many Americans have forgotten this reality.

In some ways, the disconnection is not surprising. Catherine Lutz, who has exposed the deep roots anchoring modern-day militarism in her books *Homefront* and *Empire of Bases*, notes that the Defense Department has spent billions of dollars on "decades-long work to control the messages that the American people receive and the beliefs they hold about the innocence and high civilizational goals of the US military."[3] (According to the *New York Times*, the US Army alone budgeted $1.35 billion for advertising between 2006 and 2011.)[4] Pentagon officials and the compliant corporate media have also sanitized the brutality and violence inherent in militarism's predictable products: war and occupation.[5]

But all one needs to do is to look at war's victims to understand why a militarized society should be an anachronism today. All one needs to do is to look at the wedding photo of Ty Ziegel and Renee Kline, who were married on October 7, 2006. At first glance, it appears like any other wedding photo: the beautiful bride wears a lovely white dress and holds a bouquet of roses, while the groom stands by her side, wearing the impeccable black and blue dress suit of the US Marine Corps. But a closer look reveals that Sergeant Ty Ziegel has been severely mutilated—his face is nearly unrecognizable as the result of burns from a car bombing in Iraq in 2004. (Ty Ziegel also had half of his left arm amputated.) Is he smiling? Is he frowning? The scar tissue is so thick that it is impossible to tell. Renee Kline appears stunned. Her face stares vacantly into the distance. We have no idea what she might be thinking. The photographer, Nina Berman, writes that her photo "shows how war has crept its way into the most common phase of daily life."[6] One is not sure whether to weep tears of joy for love's triumph, or tears of grief for the severe injuries inflicted upon the young man.[7]

To understand why a militarized society should be an anachronism today, all one needs to do is to hear the story of Noria Barkat, a seven-year-old girl from Farah province in Afghanistan. She and her two sisters suffered severe burns on May 4, 2009, when US helicopters bombed the small village of Granai. According to a report, "the entire left side of her body [was] a patchwork of weeping bandages," and Noria Barkat had to undergo multiple skin-graft operations in the weeks following her injury. Photos of young survivors of the air strikes are heartrending: the images of children with blistered and charred faces and suppurating wounds are nearly impossible to bear. Yet others in Granai suffered a fate far worse. The US bombing killed Noria Barkat's mother, along with as many as ninety-six other civilians, according to the Afghan Independent Human Rights Commission. The attack killed more Afghan civilians in one day than any other since the US-led invasion began in late 2001.[8]

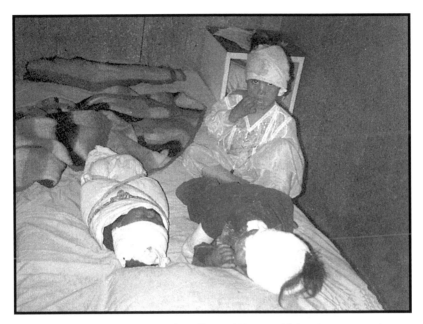

Figure 8.1: A US air raid upon the village of Karam, Afghanistan, severely injured these children, whose parents and many other villagers were killed in the October 11, 2001 attack. (Photo courtesy of RAWA/Wikimedia Commons.)

Thousands of accounts like these can be found in the tragic annals of occupied Iraq and Afghanistan, though they are largely invisible to the American public. Making them visible will be a necessary task for those hoping to change the status quo. Now more than ever before, opponents of American militarism—advocates of a pacific America—must begin "identifying and challenging the pillars of belief and the streams of profit that support business as usual within the military normal."[9]

Exploding Myths

There is much work to be done. As mentioned earlier in this book, even some social scientists who "ought to be acting as responsible and independent critics of their government's policies" (in the words of the late Senator William Fulbright) have lowered their critical faculties and decided to embed with the military "to save lives."[10]

But there are concrete measures that might eventually break the shackles of our militarizing culture, a culture that has become something of an American tradition. We might take inspiration from Franz Boas, the renowned anthropologist, who once asked: "How can we recognize the shackles that tradition has laid upon us? For when we recognize them, we are also able to break them down."[11]

Breaking down the pervasive ideology of militarism could take many forms. Shaking the "pillars of belief"—exploding the myths surrounding and perpetuating militarism—is one way of bringing about change. As points of departure, we might consider the following:

1. *Exploding the myth of generosity and goodwill.* Military recruiters (including those recruiting social scientists for embedded work) often convince potential recruits that the armed forces are primarily concerned with delivering humanitarian aid, economic development, and emergency relief abroad and at home. This has become a leading motive for many young people to join the military. Anthropologist David Graeber refers to this syndrome as an "army of altruists." He asks: "Why do working-class kids join the army anyway? Because, like any teenager, they want to escape the world of tedious work and meaningless consumerism, to live a life of adventure and camaraderie, in which they are doing something genuinely noble."[12] The military appears to offer this noble prospect to nearly all young Americans. Few other institutions do. It is striking evidence of how military institutions are sophisticated enough to co-opt the idealism of our youth and to draw them into cycles of violence. To explode this myth and decommission American society, anthropologists might engage in a renewed public anthropology, communicating with broad audiences (in print, on the airwaves, and online) about the ways in which the military-industrial-entertainment complex has harnessed youth culture to help it meet its objectives.

2. *Exploding the myth of American exceptionalism.* The idea that our society is fundamentally different from—and morally superior to—other societies is among the most entrenched and perilous ideologies lying behind militarism. Some have argued that it can be traced to the Puritans who arrived in the Americas in the early 1600s, and cite John Winthrop's famous "city on a hill" sermon as evidence. For centuries, the idea of American exceptionalism has been a powerful force in academic, legal, and popular discourses. It has also served to justify conquest, "Manifest Destiny," and military intervention on nearly every continent over the past two centuries. In essence, it is a

peculiar form of ethnocentrism—and as such, anthropologists are in a strong position to publicly critique it and to expose its pernicious consequences.

3. *Exploding the myth of war as entertainment.* More and more, media corporations present war as light entertainment. Among the most successful recruiting tools developed by the Pentagon and its corporate allies is *America's Army*, a series of video games available for free downloading on various computer platforms. The man who conceived of the idea, Colonel Casey Wardynski, noted that he envisioned it as "a virtual Soldier experience that was engaging, informative, and entertaining." Recruiters have used it at amusement parks, sports events, and other venues. According to Nick Turse, the "first person shooter" game was developed by gaming giants Epic Games and NVIDIA, with support from Lucasfilm's THX, Dolby Laboratories, and other companies. He notes: "It hits the very youth demographic the Army was targeting for potential recruits as well as their younger siblings."[13] For psychologist and former West Point professor Dave Grossman, the effects of such games (along with other factors) are insidious: "We are reaching that stage of desensitization at which the infliction of pain and suffering has become a source of entertainment: vicarious pleasure rather than revulsion. We are

Figure 8.2: War as entertainment: the video game *America's Army* has been an immensely successful recruiting tool for the US Department of Defense. (Photo courtesy of US Army.)

learning to kill, and we are learning to like it."[14] To decommission American society, anthropologists should become more involved in critical studies of media technology, and its impact on users. A new generation of social scientists, including Beatrice Jauregaui (who has done participant observation at the US Army Experience Center in Philadelphia), Robertson Allen (who has conducted interviews and participant observation among the designers and users of America's Army video game), and Matthew Sumera (who has analyzed home-made combat music videos created and posted online by US soldiers), provide refreshing examples of how critical anthropology can play a role in exposing the linkages between media, war, and technology.[15]

Although militarism is a powerful force in the United States today, exploding these and other myths that surround it might make an impact on decommissioning American society, if supported by independent (and non-commercial) media and a more autonomous university system. One thing is certain: doing nothing at all will only perpetuate our militarizing culture and its harmful effects around the world. We can take heart from the lessons that history has to offer: "The American people have the courage to fight. We have shown this a dozen times in the past, from Bunker Hill to Gettysburg, from Normandy to Guadalcanal. We also have the courage to *stop* fighting, not when someone else decides for us, but when *we* decide for ourselves."[16]

Notes

1. Jeremy Scahill, "Stunning Statistics About the War that Everyone Should Know," *CounterPunch*, December 18, 2009, http://www.counterpunch.org/scahill12182009.html (accessed March 12, 2010).

2. Lizette Alvarez, "More Americans Joining Military As Jobs Dwindle," *New York Times*, January 18, 2009; Donna Miles, "Recruiting Successes Continue in Fiscal 2009," *Armed Forces Press Service*, November 10, 2008, http://www.defenselink.mil/news/newsarticle.aspx?id=5188 (accessed March 12, 2010).

3. Catherine Lutz, "The Military Normal: Feeling at Home with Counterinsurgency in the United States," in *The Counter-Counterinsurgency Manual* (Chicago: Prickly Paradigm Press, 2009), ed. the Network of Concerned Anthropologists, 36–37.

4. Stuart Elliot, "Army to Use Webcasts from Iraq for Recruiting," *New York Times*, November 10, 2008.

AFTERWORD

5. Norman Solomon, *War Made Easy: How Presidents and Pundits Keep Spinning Us to Death* (New York: Wiley, 2006); John A. MacArthur, *Second Front: Censorship and Propaganda in the 1991 Gulf War* (Berkeley: University of California Press, 1992).

6. Nina Berman, quoted in Ron Steinman, "A Picture Really Is Worth a Thousand Words," *The Digital Journalist*, March 2007, http://digitaljournalist.org/issue0703/a-thousand-words.html (accessed December 12, 2009).

7. Ty Ziegel's troubles continued after returning to the United States from his deployment. He underwent approximately two years of rehabilitation, but he had difficulty holding a job after treatment. He hoped that monthly disability checks from the Veterans Administration might help to pay expenses, but he received much less payment than he had expected. Eventually, the VA sent him a letter that "rated" his injuries according to a cold bureaucratic calculus: "80 percent for facial disfigurement, 60 percent for left arm amputation, a mere 10 percent for head trauma and nothing for his left lobe brain injury, right eye blindness, and jaw fracture." See Emily Probst, "Wounded Warriors Face Homefront Battle with VA," *CNN News*, November 16, 2007, http://www.cnn.com/2007/HEALTH/11/15/wounded.marine/index.html (accessed December 12, 2009).

8. Guy Smallman, "Villagers' Legacy of Pain From US Air Raid," *Financial Times*, June 19, 2009; Jon Boone, Ewen MacAskill, and Mark Tran, "US Air Strikes Kill Dozens of Afghan Civilians," *The Guardian*, May 6, 2009; Patrick Cockburn, "Afghans Riot Over Air-Strike Atrocity," *The Independent*, May 8, 2009.

9. Lutz, "Military Normal," 37.

10. David Matsuda, quoted in Peter Graf, "US Deploys Latest Tactic in Iraq: Anthropology," Reuters News Service, January 9, 2008, http://www.alertnet.org/thenews/newsdesk/L06475304.htm (accessed January 20, 2008).

11. Franz Boas quoted in *Franz Boas: The Shackles of Tradition*, DVD, directed by Andre Singer (1986).

12. David Graeber, "Army of Altruists," *Harper's Magazine*, January 2007, 38.

13. Nick Turse, *The Complex: How the Military Invades Our Everyday Lives* (New York: Macmillan, 2008), 117–118.

14. Dave Grossman, *On Killing: The Psychological Cost of Learning to Kill in War and Society* (New York: Back Bay Books, 2009).

15. Beatrice Jauregui, "Military Communitas? Re-centering the Soldier-Citizen Interface at the US Army Experience Center," presented at the University of Chicago, April 25, 2009 (Chicago, IL); Robertson Allen, "The Army Rolls through Indianapolis: Fieldwork at the Virtual Army Experience," *Transformative Works and Cultures* 2 (2009); Matthew Sumera, "Music, Aesthetics, and the Technologies of Online War," presented at the annual meetings of the American Anthropological Association, December 6, 2009 (Philadelphia, PA).

16. Howard Zinn, *Vietnam: The Logic of Withdrawal* (Boston: Beacon Press, 1967), 122.

Glossary

AAA   American Anthropological Association

AFRICOM   US African Command; a US Department of Defense "unified combatant command" charged with coordinating US military operations on the African continent

BAE Systems UK military corporation responsible for recruiting, training, and administration services for the Human Terrain System

CEAUSSIC   Commission on the Engagement of Anthropology with US Security and Intelligence Communities; an ad hoc group organized by the American Anthropological Association

CIA   US Central Intelligence Agency

CORDS   Civil Operations and Revolutionary Development Support; a US Department of Defense counterinsurgency program employed during the Vietnam War

DIA   US Defense Intelligence Agency

DNI   US Director of National Intelligence

DOD   US Department of Defense

FBI   US Federal Bureau of Investigation

FM 3-24   US Army counterinsurgency field manual

HTS   Human Terrain System; experimental US Army counterinsurgency program

HTT	Human Terrain Team; five person civilian-military team embedded with US Army brigades in Iraq and Afghanistan for counterinsurgency work
HUAC	US House Un-American Activities Committee; Congressional committee charged with investigating subversion and disloyalty in the United States from 1938 to 1975
IC-CAE/IC Centers	Intelligence Community Centers of Academic Excellence; university-based academic recruiting centers funded by the US Director of National Intelligence
ICSP	Intelligence Community Scholars Program; scholarship program for university students which requires recipients to work with intelligence agencies
IGKNU	Integrated Global Knowledge and Understanding Collaboration; academic center at University of Texas-Pan American funded by US Director of National Intelligence
JROTC	Junior Reserve Officer Training Corps
NATO	North Atlantic Treaty Organization
NSA	US National Security Agency
PRISP	Pat Roberts Intelligence Scholars Program; scholarship program funded by US intelligence agencies
RAND	Research and Development Corporation; a federally funded military research company based in Santa Monica, California
ROTC	Reserve Officer Training Corps
SERE	Survival, Evasion, Resistance, Escape; a US military training program which prepares soldiers to endure capture
UTPA	University of Texas-Pan American; Intelligence Community grant recipient located in Edinburg, Texas

References

ABC News. "When Is Torture OK?" *Nightline*. June 17, 2004.

Abu-Lughod, Lila. *Veiled Sentiments: Honor and Poetry in a Bedouin Society.* Cairo, Egypt: American University in Cairo Press, 1987.

———. "Writing against Culture." In *Recapturing Anthropology: Working in the Present.* Edited by Robin Fox, 137–162. Santa Fe, NM: School of American Research Press, 1991.

Agee, Phillip. *Inside the Company: CIA Diary.* New York: Bantam, 1984.

Aguilar-Moreno, Manuel. *Handbook to Life in the Aztec World.* Oxford, UK: Oxford University Press, 2007.

Al-Ali, Nadje, and Nicola Pratt. *What Kind of Liberation? Women and the Occupation of Iraq.* Berkeley: University of California Press, 2009.

Allen, Robertson. "The Army Rolls through Indianapolis: Fieldwork at the Virtual Army Experience." *Transformative Works and Cultures* 2 (2009). http://journal.transformativeworks.org/index.php/twc/article/view/80/97.

———. "Games without Tears, Wars without Frontiers." Presented at the annual meetings of the American Anthropological Association (December 6, 2009), Philadelphia, PA.

Alvarez, Lizette. "More Americans Joining Military As Jobs Dwindle." *New York Times.* January 18, 2009.

American Anthropological Association. "Statement on Torture." June 2007. http://aaanet.org/issues/policy-advocacy/Statement-on-Torture.cfm.

———. "Statement on the US Occupation of Iraq." June 2007. http://aaanet.org/issues/policy-advocacy/Statement-on-the-US-Occupation-of-Iraq.cfm.

American Anthropological Association Commission on the Engagement of Anthropology with US Security and Intelligence Communities. *Final Report on The Army's Human Terrain System Proof of Concept Program.* October 14, 2009. http://www.aaanet.org/cmtes/commissions/CEAUSSIC/upload/CEAUSSIC_HTS_Final_Report.pdf.

American Anthropological Association Executive Board. "Statement on the Human Terrain System Project." October 31, 2007. http://www.aaanet.org/pdf/EB_Resolution_110807.pdf.

Anderson, Craig A., et al. "The Influence of Media Violence on Youth." *Psychological Science in the Public Interest* 4(3), December 2003:81–110.

"Anthropology and War." *The Diane Rehm Show* (American University Radio). October 10, 2007. http://thedianerehmshow.org/shows/2007-10-10/anthropologists-and-war.

Aspden, Rachel. "Read and Digest, Mr. Blair." *The Guardian*. September 3, 2006. http://www.guardian.co.uk/books/2006/sep/03/biography.features.

Axe, David. "After Setbacks, Human Terrain System Rebuilds." *World Politics Review*. November 25, 2009. http://www.worldpoliticsreview.com/article.aspx?id=4697.

Bacevich, Andrew J. *The New American Militarism: How Americans Are Seduced by War*. New York: Oxford University Press, 2005.

Bagaric, Mirko, and Julie Clarke. *Torture: When the Unthinkable Is Morally Permissible*. Albany, NY: SUNY Press, 2007.

Baker, Peter, et al. "Among Top Officials, 'Surge' Has Sparked Dissent, Infighting." *Washington Post*. September 9, 2007.

Baram, Amatzia. "Victory in Iraq, One Tribe at a Time." *New York Times*. October 28, 2003.

Barclay, Paul. "'They Have for the Coast Dwellers a Traditional Hatred': Governing Igorots in Northern Luzon and Central Taiwan, 1895–1915." In *The American Colonial State in the Philippines*. Edited by Julian Go and Anne L. Foster, 217–255. Durham, NC: Duke University Press, 2003.

Barrows, David P. *Report of the Bureau of Non-Christian Tribes of the Philippine Islands for the Year Ended August 31, 1902*. Washington DC: Report of the Philippine Commission, Bureau of Insular Affairs, War Department, 1902.

Bass, Thomas A. "Counterinsurgency and Torture." *American Quarterly* 60, no. 2 (2008): 233–240. BBC World Service. "World Citizens Reject Torture, Global Poll Reveals." October 19, 2006. http://www.globescan.com/news_archives/bbc-torture06/BBCTorture06.pdf.

Beeman, William O. "The US-Shi'ite Relationship in a New Iraq: Better than the British?" *Strategic Insights*, May 2004:1–8. http://www.ccc.nps.navy.mil/si/2004/may/beemanMay04.asp.

Bhatia, Michael V. *War and Intervention: Issues for Contemporary Peace Operations*. Sterling, VA: Kumarian, 2003.

——, ed. *Terrorism and the Politics of Naming*. New York: Routledge, 2007.

——, et al., eds. *Afghanistan, Arms, and Conflict*. New York: Routledge, 2008.

Bhattacharjee, Yudhijit. "Pentagon Asks Academics for Help in Understanding Enemies." *Science* 316 (2007): 534–535.

Boas, Franz. Letter to the Editor. *New York Times.* January 7, 1916.

Bogan, Jesse. "Intelligence Grants in Valley Rile Some." *San Antonio Express-News.* December 2, 2006. http://www.mysanantonio.com/news/MYSA120306_04B_intelligencealert_2715c86_html8625.html.

Bok, Derek. *Universities in the Marketplace: The Commercialization of Higher Education.* Princeton, NJ: Princeton University Press, 2004.

Boone, Jon, Ewen MacAskill, and Mark Tran. "US Air Strikes Kill Dozens of Afghan Civilians." *The Guardian.* May 6, 2009. http://www.guardian.co.uk/world/2009/may/06/us-air-strikes-afghan-civilians.

Boot, Max. "Navigating the 'Human Terrain." *Los Angeles Times.* December 7, 2006.

Booth, Ken. *Strategy and Ethnocentrism.* London: Croom Helm, 1979.

Brecher, Bob. *Torture and the Ticking Bomb.* San Francisco: Wiley-Blackwell, 2007.

Burger King Corporation. "News Release: Burger King Corp. Beams Up Movie Tie-Ins with Paramount Pictures." May 4, 2009. http://investor.bk.com/phoenix.zhtml?c=87140&p=irol-newsArticle&ID=1283540&highlight=.

Bruno, Greg. "A Tribal Strategy for Afghanistan." *Washington Post.* November 11, 2008.

Buchan, James. "Miss Bell's Lines in the Sand." *Guardian.* March 12, 2003. http://www.guardian.co.uk/world/2003/mar/12/iraq.jamesbuchan.

Bybee, Jay. "Memorandum for Alberto R. Gonzales." August 1, 2002. http://news.findlaw.com/wp/docs/doj/bybee80102mem.pdf.

"Center for Academic Excellence Creates New Opportunities for Valley Students." *Los Arcos: University of Texas Pan-American.* Fall 2007:18.

Chabris, Margaret. "'GI Joe: The Rise of Cobra' Advances on 7-Eleven Stores." *7-11 News Room.* June 30, 2009. http://www.7-eleven.com/NewsRoom/GIJoeTheRiseOfCobraAdvancesOn7Eleven/tabid/316/Default.aspx.

Chamberlain, Alexander F. "Review of *The Bontoc Igorot* by Alfred E. Jenks." *American Anthropologist* 7 (1905): 696–701.

Chomsky, Noam. *American Power and the New Mandarins.* New York: Pantheon, 1969.

"Cloak and Gown." *Texas Observer.* April 21, 2006. http://www.texasobserver.org/archives/item/14790-2188-political-intelligence-marchers-mccain-y-mas.

Cockburn, Patrick. "Afghans Riot Over Air-Strike Atrocity." *Independent.* May 8, 2009. http://www.independent.co.uk/news/world/asia/afghans-riot-overairstrike-atrocity-1681070.html.

Cole, Juan. "Petraeus, Iraq and the Lebanon Analogy." *Informed Comment.* April 9, 2008. http://www.juancole.com/2008/04/petraeus-iraq-and-the-lebanon-analogy.html.

Cook, Fred J. *The Warfare State*. New York: Macmillan, 1962.

Cooper, Helene, and Sheryl Gay Stolberg. "Obama Ponders Outreach to Elements of Taliban." *New York Times*. March 7, 2009.

Crumpton, Henry. "Intelligence and Homeland Defense." In *Transforming US Intelligence*. Edited by Jennifer Sims and Burton Gerber, 198–219. Washington DC: Georgetown University Press, 2005.

Cumings, Bruce. "Boundary Displacement: Area Studies and International Studies during and after the Cold War." *Bulletin of Concerned Asia Scholars* 29, no. 1 (1999): 6–26.

Danzig, David. "An Open Letter to Antonin Scalia." June 27, 2007. http://www. humanrightsfirst.info/pdf/07622-etn-danzig-scalia-24.pdf.

Dartmouth College Laboratory for Human Terrain. "Approach." *Laboratory for Human Terrain*. http://www.dartmouth.edu/%7Ehumanterrain/Approach.html.

——. *Laboratory for Human Terrain*. http://www.dartmouth.edu/~humanterrain/.

Dawson, Mark. "Some Thoughts As My Additions to Ethnography.com Wind Down." *Ethnography.com*. June 2008. http://www.ethnography.com/2008/07/ some-thoughts-as-i-head-overseas/.

DeAtkine, Norvell B. "Foreword." In *The Arab Mind*. By Raphael Patai, i–xviii. Revised edition. New York: Hatherleigh Press, 2002.

Dehghanpisheh, Babak, and Evan Thomas. "Scions of the Surge." *Newsweek*. March 14, 2008:28–34.

Deloria, Vine. *Custer Died for Your Sins*. New York: Macmillan, 1969.

DeYoung, Karen, and Walter Pincus. "CIA Releases Files on Past Misdeeds." *Washington Post*. June 27, 2007. http://www.washingtonpost.com/wp-dyn/content/ article/2007/06/26/AR2007062600861.html.

Der Derian, James. *Virtuous War: Mapping the Military-Industrial-Media-Entertainment Network*. New York: Routledge, 2001

Dershowitz, Alan M. "Want to Torture? Get a Warrant." *San Francisco Chronicle*. January 22, 2002.

Diamond, Stanley. "War and the Dissociated Personality." In *War: The Anthropology of Armed Conflict and Aggression*. Edited by Morton Fried, Marvin Harris, and Robert Murphy, 181–188. Garden City, NY: Natural History Press, 1968.

"Does Torture Work?" *Economist*. January 27, 2009:12. http://www.economist. com/blogs/democracyinamerica/2009/01/does_torture_work_1.

Dreyfuss, Robert. *Devil's Game: How the United States Helped Unleash Fundamentalist Islam*. New York: Metropolitan Books, 2005.

"Dubble Bubble Product Placement in GI Joe." *Product Placement News.* September 9, 2009. http://www.productplacement.biz/200909103220/News/Movies/dubble-bubble-product-placement-in-gi-joe.html.

Dunn, Timothy, and Jose Palafox. "Militarization of the Border." In *Oxford Encyclopedia of Latinos and Latinas in the United States, Volume 3.* Edited by Suzanne Oboler and Deana J. Gonzalez, 150–155. Oxford, UK: Oxford University Press, 2005.

Eban, Katherine. "Rorschach and Awe." *Vanity Fair.* July 17, 2007. http://www.vanityfair. com/politics/features/2007/07/torture200707.

Edwards, David B. *Before Taliban: Genealogies of the Afghan Jihad.* Berkeley: University of California Press, 2002.

Eggan, Fred. "Applied Anthropology in the Mountain Province, Philippines." In *Social Organization and the Applications of Anthropology: Essays in Honor of Lauriston Sharp.* Edited by Robert J. Smith, 196–209. Ithaca, NY: Cornell University Press, 1975.

Eickelman, Dale. "First, Know the Enemy, Then Act." *Los Angeles Times.* December 9, 2001.

Eidelson, Roy. "An Individual-Group Belief Framework." *Peace and Conflict* 15 (2009): 1–26.

———. "How Americans Think about Torture-and Why." *Truthout.* May 11, 2009. http://www.truthout.org/051209C.

———. "Self and Nation: A Comparison of Americans' Beliefs Before and After 9/11." *Peace and Conflict* 11 (2005): 153–175.

Eisenstadt, Michael. "Tribal Engagement: Lessons Learned." *Military Review,* May 2007:16–31.

El-Haj, Nadia Abu. "Edward Said and the Political Present." *American Ethnologist* 32, no. 4 (2005): 538–555.

Electronic Arts Inc. "EA Calls All GI Joe Fans to Report for Duty." August 4, 2009. http://investor.ea.com/releasedetail.cfm?releaseid=400911.

Eller, Claudia, and Ben Fritz. "Paramount Pictures Waves the Flag for 'GI Joe." *Los Angeles Times.* August 3, 2009.

Elliot, Stuart. "Army to Use Webcasts from Iraq for Recruiting." *New York Times.* November 10, 2008.

Ewen, Stuart. *Captains of Consciousness: Advertising and the Social Roots of Consumer Culture.* New York: McGraw-Hill, 1976.

"Exclusive Report from Iraq." *Democracy Now!* (syndicated by Pacifica Radio). September 11, 2007. http://www.democracynow.org/2007/9/11/exclusive_report_from_iraq_u_s.

Faris, James. "Pax Britannica and the Sudan: S. F. Nadel." In *Anthropology and the Colonial Encounter*. Edited by Talal Asad, 153–170. New York: Humanity Books, 1971.

Fay, George R. Article 15-6 Investigation of the Abu Ghraib Facility and 205th Military Intelligence Brigade. August 2004. http://news.findlaw.com/hdocs/docs/dod/fay82504rpt.pdf.

Ferguson, R. Brian. "Ten Points on War." *Social Analysis* 52, no. 2 (2008): 32–49.

Fernea, Elizabeth. *Guests of the Sheik: An Ethnography of an Iraqi Village*. Garden City, NY: Doubleday, 1965.

Fernea, Robert. "Why If We Don't Leave Iraq Now We May Bring on a Civil War." *History News Network*. January 10, 2005. http://hnn.us/articles/9517.html.

Fisk, Robert. "Let Us Rebel Against Poisonous Academics and Their Preposterous Claptrap of Exclusion." *The Independent*. May 14, 2005. http://www.independent.co.uk/opinion/commentators/fisk/robert-fisk-let-us-rebel-againstpoisonous-academics-and-their-preposterous-claptrap-of-exclusion-490624.html.

"For the First Time, Americans Oppose Afghan War." *Angus Reid Global Monitor*. January 25, 2007. http://www.angus-reid.com/polls/view/14497.

Franz Boas: The Shackles of Tradition. DVD. Directed by Andre Singer. Hamilton, NJ: Films for the Humanities and Sciences, 1986.

Freeman, Samuel. "Intelligence Agencies Are Penetrating Our Universities Today." *Rio Grande Guardian* (McAllen, Texas). April 10, 2007. http://www.riograndeguardian.com/index.asp.

———. "PACE and the 'Spy Center's' Shills." *Rio Grande Guardian* (McAllen, Texas). January 30, 2009. http://www.riograndeguardian.com/index.asp.

Fried, Morton. *The Notion of Tribe*. Menlo Park, CA: Cummings, 1975.

Fritz, Ben, "'GI Joe' Opens to $100 Million Worldwide, But Will It Hold?" *Los Angeles Times*. August 9, 2009.

Fry, Douglas. *Beyond War: The Human Potential for Peace*. New York: Oxford University Press, 2007.

Fulbright, J. William. "A Point of View." *Science* 158 (1967): 1555.

Furner, Mary O. *Advocacy and Objectivity: A Crisis in the Professionalization of American Social Science, 1865–1905*. Lexington: University of Kentucky Press, 1975.

Gallup. "Slim Majority Wants Bush-Era Interrogations Investigated." April 27, 2009. http://www.gallup.com/poll/118006/Slim-Majority-Wants-Bush-Era-Interrogations-Investigated.aspx.

Galuszka, Peter. "Black Colleges Involved in Efforts to Boost Intelligence Community Talent Pool." *Diverse Online*. January 11, 2007. http://diverseeducation.com/article/6874/black-colleges-involved-in-efforts.html.

Garner, Joshua. "University's 'Spy Camp' Lets Teens Learn about Intelligence Gathering." *Catholic News Service.* July 17, 2007. http://www.catholicnews.com/data/briefs/cns/20070717.htm.

Gebauer, Matthias. "Germany Issues Arrest Warrants for 13 CIA Agents in El-Masri Case." *Spiegel Online.* January 31, 2007. http://www.spiegel.de/international/0,1518,463385,00.html.

Gentile, Gian P. "A (Slightly) Better War: A Narrative and Its Defects." *World Affairs Journal* 171, no. 1 (2008): 57–64.

GfK Roper Public Affairs & Media. "The AP-GfK Poll." June 2009. http://www.apgfkpoll.com/pdf/AP-GfK_Poll_Supreme_Court_Final_Topline.pdf.

Ghosh, Amitav. "Theater of Cruelty: Reflections on the Anniversary of Abu Ghraib." *The Nation.* July 18–25, 2005:31–32. http://www.thenation.com/doc/20050718/ghosh.

Ginbar, Yuval. *Why Not Torture Terrorists?* Oxford, UK: Oxford University Press, 2008.

Giroux, Henry A. *The University in Chains: Confronting the Military-Industrial-Academic Complex.* Boulder, CO: Paradigm Publishers, 2007.

Glenn, David. "Anthropologists Vote to Clamp Down on Secret Scholarship." *Chronicle of Higher Education News Blog.* December 1, 2007:8–11. http://chronicle.com/news/article/3532/anthropologists-vote-toclamp-down-onsecretscholarship.

———. "Former Human Terrain System Participant Describes Program in Disarray." *Chronicle of Higher Education.* December 5, 2007. http://chronicle.com/article/Former-Human-Terrain-System/285/.

———. "Social Scientist in Army's 'Human Terrain' Program Dies in Afghanistan." *Chronicle of Higher Education.* May 9, 2008:9. http://chronicle.com/article/Social-Scientist-in-Army-s/40946.

Go, Julian, and Anne L. Foster, eds. *The American Colonial State in the Philippines.* Durham, NC: Duke University Press, 2003.

Golden, Mark. "Childhood in Ancient Greece." In *Coming of Age in Ancient Greece.* Edited by Jenifer Neils and John H. Oakley, 13–29. New Haven, CT: Yale University Press, 2003.

Goldman, Jim. "Cisco Reports for Duty in 'GI Joe.'" *CNBC Business News.* August 11, 2009. http://www.cnbc.com/id/32375230.

Goldstein, Harry. "Modeling Terrorists." *IEEE Spectrum* 43, no. 9 (2006): 26–34. http://www.spectrum.ieee.org/sep06/4424.

Gompert, David. *Heads We Win: Improving Cognitive Effectiveness in Counterinsurgency.* Santa Monica, CA: RAND Corporation, 2007.

González, Roberto J. "Standing Up against Torture and War," *Anthropology News* 48, no. 3 (2007): 5.

——, Hugh Gusterson, and David Price. "Introduction: War, Culture, and Counterinsurgency." In *The Counter-Counterinsurgency Manual*. Edited by the Network of Concerned Anthropologists, 1–20. Chicago: Prickly Paradigm Press, 2009.

Graeber, David. "Army of Altruists." *Harper's Magazine*. January 2007:31–38.

Graf, Peter. "US Deploys Latest Tactic in Iraq: Anthropology." Reuters News Service. January 9, 2008. http://www.alertnet.org/thenews/newsdesk/L06475304.htm.

Greenberg, Karen J., and Joshua L. Dratel, eds. *The Torture Papers: The Road to Abu Ghraib*. Cambridge, UK: Cambridge University Press, 2005.

Griffin, Marcus. "Going Native." *From an Anthropological Perspective*. July 10, 2007. http://web.archive.org/web/20071021082810/marcusgriffin.com/blog/2007/07/going_native.html#more.

Grossman, Dave. *On Killing: The Psychological Cost of Learning to Kill in War and Society*. New York: Back Bay Books, 2009.

——, and Gloria DeGaetano. *Stop Teaching Our Kids to Kill*. New York: Crown, 1998.

Gusterson, Hugh. "Anthropology and the Military—1968, 2003, and Beyond?" *Anthropology Today* 19, no. 3 (2003): 25–26.

——. "The US Military's Quest to Weaponize Culture." *Bulletin of the Atomic Scientists*. June 20, 2008. http://www.thebulletin.org/web-edition/columnists/hugh-gusterson/the-us-militarys-quest-to-weaponize-culture.

——. "Why the War in Afghanistan Cannot Be Won." *Bulletin of the Atomic Scientists*. September 21, 2009. http://www.thebulletin.org/web-edition/columnists/hugh-gusterson/why-the-war-afghanistan-cannot-be-won.

——, and David Price. "Spies in Our Midst." *Anthropology News* 46, no. 6 (2005): 39–40.

Halper, Katie. "US is Paying Off Iraq's Worst War Criminals." *Alternet*. September 18, 2007. http://www.alternet.org/world/62827/.

Hamady, Sania. *Temperament and Character of the Arabs*. New York: Twayne Publishers, 1960.

Hamilton, William. "Toying with War." *The Age* (Melbourne, Australia). May 4, 2003. http://www.theage.com.au/articles/2003/05/03/1051876901536.html.

Hedges, Chris. *War Is a Force That Gives Us Meaning*. New York: Anchor, 2003.

Helbig, Zenia. "Personal Perspective on the Human Terrain System." Presentation, annual meetings of the American Anthropological Association, Washington DC, November 29, 2007. http://www.wired.com/images_blogs/dangerroom/files/aaa_helbig_hts.pdf.

Hersh, Seymour. "The Gray Zone." *New Yorker.* May 25, 2004:38–44. http://www.newyorker.com/fact/content/?040524fa_fact.

Hodge, Nathan. "Help Wanted: 'Human Terrain' Teams for Africa." *Danger Room (Wired Blog).* January 12, 2009. http://www.wired.com/dangerroom/2009/01/help-wanted-hum/.

Holman, Kimberly. "Yo, Joe! Guard Adds Real-Life Heroes to GI Movie." *Grizzly: Official Newsmagazine of the California National Guard.* September 2009:4.

Horton, Scott. "How Hollywood Learned to Stop Worrying and Love the (Ticking) Bomb." *Harper's Magazine.* March 2008. http://www.harpers.org/archive/2008/03/hbc-90002531.

Howell, Georgina. "The Remarkable Life of Gertrude Bell." *Guardian.* September 3, 2006.

"In the Dark." *Economist.* February 2, 2009:49.

"Intelligence Studies Initiative." *Trinity Magazine.* Fall 2005. http://www.trinitydc.edu/news_events/mags/fall05/intelligence_studies_initiative.php.

"Iraq Has Really Become Somalia." *Democracy Now!* (syndicated by Pacifica Radio). April 1, 2008. http://www.democracynow.org/2008/4/1/iraq_has_become_somaliaa_collection_of.

"Is Torture on Hit Fox TV Show '24' Encouraging US Soldiers to Abuse Detainees?" *Democracy Now!* (syndicated by Pacifica Radio). February 22, 2007. http://www.democracynow.org/2007/2/22/is_torture_on_hit_fox_tv.

Jager, Sheila Miyoshi. *On the Uses of Cultural Knowledge.* Washington DC: Strategic Studies Institute, 2007.

Jannarone, Greg. *Behavioral Influences Analysis: Mission and Methodology Overview.* Presentation, US Air Force Behavioral Influences Analysis Center, Maxwell Air Force Base, Alabama. March 18, 2008. http://www.au.af.mil/bia/slides/bia_msn_bfg.pdf.

Jauregui, Beatrice. "Military Communitas? Re-centering the Citizen-Soldier Interface at the US Army Experience Center." Presented at the conference "Reconsidering American Power" at the University of Chicago (April 24, 2009).

Jeffreys, Derek S. *Spirituality and the Ethics of Torture.* New York: Palgrave Macmillan, 2009.

Jenks, Alfred E. "Building a Province." *Outlook.* May 21, 1904:170–177.

Jones, Matt, and Isabel Dupre. "Military Tactics." *Marie Claire.* March 2010:160–169.

Kadidal, Shayana. "NSA Surveillance: More Muck from the Bowels of AT&T." *Huffington Post.* April 14, 2006. http://www.huffingtonpost.com/shayana-kadidal/nsa-surveillance-more-muc_b_19128.html.

Kenyatta, Jomo. *Facing Mount Kenya*. London: Secker and Warburg, 1938.

Kilcullen, David. "Anatomy of a Tribal Revolt." *Small Wars Journal Blog*. August 29, 2007.

———. "Counterinsurgency Redux." *Survival* 48, no. 4 (2006): 111–130.

———. "Political Consequences of Military Operations in Indonesia 1945–2000: A Fieldwork Analysis of the Political Power-Diffusion Effects of Guerrilla Conflict." PhD dissertation, School of Politics, University of New South Wales, 2000.

———. "Twenty-Eight Articles: Fundamentals of Company-Level Counterinsurgency." *Military Review*. May–June 2006:105–107. http://usacac.army.mil/cac2/COIN/repository/28_Articles_of_COIN-Kilcullen(Mar06).pdf.

Kinzer, Stephen. *Overthrow: America's Century of Regime Change from Hawaii to Iraq*. New York: Times Books, 2007.

Kipp, Jacob, et al. "The Human Terrain System: A CORDS for the 21st Century." *Military Review*. September–October 2006:8–15.

Klein, Joe. "Good General, Bad Mission." *Time*. January 12, 2007:25.

Klein, Naomi. "Torture's Dirty Secret: It Works." *The Nation*. May 12, 2005:10. http://www.thenation.com/doc/20050530/klein.

Kohn, Richard H. "The Danger of Militarization in an Endless 'War' on Terrorism." *Journal of Military History*. January 2009:177-208.

Lagouranis, Tony, and Allen Mikaelian. *Fear Up Harsh: An Army Interrogator's Dark Journey through Iraq*. New York: NAL Caliber, 2007.

Landis, Frank. "Moscow Rules Moss's Mind." *Covert Action Information Bulletin* 24, no. 14 (1985).

Lathrop, Stacy. "Human Nature, Rights, and Ethics." *Anthropology News* 45, no. 6 (2005): 8.

Lawrence, T. E. "Twenty-Seven Articles." *Arab Bulletin*. August 20, 1917.

Leach, E. R. *Political Systems of Highland Burma*. Cambridge, MA: Harvard University Press, 1954.

Libicki, Martin, et al. *Byting Back: Regaining Information Superiority against 21st Century Insurgents*. Santa Monica, CA: RAND Corporation, 2007.

Lindner, Evelin. *Making Enemies: Humiliation and International Conflict*. Santa Barbara, CA: Praeger Security International, 2006.

Lococo, Edmond. "Lockheed, Sikorsky Grab Villain's Roles in Film 'Transformers.'" *Bloomberg News Service*. July 3, 2007. http://www.bloomberg.com/apps/news?pid=20601109&sid=aeNvfvWH13yY&refer=news.

Lutz, Catherine. *Homefront: A Military City and the American 20th Century.* Boston: Beacon Press, 2001.

——. "The Military Normal: Feeling at Home with Counterinsurgency in the United States." In *The Counter-Counterinsurgency Manual.* Edited by the Network of Concerned Anthropologists, 23–37. Chicago: Prickly Paradigm Press, 2009.

MacArthur, John A. *Second Front: Censorship and Propaganda in the 1991 Gulf War.* Berkeley: University of California Press, 1992.

Mackey, Chris, and Greg Miller. *The Interrogators: Task Force 500 and America's Secret War against Al Qaed a.* New York: Back Bay Books, 2004.

Martin, Emily. *Flexible Bodies.* Boston: Beacon Press, 1994.

Mayer, Jane. *The Dark Side.* New York: Doubleday, 2008.

——. "Whatever It Takes: The Politics of the Man behind *24.*" *New Yorker.* February 19, 2007: 66–82. http://www.newyorker.com/reporting/2007/02/19/070219fa_fact_mayer.

McConnell, Richard, Christopher Matson, and Brent Clemmer. "MiTT and Its 'Human Terrain.'" *Field Artillery.* January–February 2007:11–14.

McCoy, Alfred. *A Question of Torture: CIA Interrogation from the Cold War to the War on Terror.* New York: Metropolitan Books, 2006.

——. "The Myth of the Ticking Time Bomb." *The Progressive.* October 2006:20–24. http://www.progressive.org/mag_mccoy1006.

McFate, Montgomery. "Anthropology and Counterinsurgency: The Strange Story of Their Curious Relationship." *Military Review.* March–April 2005:24–38.

——. "The 'Memory of War': Tribes and the Legitimate Use of Force in Iraq." In *Armed Groups.* Edited by Jeffrey H. Norwitz, 291–310. Newport, RI: US Naval War College, 2008.

——. "The Military Utility of Understanding Adversary Culture." *Joint Force Quarterly* 38 (2005): 42–48.

——, and Andrea Jackson. "An Organizational Solution for DOD's Cultural Knowledge Needs." *Military Review.* July–August 2005:18–21.

McIlwraith, Robert. "I'm Addicted to Television: The Personality, Imagination, and Watching Patterns of Self-Identified TV Addicts." *Journal of Broadcasting and Electronic Media* 42(3)(1998): 371–387.

McNamara, Laura. "Culture, Torture, Interrogation, and the Global War on Terrorism." Presentation, annual meetings of the Society for Applied Anthropology, Santa Fe, NM, March 17–21, 2009. http://sfaapodcasts.net/2009/05/10/scholars-security-and-citizenship-part-i-sar-plenary/.

Mead, Margaret. "Warfare Is Only an Invention—Not a Biological Necessity." *Asia* 40 (1940).

Mechanic, Michael. "Voluntary Confinement." *Mother Jones*. March/April 2008:50–52, 96. http://motherjones.com/politics/2008/03/voluntary-confinement.

Meek, C. K. *Law and Authority in a Nigerian Tribe: A Study in Indirect Rule.* Oxford, UK: Oxford University Press, 1937.

Milbank, Dana, and Claudia Deane. "Poll Finds Dimmer View of Iraq War, 52% Say U.S. Has Not Become Safer." *Washington Post.* June 8, 2005.

Miles, Donna. "Recruiting Successes Continue in Fiscal 2009." *Armed Forces Press Service.* November 10, 2008. http://www.defenselink.mil/news/newsarticle. aspx?id=5188.

Milgram, Stanley. *Obedience to Authority: An Experimental View.* New York: Harper and Row, 1974.

Miller, Greg. "Obama Preserves Renditions as Counterterrorism Tool." *Los Angeles Times.* February 1, 2009.

Mondino, Jean-Baptiste. "Combat Ready: Fashion Deploys for Action, Ready March!" *T-Magazine.* March 2010:162–167.

Monoky, Anne. "Utilitarian Chic." *Harper's Bazaar.* January 2010:142–143.

Morris, Michael. "Al Qaeda As Insurgency." *Joint Force Quarterly* 39 (2005): 41–50.

Moss, Robert. *The War for the Cities.* New York: Coward, McCann, and Geoghegan, 1972.

Mulrine, Anne. "Culture Warriors." *US News and World Report.* December 10, 2007:34–37.

Nadel, S. F. *The Foundations of Social Anthropology.* London: Cohen & West, 1951.

——. *The Nuba.* London: Oxford University Press, 1947.

Nader, Laura. "Controlling Processes: Tracing the Dynamic Components of Power." *Current Anthropology* 38, no. 5 (1997): 711–737.

——. *Harmony Ideology: Justice and Control in a Zapotec Mountain Village.* Stanford, CA: Stanford University Press, 1991.

——. "Iraq and Democracy." *Anthropological Quarterly* 76, no. 3 (2003): 479–483.

——. "The Phantom Factor: Impact of the Cold War on Anthropology." In *The Cold War and the University.* Edited by Andre Schiffrin, 107–148. New York: The New Press, 1997.

——. "*1984* and *Brave New World*: The Insidious Threat of Covert Control." *Radcliffe Quarterly.* December 1983:2–3.

Naffsinger, Paul A. "'Face' among the Arabs." *CIA Studies in Intelligence* 8, no. 3 (1964).

Nakashima, Ellen. "A Story of Surveillance." *Washington Post.* November 7, 2007. http://www.washingtonpost.com/wp-dyn/content/article/2007/11/07/AR20071107 00006.html.

Newfield, Christopher. *Unmaking the Public University: The Forty-Year Assault on the Middle Class.* Cambridge, MA: Harvard University Press, 2008.

Nimri Aziz, Barbara. *Swimming Up the Tigris.* Gainesville: University Press of Florida, 2007.

Noble, David. *America by Design: Science, Technology, and the Rise of Corporate Capitalism.* New York: Oxford University Press, 1979.

"NSA Whistleblower Warns Domestic Spying Program Is Sign the US Is Decaying into a 'Police State.'" *Democracy Now!* (syndicated by Pacifica Radio). January 3, 2006. http://www.democracynow.org/2006/1/3/exclusive_national_security_agency_ whistleblower_warns.

Oppel, Richard A. "Iraq Takes Aim at US-tied Sunni Groups' Leaders." *New York Times.* August 22, 2008.

Orwell, George. "Politics and the English Language." In *A Collection of Essays.* Edited by George Orwell, 156–170. New York: Harcourt Brace Jovanovich, 1953.

Packer, George. "Knowing the Enemy." *New Yorker.* December 18, 2006:60–69. http://www.newyorker.com/archive/2006/12/18/061218fa_fact2.

Panasitti, Mike, and Natasha Schull. "Re-articulating the Moral Economy of Gambling." *Kroeber Anthropological Society Papers* 77 (1994).

Patai, Raphael. *The Arab Mind.* New York: Scribner, 1973.

Patterson, Margot. "The Mission of Ray McGovern." *National Catholic Reporter.* October 27, 2006:11.

Paust, Jordan. "Executive Plans and Authorizations to Violate International Law Concerning Treatment and Interrogation of Detainees." *Columbia Journal of Transnational Law* 43, no. 3 (2005): 811–863.

Peattie, Lisa. "Normalizing the Unthinkable." *Bulletin of the Atomic Scientists.* March 1984:32–36.

Pels, Peter. "The Rise and Fall of the Indian Aborigines: Orientalism, Anglicism, and the Emergence of an Ethnography of India, 1833–1869." In *Colonial Subjects: Essays on the Practical History of Anthropology.* Edited by Peter Pels and Oscar Salemink, 82–116. Ann Arbor: University of Michigan Press, 1999.

Pérez, Gina. "JROTC, Citizenship, and Puerto Rican Youth in Lorain, Ohio." Presentation, annual meetings of the American Anthropological Association, Philadelphia, PA, December 6, 2009.

——. "JROTC and Latina/o Youth in Neoliberal Cities." In *Rethinking America*. Edited by Jeff Maskovsky and Ida Susser, 31–48. New York: Paradigm Publishers, 2009.

Perry, Daniel. "The China Connection: UTPA Students Experience Chinese Culture, Academics." *Monitor* (McAllen, Texas). July 24, 2007. http://www.themonitor.com/articles/china-4002-students-center.html.

Peters, Ralph. "Blood Borders." *Armed Forces Journal*. June 2006. http://www.afji.com/2006/06/1833899/.

——. "Constant Conflict." *Parameters*. Summer 1997:4–14.

——. "The Human Terrain of Urban Operations." *Proceedings* 30, no. 1 (2000): 4–12.

Peterson, Scott. "US Army's Strategy in Afghanistan: Better Anthropology." *Christian Science Monitor*. September 7, 2007.

Petraeus, David. "Report to Congress on the Situation in Iraq." Testimony to US Congress. September 10–11, 2007. http://www.defense.gov/pubs/pdfs/Petraeus-Testimony20070910.pdf.

"Petraeus Says Afghan Tribes Could Help Fight Militants." *International Herald Tribune*. November 6, 2008. http://www.iht.com/articles/ap/2008/11/06/asia/AS-Afghanistan-Petraeus.php.

Pew Research Center. *America's Place in the World 2005*. November 2005. http://people-press.org/reports/pdf/263.pdf.

——. "Public Remains Divided over Use of Torture." April 2009. http://people-press.org/reports/pdf/510.pdf.

Pincus, Walter. "Howard, Virginia Tech Join US Intelligence Program." *Washington Post*. September 7, 2009.

Plascencia, Luis F. B. "The Military Gates of Non-Citizenship: Latino 'Aliens' and Non-citizen Nationals Performing Military Work in the US Homeland." Presentation, annual meetings of the American Anthropological Association, Philadelphia, PA, December 6, 2009.

Platt, Kamala. "How Can We Sleep? The Birthing of an Intelligence Center on University Grounds." *La Voz de Esperanza* (San Antonio, Texas). May 2007:6–7.

——. "Latino/a Students and Covert 'Securities': The Integration of Academic and Intelligence Communities." *Latino Studies* 6:456–465.

Poulous, Ryan. "UTEP Camp Shows the World of Intelligence." *El Paso Inc.* http://www.elpasoinc.com/showArticle.asp?articleId=1471.

Priest, Dana. "CIA Holds Terror Suspects in Secret Prisons." *Washington Post*. November 2, 2005.

——, and Barton Gellman. "US Decries Abuse but Defends Interrogations." *Washington Post*. December 26, 2002.

Price, David. *Anthropological Intelligence: The Deployment and Neglect of Anthropology in the Second World War.* Durham, NC: Duke University Press, 2008.

——. "Gregory Bateson and the OSS." *Human Organization* 57, no. 4 (1998): 379–384.

——. "Obama's Classroom Spies." *CounterPunch.* June 23, 2009. http://www.counterpunch.org/price06232009.html.

——. "Pilfered Scholarship Devastates General Petraeus's Counterinsurgency Manual." *CounterPunch.* October 30, 2007. http://www.counterpunch.org/price10302007.html.

——. "Silent Coup: How the CIA Is Welcoming Itself Back onto American University Campuses." *CounterPunch.* January 16–31, 2010:1–5.

——. "The CIA's Campus Spies." *CounterPunch.* March 12–13, 2005. http://www.counterpunch.org/price03122005.html.

——. "The Spook School Program." *CounterPunch.* February 1–15, 2010:6–7.

"Professor McCoy Exposes the History of CIA Interrogation." *Democracy Now!* (syndicated by Pacifia Radio). February 17, 2006. http://www.democracynow.org/2006/2/17/professor_mccoy_exposes_the_history_of.

Probst, Emily. "Wounded Warriors Face Homefront Battle with VA." *CNN News.* November 16, 2007. http://www.cnn.com/2007/HEALTH/11/15/wounded.marine/index.html.

Qureshi, Emram. "Misreading *The Arab Mind.*" *Boston Globe.* May 30, 2004. http://www.boston.com/news/globe/ideas/articles/2004/05/30/misreading_the_arab_mind/.

Renzi, Fred. "Terra Incognita and the Case for Ethnographic Intelligence." *Military Review* (May 2006): 16–23.

Ribeiro, Gustavo Lins. "Security for Whom? Anthropologists and Repressive State Elites." *Focaal* 50 (2007): 146–154.

Ricks, Thomas. "Officers with PhDs Advising War Effort." *Washington Post.* February 5, 2007.

Ridgeway, James, Daniel Schulman, and David Corn. "There's Something about Mary." *Mother Jones.* July 30, 2008. http://www.motherjones.com/news/feature/2008/07/mary-mcfate-sapone-gun-lobby-nra-spy.html.

Risen, James, and Eric Lichtblau. "Bush Lets US Spy on Callers without Courts." *New York Times.* December 16, 2005.

Robben, Antonius C. G. M. "Anthropology and the Iraq War: An Uncomfortable Engagement." *Anthropology Today* 25, no. 1 (2009): 1–3.

Rodriguez, Rene. "*GI Joe: The Rise of Cobra*: It's More Toy Commercial Than Movie." *Miami Herald*. August 7, 2009. http://miamiherald.typepad.com/reeling/2009/08/review-gi-joe-the-rise-of-cobra.html.

Rohde, David. "Army Enlists Anthropology in War Zones." *New York Times*. October 5, 2007.

Rosen, Nir. "The Myth of the Surge." *Rolling Stone*. March 6, 2008.

Roth, Kenneth, Minky Worden, and Amy D. Bernstein. *Torture: Does It Make Us Safer? Is It Ever OK?* New York: New Press, 2005.

Rubinstein, Robert A. *Peacekeeping under Fire: Culture and Intervention*. New York: Paradigm Publishers, 2008.

Said, Edward. *Orientalism*. New York: Vintage, 1978.

———. "A Window on the World." *Guardian*. August 2, 2003. http://www.guardian.co.uk/books/2003/aug/02/alqaida.highereducation.

Salemink, Oscar. "Ethnography as Martial Art: Ethnicizing Vietnam's Montagnards, 1930–1954." In *Colonial Subjects: Essays on the Practical History of Anthropology*. Edited by Peter Pels and Oscar Salemink, 282–325. Ann Arbor: University of Michigan Press, 1999.

Sánchez, Leonel. "Hero Worship Puts Focus on Sailor Dad." *San Diego Union-Tribune*. August 6, 2009.

Sánchez, Ricardo. "CJTF-7 Interrogation and Counter-Resistance Policy." Unpublished memorandum. October 2003. http://www.aclu.org/safefree/general/175611g120050329.html.

Santos, Eugene, and Qunhua Zhao. "Adversarial Models for Opponent Intent Inferencing." In *Adversarial Reasoning*. Edited by Alexander Kott and William McEneaney, 1–22. Boca Raton, FL: Chapman and Hall, 2006.

Scahill, Jeremy. "Stunning Statistics About the War that Everyone Should Know." *CounterPunch*. December 18, 2009. http://www.counterpunch.org/scahill12182009.html.

Scales, Robert H. "Army Transformation: Implications for the Future." Testimony before the US House Armed Services Committee. July 15, 2004. http://www.au.af.mil/au/awc/awcgate/congress/04-07-15scales.pdf

Schein, Edward H. *Coercive Persuasion*. New York: H. H. Norton, 1971.

Schetter, Conrad, Rainer Glassner, and Masood Karokhail. "Beyond Warlordism: The Local Security Architecture in Afghanistan." *Internationale Politik und Gesellschaft* 2 (2007): 136–152.

Schuman, Howard. *Method and Meaning in Polls and Surveys*. Cambridge, MA: Harvard University Press, 2008.

Scott, James C. *Seeing Like a State.* New Haven, CT, and London: Yale University Press, 1998.

Shachtman, Noah. "'Sim Iraq' Sent to Battle Zone." *Danger Room (Wired Blog).* November 19, 2007. http://blog.wired.com/defense/2007/11/mathematicalmo.html.

Shamsi, Hina. "General Miller Takes the Stand." *Human Rights First.* May 2006. http://www.humanrightsfirst.org/blog/cardona/2006/05/general-millertakes-stand.aspx).

Shapiro, Ari. "Mukasey Refuses to Call Waterboarding Torture." *All Things Considered* (National Public Radio). October 18, 2007. http://www.npr.org/templates/story/story.php?storyId=15413635.

Shapiro, H. A. "Fathers and Sons, Men and Boys." In *Coming of Age in Ancient Greece.* Edited by Jenifer Neils and John H. Oakley, 85–111. New Haven, CT: Yale University Press, 2003.

Sheftick, Gary, and Grafton Pritchartt. "Face of Defense: Soldiers Bring Life to 'GI Joe." *American Forces Press Service.* August 11, 2009. http://www.defenselink.mil/news/newsarticle.aspx?id=55441.

Silliman, Stephen. "The 'Old West' in the Middle East: US Military Metaphors in Real and Imagined Indian Country." *American Anthropologist* 110, no. 2 (2008): 237–247.

Silverman, Barry. "Human Terrain Data: What Should We Do with It?" In *Proceedings of 2007 Winter Simulation Conference.* Edited by S. G. Henderson. 2007. http://repository.upenn.edu/cgi/viewcontent.cgi?article=1330&context=ese_papersilv.

Simon, Steven. "The Price of the Surge." *Foreign Affairs.* May–June 2008:57–76.

Simpson, Christopher, ed. *Universities and Empire: Money and Politics in the Social Sciences during the Cold War.* New York: The New Press, 1999.

Smallman, Guy. "Villagers' Legacy of Pain From US Air Raid." *Financial Times.* June 19, 2009.

"Social Scientists in War Zones." *Here and Now* (National Public Radio). October 12, 2007. http://www.hereandnow.org/2008/07/show-rundown-for-7282008/.

Solomon, Norman. *War Made Easy: How Presidents and Pundits Keep Spinning Us to Death.* New York: Wiley, 2006.

"Special Events: Scavenger Hunts." *International Spy Museum.* http://www.spymuseum.org/special/hunts.php.

Sponsel, Leslie E. "Reflections on the Possibilities of a Nonkilling Society." In *Toward a Nonkilling Paradigm.* Edited by Joam Evans Pim, 35–72. Honolulu: Center for Global Nonkilling, 2009.

Starrett, Gregory. "Culture Never Dies: Anthropology at Abu Ghraib." *Anthropology News* 45, no. 6 (2004): 10–11.

Steinman, Ron. "A Picture Really Is Worth a Thousand Words." *The Digital Journalist.* March 2007. http://digitaljournalist.org/issue0703/a-thousand-words.html.

Sterling, Joe. "American Grad Student Dies in Iraq." *CNN News.* June 26, 2008. http://www.cnn.com/2008/WORLD/meast/06/26/iraq.american.death/.

Stockman, Farah. "Anthropologist's War Death Reverberates." *Boston Globe.* February 12, 2009. http://www.boston.com/news/world/middleeast/articles/2009/02/12/anthropologists_war_death_reverberates/.

Taguba, Antonio. *Article 15-6 Investigation of the 800th Military Police Brigade.* May 2004. http://www.npr.org/iraq/2004/prison_abuse_report.pdf.

Tapper, Richard. "Anthropologists, Historians, and Tribespeople." In *Tribes and State Formation in the Middle East.* Edited by Philip S. Khoury and Joseph Kostiner, 48–73. Berkeley: University of California Press, 1990.

Testino, Mario. "Military Issue." *Vogue.* March 2010:446–458.

Thomas, Evan, and Michael Hirsh. "The Debate over Torture." *Newsweek.* November 21, 2005:26–33.

Todd, Lin, et al. *Iraq Tribal Study: al-Anbar Governorate.* Unpublished report. http://turcopolier.typepad.com/the_athenaeum/files/iraq_tribal_study_070907.pdf.

"The Torture Question." *PBS Frontline.* October 18, 2005. http://www.pbs.org/wgbh/pages/frontline/torture/interviews/lagouranis.html#4.

Tripp, Charles. "Iraq: The Imperial Precedent." *Le Monde Diplomatique* (English edition). January 3, 2003. http://mondediplo.com/2003/01/02empire.

Tuchman, Gaye. *Wannabe U: Inside the Corporate University.* Chicago: University of Chicago Press, 2009.

Turnbull, Stephen. *Mongol Warrior 1200–1350.* London: Osprey Publishing, 2003.

Turse, Nick, *The Complex: How the Military Invades Our Everyday Lives.* New York: Metropolitan Books, 2008.

"University of Texas-Pan American Faculty Senate Minutes." April 26, 2006. https://portal.utpa.edu/portal/page/portal/utpa_main/daa_home/senate_home/senate_imagesfiles/fs_060426_lm.pdf.

US Air Force. "Mitigate IED Threat by Leveraging an Effect-Based Approach." *SITIS Archives.* http://www.dodsbir.net/sitis/archives_display_topic.asp?Bookmark=32088.

US Army. *Counterinsurgency: Field Manual 3-24.* Washington DC: Government Printing Office, 2006.

——. *Intelligence Interrogation: Field Manual 34-52.* Washington DC: Government Printing Office, 1992.

US Army Human Terrain System Reachback Research Center. "My Cousin's Enemy Is My Friend: A Study of Pashtun 'Tribes' in Afghanistan." Unpublished report. September 2009. http://easterncampaign.files.wordpress.com/2009/11/mycousins-enemy-is-my-friend-a-study-of-pashtun-tribes.pdf.

US Department of Defense Office of the Inspector General. *Review of DoD-Directed Investigations of Detainee Abuse.* August 2006. http://www.fas.org/irp/agency/dod/abuse.pdf.

US House Intelligence Committee. "Building Capabilities: The Intelligence Community's National Security Requirements for Diversity of Language, Skills, and Ethnic and Cultural Understanding." November 5, 2003. http://www.fas.org/irp/congress/2003_hr/110503hpsci.pdf.

US House Un-American Activities Committee. *Guerrilla Warfare Advocates in the United States.* Washington DC: Government Printing Office, 1968.

US Office of the Director of National Intelligence. "Intelligence Community Centers of Academic Excellence Program." *Intelligence Community Centers of Academic Excellence.* http://www.dni.gov/cae/institutions.htm.

——. *United States Intelligence Community Centers of Academic Excellence in National Security Studies: Program Plan for Fiscal Years 2005–2015.* Washington DC: Office of the Director of National Intelligence, 2005. http://www.trinitydc.edu/programs/intel_center/IC CAE Application April05 seal.pdf.

US Office of Secretary of Defense. *OSD RDT&E Budget Item Justification.* http://www.dtic.mil/descriptivesum/Y2008/OSD/0603648D8Z.pdf.

Valentine, Douglas. *The Phoenix Program.* New York: Morrow, 1990.

Virilio, Paul. *War and Cinema.* New York: Verso, 1989.

War Is Sell. DVD. Directed by Brian Standing. Madison, WI: Prolefeed Studios, 2004.

Wilcox, John. *Precision Engagement—Strategic Context for the Long War.* Presentation, Precision Strike Winter Roundtable, US Department of Defense, February 1, 2007. http://www.dtic.mil/ndia/2007psa_winter/wilcox.pdf.

Wilkinson, Tracy, and Maria De Cristofaro. "Italy Indicts CIA Agents in Kidnapping." *Los Angeles Times.* February 17, 2007. http://articles.latimes.com/2007/feb/17/world/fg-cia17.

Willing, Richard. "Intelligence Agencies Invest in College Education." *USA Today.* November 27, 2006.

Wisnewski, J. Jeremy, and R. D. Emerick. *The Ethics of Torture.* London: Continuum, 2009.

Wolf, Eric R. *Sons of the Shaking Earth.* Chicago: University of Chicago Press, 1957.

Zimbardo, Philip G. *The Lucifer Effect: Understanding How Good People Turn Evil.* New York: Random House, 2007.

Zinn, Howard. *Vietnam: The Logic of Withdrawal.* Boston: Beacon Press, 1967.

Zogby, John. "War, Peace, and Politics." *The Way We'll Be.* September 26, 2009. http://www.zogby.com/blog2/index.php/category/war/.

Index

AAA (American Anthropological
  Association)
  code of ethics, 88, 92n29
  newsletter, 96
  statements
    on Human Terrain System,
      112–113
    on torture, 70, 89, 92–93n31
    on US occupation of Iraq, 89,
      92–93n31
Abu Ghraib
  anthropologists' responses to, 96–99
  and *The Arab Mind*, 95–109
  dehumanization at, 99–101, 104, 106
  torture of prisoners at, 95–101
  training of intelligence agents at,
    99–101
Afghanistan
  civilian casualties, 173, 174–175
  counterinsurgency in, 77–93, 166–169
  prisoner torture in, 70
  social scientists in, 28, 111–131
  subcontractors in, 173
  tribes
    and US military, 22, 153–156,
      166–167
  US military occupation of, 173
  war in, 19, 173–174
Al-Ali, Nadje, 149
al-Anbar (Iraqi province), 155, 156, 157,
  161–163, 166
al-Qaeda, 45, 85, 86, 92n28, 95, 115
  in Iraq, 155, 157, 158, 159, 161, 164, 166
alternative dispute resolution, 61
American Anthropological Association.
  See AAA
American exceptionalism, 28, 68,
  168–169, 176
Anglo-Egyptian Sudan. *See* Sudan
anthropology
  anti-imperial, 147–150
  applied, 140, 146
  colonial
    in Afghanistan, 111–127, 167–168
    in Iraq, 85–88, 111–127, 142–145,
      153, 161–163, 167-168, 183
    in Nigeria, 145–146

in Philippines, 136–141
in Sudan, 146–147
in Taiwan, 140–141
in Vietnam, 141–142
dilemmas of, 88–90, 104–106, 125–
  127, 135–136, 149–150, 168
Latin American, 168
mercenary, 89
pilfering of
  by CIA, 98
  by military, 79, 141–143
tribal concept in, 139–140, 142, 146,
  153, 155–156, 166, 169n1
Arab Mind, The
  and Abu Ghraib, 95–109
  and dehumanization, 96, 99–106
  as justification for military occupa-
    tion, 104–106
  as orientalist, 101–103, 105
  as preferred military text, 96, 99–101,
    102–103, 104–106, 106–107n6,
    109n33
  Seymour Hersh on, 95–99
Aztec society
  childhood in, 24–25
  family life in, 24
  history of, 24
  militarism in, 24–25
  women in, 25
Bacevich, Andrew
  on militarism, 20
BAE Systems, 86, 118, 124, 126, 131n55
Barrows, David P., 140, 142, 149
Bell, Gertrude
  on Arab independence, 144
  in Mesopotamia, 144, 145, 146
Blackwater, 77, 173
Boas, Franz
  on American imperialism, 147–148
  on "shackles of tradition," 175
Bontoc Igorot. *See* Igorot
British Mandate. *See* colonialism, British
Burger King Corporation, 15–16, 17
Bush, George W.
  and Iraq war, 83–84, 103, 157–158,
    165–166
  legal counsel of, 61–62

at Abu Ghraib, 99–101, 104–105
in *The Arab Mind*, 96, 101–102, 105–106
and "human terrain," 116
of Iraqis, 149
Dershowitz, Alan, 65–67
DIA (Defense Intelligence Agency), 35–39
DNI. *See* US Director of National
Intelligence
education
commercialization of, 51–53
and intelligence agencies, 35–53
militarization of
in Aztec society, 24, 25
in Sparta, 22, 25
in United States, 19, 27, 35–41,
47–53
Eggan, Fred, 140
Eidelson, Roy, 67–68
Eisenhower, Dwight D.
on military-industrial complex, 15, 27
entertainment
and militarism, 13–21, 38, 62–65,
101, 177–178
violence as
in motion pictures, 16–17, 18–19, 101
on television, 62–65, 101
in video games, 177–178
ethnography
as intelligence source, 104–106
and mapping, 118–126, 142, 153
of Middle East, 102–103
militarization of, 113, 115, 116–117,
118, 141
and warfare, 141–142
ethics, professional, 48, 77, 88–89,
92n29, 105, 112–113, 167–168
Ewen, Stuart, 57–58
Facing Mt. Kenya, 148
families
militarization of
in Aztec society, 25
in Mongolian society, 23, 25
in Sparta, 22–23, 25
in United States, 14–15, 18–19, 27
fashion
militarization of, 19, 21, 25, 30n15
FBI (Federal Bureau of Investigation),
35–39, 42, 44–45, 49–51, 62
Fear Up Harsh, 99–101
Feisal I, 143–145
Ferguson, R. Brian, 26–27
Fernea, Elizabeth, 103
Fernea, Robert, 149, 155
films, 16–17, 18–19, 101
Finnegan, Patrick, 62–64
Fisk, Robert

on academics, 149
FM 3-24 (counterinsurgency field
manual), 77–93
Fondacaro, Steve, 126, 167–168
Fox Television, 62–63
Fry, Douglas, 26
Fulbright, William, 52–53
Galliéni, Joseph, 142
Gates, Robert, 51, 154
Genghis Khan, 23
Gentile, Gian
on Vietnam War, 164–165
GI Joe: The Rise of Cobra (motion picture), 14–18
GI Joe (toy), 15
Great Britain
and colonialism
in Africa, 117, 145–148
in India, 97, 117
in Malaya, 83, 85, 145
in Mesopotamia, 79–80, 85,
142–145, 162–163
counterinsurgency tactics, 85
divide and conquer, 162–164
indirect rule, 142–147
recruitment of "Gurkhas" by, 139
and T. E. Lawrence, 79–83, 142–145
Guantánamo Bay
and Barack Obama presidency, 70
as behavioral research laboratory, 97,
98
torture at, 70, 97, 109n30
Gusterson, Hugh, 18, 40–41, 88–89,
92n29, 149
Harman, Jane, 35–36
harmony, coercive, 60–61
Hasbro, 15–17
Hersh, Seymour
and Abu Ghraib scandal, 95–99
and *The Arab Mind*, 95–96, 99
Hollywood, 13, 15, 16, 18, 62, 101
Human Social Culture Behavioral Modeling, 121
Human Terrain System
AAA statement on, 112–113
and BAE Systems, 118, 126, 131n55
CEAUSSIC report on, 113, 127n7
cost of, 112, 117, 122
ethical implications of, 124–127
future of, 124–127
history of, 113–122
as intelligence program, 111, 126
and modeling and simulation programs, 120–122
Network of Concerned Anthropologists' response to, 112

About the Author

Roberto J. González is Associate Professor of Anthropology at San José State University. After receiving a bachelor's degree from the University of Texas, Austin, in 1992, he began his graduate studies in anthropology at the University of California, Berkeley. He received his PhD there in 1998. His doctoral research analyzed the agricultural theories and practices of subsistence farmers in southern Mexico. His first book, *Zapotec Science: Farming and Food in the Northern Sierra of Oaxaca* (2001) is based upon this work, and it won the first annual Julian Steward Award from the Anthropology and Environment Section of the American Anthropological Association. More recently, Dr. González has published an edited volume, *Anthropologists in the Public Sphere: Speaking Out on War, Peace, and American Power* (2004) and the book *American Counterinsurgency: Human Science and the Human Terrain* (2009). He has written many articles in academic journals and other periodicals, including the *Los Angeles Times*, the *San Francisco Chronicle*, *In These Times*, and *Z Magazine*, and he has been interviewed for programs produced by National Public Radio and the British Broadcasting Corporation, among others. He is a founding member of the Network of Concerned Anthropologists.